geek

SILICON VALLEY

the inside gu
palo alto | sta
mountain view | santa clara
sunnyvale | san jose | san francisco

To buy books in quantity for corporate use
or incentives, call **(800) 962–0973**
or e-mail **premiums@GlobePequot.com.**

INSIDERS' GUIDE®

Text design: M.A. Dubé
Maps created by M.A. Dubé © Morris Book Publishing, LLC
Spot photos © iStockphoto.com

Library of Congress Cataloging-in-Publication Data is available on request.
ISBN: 978-0-7627-4239-4

Manufactured in the United States of America
First Edition/Second Printing

SILICON VALLEY

geek

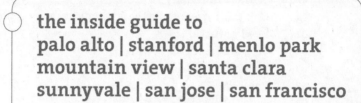

the inside guide to
palo alto | stanford | menlo park
mountain view | santa clara
sunnyvale | san jose | san francisco

ashlee vance

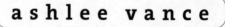

The Globe Pequot Press | Guilford, Connecticut

How to Use This Book

WHAT YOU WILL FIND IN THIS VOLUME IS A PLACE-BASED tour of the Silicon Valley by geeks, for geeks (and really, anyone with even a passing interest in the world of technology). We've focused on the companies and institutions that make this Valley what it is—the major corporate players, the universities and research institutions, the museums and venture capitalists. You'll read their stories, learn how (and if) you can visit their facilities, and come to understand their place in Silicon Valley past, present, and future. We've also included side trips into attractions, eateries, and other establishments of particular interest to geeks and geek-watchers.

What you won't find here is an exhaustive guide to sightseeing the Valley. For that we recommend you turn to *Southern California Off the Beaten Path, Northern California Off the Beaten Path, Driving the Pacific Coast California,* or *Quick Escapes San Francisco.*

Look for the grey boxes dotting the pages to tell you exactly where you'll find each facility. As befits a geek guide, we've added Web addresses where you can learn more about just about every possible topic here.

Sidebars throughout the book delve into the specifics of Valley lore and culture. Others point you toward great geek gathering spots and profile some of the area's most famous and infamous personalities.

Because the book is arranged around places, not chronology or topics, many of Silicon Valley's most interesting people and institutions are described in more than one spot. You'll find information on the legendary Robert Noyce, for instance, in sections on Sand Hill Road as well as on Fairchild Semiconductor, Shockley Semiconductor, Intel, and more. If there's a subject you particularly want to pursue here, then, we urge you to take a look at this book's index (again by geeks, for geeks) to find our every reference.

Given the pace of life out here, we fully expect parts of this book to be outdated before it even hits the bookshelves. Such is life in Silicon Valley.

Introduction:
Thank You, Mama Shockley

BUREAUCRATS, GIANT CORPORATIONS, AND UNIVERSITIES scattered around the globe have spent billions of dollars trying to replicate Silicon Valley. Researchers, too, have dug deep into the region's history, hoping to unlock the secrets behind this technophiles' paradise. All of this effort, however, seems wasted for one simple reason. William Shockley's mother lived in Palo Alto.

Shockley, a brilliant physicist, could have set up his new transistor lab just about anywhere, and, in fact, his financial backer would have preferred to see the company begin in Southern California. But, reeling from a divorce and professional tensions, Shockley cared less about placating his investor than preserving his mental health. He needed his dear old mom and the comforting surroundings of his boyhood home near Stanford University.

Shockley Semiconductor Laboratory officially opened for business in 1956 at 391 San Antonio Road in Mountain View, just a few miles from where Shockley grew up. In what would turn out to be a most symbolic gesture, Shockley cleared out the remnants of a fruit-packing plant that had been on the site and started filling the building with scientific equipment. He then took a risk by ordering the team of young, bright researchers he had assembled to focus on using silicon as the key material for the company's transistors and other devices. Shockley literally brought the silicon to Silicon Valley.

Or at least that's one version of Silicon Valley's origins. Plenty of historians, on the other hand, reject the idea of hanging the region's birth and development on Shockley. Most often, researchers point to the budding electronics industry that already existed here. The San Francisco Bay Area had been attracting a large crop of radio enthusiasts since the early 1900s, and a number of these hobbyists and well-educated researchers would create a vibrant electronics community that touched San Francisco, Redwood City, Palo Alto, and San Jose.

The area had a lot to offer the burgeoning electronics field. While still young when compared with eastern rivals, Stanford University did a great deal to contribute to the fledgling economy by supplying the talent needed to fuel companies. In return, the companies provided the jobs that made it possible for Stanford graduates to stay in the area rather than heading to the Midwest or East Coast to work for large, established players.

Stanford also had a key player in Professor Fred Terman, who was critical to nurturing the network forming between students and entrepreneurs. He would, for instance, encourage Stanford students Bill Hewlett and Dave Packard to form their own venture. Hewlett-Packard would turn into the premier electronics company in the region and provide tens of thousands of jobs.

It certainly didn't hurt, either, that the San Francisco Midpeninsula offered clear lifestyle benefits. Locals had quick access to a world-class city in San Francisco. They could travel to either ocean or mountains within minutes and had a ready supply of sunshine to enjoy the outdoors. Right up to the 1960s, residents could buy homes surrounded by orchards and lush, rolling hills with relative ease.

Those inclined toward starting a business had major advantages in Santa Clara County. Unlike in San Francisco, unions were not powerful here, which helped keep wages down. The county government had tax policies in place that promoted the creation of new businesses and factories in the suburbs. Beyond all that, local universities, the military, and private industries did their part to secure large government contracts for research and development.

The region had been known as the Valley of Heart's Delights for its vast supply of orchards, complemented by beautiful grasslands, forests, and abundant wildlife. By the mid–twentieth century, the conditions had clearly been set for this all to change on a grand scale.

For better or for worse, the Valley of Heart's Delights was poised to be conquered.

That's what makes Shockley's gutting of the fruit-packing plant on San Antonio Road so fitting. He delivered the idea that sealed the orchards' demise.

Never a successful businessman, Shockley secured his place in Silicon Valley history in an unusual way: by hiring the brightest scientists and engineers he could find and then scaring them off with his unorthodox management style. About a year after the Shockley lab opened, Robert Noyce, Gordon Moore, and six other employees broke away to start Fairchild Semiconductor. The group obtained outside funding for their new company, kicking off in earnest the region's venture capital economy. Fairchild went on to become a major supplier of the integrated circuits that would fuel the dramatic growth in computing. The company could not capitalize on all its innovations, however, prompting many "Fairchildren" to start their own companies and make Santa Clara County the epicenter of the silicon-based semiconductor industry. Noyce and Moore later created their own start-up—Intel.

Almost all of the great Silicon Valley companies are in some way tied to the integrated circuit and processor innovations of Fairchild's offspring. Companies such as Apple Computer, Cisco Systems, Sun Microsystems, and Silicon Graphics were among the first wave of success stories. Years later the likes of Netscape, Yahoo!, eBay, and Google would piggyback on the foundation laid by the hardware heavies.

Today Silicon Valley lives up to its reputation. The headquarters of multibillion-dollar giants are common sights in Palo Alto, Mountain View, Sunnyvale, Santa Clara, and San Jose. Even more common are the myriad start-ups packed into the business centers dominating the suburban landscape. Perhaps no other place on earth can claim a brighter, more diverse collection of individuals all grasping for similar goals. The entire region has been sculpted to make doing business and exchanging ideas as simple as possible. That's why the people here tolerate the region's traffic, astronomical housing prices, and lost orchards. Silicon Valley is a type of candy land for engineers and entrepreneurs.

It is, ultimately, too simplistic to give Shockley credit for all the region has become. One man's presence cannot account for organizations as diverse as NASA, Google, Intel, and Lockheed Martin setting up shop just miles from one another. Representatives from HP and Stanford would surely cringe at the suggestion that Shockley did all the tough work.

To that point, this book will trace many of the places, figures, organizations, and companies that made and continue to make Silicon Valley what it is. You'll encounter the early elements that primed the region for growth, the hardware behemoths that capitalized on that foundation, and the flashy Internet, biotech, and nanotech firms that hope to create a new wave of innovation.

More than anything, this book will give you a glimpse of just how multifaceted the area is with its unique mix of business and culture. Many of the people who live here are convinced they could not feed their brains and souls in the same way anywhere else on the planet, and you'll get an idea why.

As you travel around, however, think about why Silicon Valley occurred here instead of in New York, Dallas, Chicago, or Los Angeles. Consider the efforts of hundreds of people to develop Silicon Valley clones in Europe, Russia, and Asia. And then meditate on the reasons why every other region has failed—largely miserably—to copy the San Francisco Midpeninsula's success.

There's a reason journalist Don Hoefler coined the term Silicon Valley for this area in a 1971 article for Microelectronics News. It wasn't because of the success of Stanford, HP, or any other organization. It was because of the rise of the semiconductor industry.

You can thank William Shockley's mother for that.

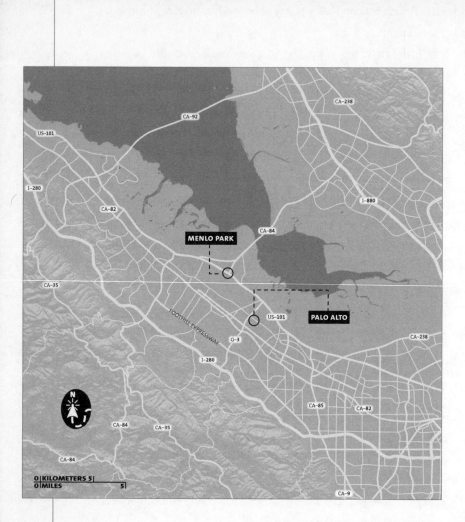

CA–238

CA–92

US–101

I–280

CA–82

I–880

CA–84

MENLO PARK

CA–35

FOOTHILL EXPRESSWAY

US–101

PALO ALTO

CA–238

G–3

I–280

N

CA–85

CA–82

CA–84

CA–35

CA–84

| 0 | KILOMETERS 5 | |
| 0 | MILES | 5 |

CA–9

PALO **ALTO** *and* MENLO **PARK**

PALO ALTO *and* MENLO PARK

PALO ALTO AND MENLO PARK HAND Silicon Valley a pair of idyllic suburbs that serve as engines for much of the local economy. Crucially, the former is home to Stanford University—without question the epicenter of this part of Silicon Valley. The school has been humming away since 1891, educating thousands of bright students. The college-town vibe permeates both Palo Alto and the neighboring Menlo Park.

Luckily for locals, Stanford has been judicious in the use of its sprawling grounds. The university's founder set aside thousands of acres of what has become prime real estate. During a couple of cash-strapped periods, it had to lease out some of this land to form the Stanford Shopping Center and Stanford Research Park. Overall, however, the university has done a remarkable job of preserving much of its acreage to give students a bucolic setting for learning. The Stanford campus also boasts a number of areas open to the public, including the elegant Rodin Sculpture Garden and "The Dish," which offers a vast, lush expanse for walkers and joggers. Such scenic areas provide a welcome respite from the strip malls and office parks that dominate so much of Silicon Valley.

Locals benefit from their own enterprise as well. Residents of Menlo Park, Palo Alto, and nearby Atherton make up one of the most affluent and well-educated collections of people in the country. Such good fortune is reflected by the comfortable—often breathtaking—houses along the tree-lined streets.

As you might expect, numerous shopping areas have sprung up to help separate these workers from their ample incomes. The Stanford Shopping Center is one of the highest-end malls in Silicon Valley. Meanwhile the shops, eateries, and bars along University and California Avenues cater to the college crowd and locals. Whether you're in the pricey shops, a bar, or a deli, Palo Alto gives off an upscale air that you won't find in some of the other suburbs.

Even in such a rarefied environment, however, it's impossible to escape Silicon Valley's business roots. After all, the town has been hosting electronics pioneers for more than a hundred years. In the span of a couple of blocks, you'll find the research lab of Federal Telegraph, which did much of the early work on vacuum tube technology, and the HP Garage where Bill Hewlett and David Packard started an

electronics giant. The latter is indeed Palo Alto's main claim to being the "Birthplace of Silicon Valley," although the old Fairchild Semiconductor headquarters down the road could fight for such a title as well.

Right next to Stanford is an industrial park packed full of company headquarters spanning the hardware, software, and biotech industries. Keeping technology-focused businesses close to campus has long been Stanford's preferred method of increasing interactions between students and enterprise.

Step into Menlo Park next door and you'll find the famed Sand Hill Road, where myriad venture capital companies operate. Just across the street from the venture dandies lies the atom-smashing Stanford Linear Accelerator, home to numerous scientific breakthroughs over the years.

Of late, Stanford and Palo Alto have specialized in producing billionaires—the founders of Sun Microsystems, Cisco Systems, Yahoo!, and Google all attended the university. Stanford graduates have managed to touch every era of Silicon Valley's development.

While not geographically in the center of Silicon Valley, it's not difficult to paint Palo Alto and Menlo Park as the lifeblood of the region.

THE STORY OF SILICON VALLEY USUALLY BEGINS AT BILL Hewlett and Dave Packard's garage. Another Palo Alto laboratory, however, made some lasting contributions to the region's reputation as an electronics hub well before Hewlett and Packard got going.

The Federal Telegraph Company helped push electronics work in San Francisco and the Midpeninsula area on three major fronts. It aided the development of wireless communications in the early part of the twentieth century, pioneered vacuum tube technology, and provided young engineers and electronics buffs with an opportunity to stay in Northern California and pursue the work that interested them—no small feat at the time.

PIONEERING THE AIRWAVES

Federal Telegraph dates back to the Australian-born and Stanford-educated Cyril Elwell. With help from some Stanford cohorts, Elwell sought and received the rights to Danish engineer Valdemar Poulsen's invention of an improved arc transmitter that could send speech through the air in a radius of up to 150 miles. Technology in hand, Elwell created what would become the Federal Telegraph Company in 1909 with some partners; they'd set up transmitters in San Francisco by 1910. One large transmitter was located on 48th Avenue between Noriega and Ortega Streets, while another was later placed in San Bruno

All that's left now of the Federal Telegraph Company is a historical marker, which sits close to 913 Emerson Street. You'll find it between some overgrown bushes near the corner of Channing Avenue and Emerson Street in a part of Palo Alto that's a mix of small shops and houses. While you're in the neighborhood, stop by the Peninsula Creamery Dairy Store at 566 Emerson; (650) 323-3175. Open Monday through Friday, this spot delivers old-time milk shakes and homemade everything else.

Early Electronics Companies

IN THE EARLY TWENTIETH CENTURY, THE San Francisco Bay Area had an unusual glut of amateur radio enthusiasts. While these radio aficionados are often ignored in the story of Silicon Valley, they actually paved the wave for the innovations that would occur decades later.

It's hard to pinpoint why the Bay Area attracted such a high quotient of radio experimenters. Historians, however, speculate that the city's role as a port and ties to the Navy put an early focus on the technology used for communication between ships.

A number of small radio and electronics companies began to crop up in the early years of the last century, most notably Federal Telegraph. The firm was also an incubator of sorts for three young electronics engineers: William Eitel, Jack McCullough, and Charles Litton.

The Bay Area companies had struggled to attract top talent and to match the support structure afforded to larger East Coast manufacturing rivals. This meant that the young electronics equipment firms—plagued by the Great Depression—had to make the most of their founders' skills and the skills of local enthusiasts. In some ways, the hardships turned out to be blessings.

In the lean years of the Depression, Litton left to found Litton Engineering Laboratories in 1932; Eitel and McCullough started their eponymous company in 1934. Both firms focused on producing high-quality, innovative products that East Coast giants could not match. In addition, they were able to snatch up homegrown talent from Stanford University, which zeroed in on electrical engineering early and churned out a number of bright young minds.

The Bay Area of the 1930s provided all these entrepreneurs with a unique setting where there was fierce competition among hungry firms but also a lot of sharing of ideas as the companies tried to make the most of what they had. This idea-swapping spirit would live on in Silicon Valley for decades—arguably up to today.

Stanford's Russell and Sigurd Varian provided the next major boost to the Bay Area electronics industry with their 1937 invention of the klystron, a key component of products ranging from radar devices to cancer treatments. After starting his own company, Russell Varian hired a youngster named Dave Packard to work on vacuum tubes. Packard was a friend of the venerable Charles Litton, too, remembering the inventor as the man "able to do everything better than anyone else."

Clearly the Bay Area was a small world. Varian Associates eventually acquired the first lease at the Stanford Research Park. In 1939 Hewlett-Packard opened for business—and the rest, as they say, is history.

Technophiles' passion for radio technology is an enduring theme in Silicon Valley. A hundred years ago radio hobbyists began morphing into electronics entrepreneurs. Later, multiple generations of Silicon Valley CEOs, executives, and engineers first tasted technology by toying with and building radios in their parents' basements. Such dabbling seems to have a profound effect on young minds.

near the current location of the San Francisco International Airport. The US Navy would go on to take over these stations during World War I.

More important for the future of Silicon Valley was Federal Telegraph's Palo Alto research laboratory. This lab let local workers not only hammer away on communications technology of the time but also experiment in new areas. Inventor Lee De Forest made the most of the opportunity. An audion is a type of vacuum tube device that amplifies electrical signals; while at the lab De Forest improved the technology to create a three-electrode version, now known as a triode. Described as one of the major inventions of the twentieth century, the triode or vacuum tube amplifier made it possible to set up long-distance telephone, radio, and radar networks. It also became a key component in other digital electronics.

About forty-five years later, in a factory just a few miles from the Federal Telegraph lab, Palo Alto–based Fairchild Semiconductor would begin mass-producing the silicon transistors that replaced vacuum tube technology.

Federal Telegraph's fortunes declined in the subsequent years, but its early contributions made a real impact on the area. Historians have pointed to the Federal Telegraph Company and Heiniz and Kaufman Incorporated as the top early electronics firms in the Bay Area and just about the only two with enough going on to keep talented youngsters at home.

STANFORD UNIVERSITY

STANFORD UNIVERSITY NEEDS LITTLE INTRODUCTION. IT has secured a spot as one of the top US colleges—not to mention the academic force behind the success of Silicon Valley. Be it HP's Bill Hewlett and Dave Packard, Sun Microsystems' Scott McNealy, Andy

Bechtolsheim, and Vinod Khosla, or Google's Larry Page and Sergey Brin, many of the dominant figures in the technology industry made their way to the business world via Stanford. The school has pumped out a seemingly endless stream of standout entrepreneurs, MBAs, engineers, and scientists.

Even aside from the academic excellence, Stanford holds its own as one of the most beautiful universities anywhere, with thousands of acres of land sweeping through the heart of Silicon Valley. Walk or drive through the Stanford campus today and you'll find reminders of the university's influence and prestige everywhere.

Most visitors start by cruising the mile-long Palm Drive—the impressive central artery of the campus. As you might guess, Palm Drive is flanked by two rows of towering palm trees. From this broad roadway you're free to head off to campus buildings, parking lots, athletic facilities, and scenic quads.

The major landmark that you'll see while on campus or even driving around Silicon Valley is the Hoover Tower, named for Stanford alumnus Herbert Hoover. Built in 1941, the structure juts up 285 feet and has an observation deck open 10:00 a.m. to 4:30 p.m.

Unlike the ostentatious tower, most of Stanford's campus is made up of rustic, foliage-rich grounds and a wide variety of Mission-style buildings. Century-old palms, ancient redwoods, and eucalyptus trees dominate the landscape. Without question the grounds give off a less manicured feel than other idyllic California campuses, such as Berkeley or Pomona College near Los Angeles. Here thin, dry grass lines the earth below the magnificent trees.

With its thousands of acres, Stanford can claim much more diverse landscapes than just about any other university, and the various nooks and crannies are worth a visit whether you're marching up to the pastoral Dish for a jog or heading to the Stanford Shopping Center to pick up some new clothes. Technology-minded types will want to aim straight for the Science and Engineering Quad (SEQ) and its William R. Hewlett Teaching Center, William Gates Computer Science Building, Paul Allen Center for Integrated Systems, and David Packard Electrical Engineering Building. You have to be a technology pioneer—and filthy rich—to have a building named for you on this lot of land.

HP founders and Stanford graduates Bill Hewlett and Dave Packard put down most of the $120 million to pay for the SEQ project. A good chunk of the funds for the other buildings came from Microsoft's founders Gates and Allen—neither of whom attended Stanford or, in fact, completed college at all.

The HP-themed buildings prove more striking than their Microsoft counterparts with their sleek lines, angles, and silvery finish. Both the Gates and Allen buildings seem to fit in better with the more traditional Stanford architecture. Those able to sneak into the Gates building courtesy of a friendly student will find numerous displays detailing Stanford's rich computing history. The displays—including such treasures as early Sun and Google computers—are managed by Stanford professors and the Computer History Museum in Mountain View.

After visiting the SEQ, a five-minute walk will take you to the Cantor Rodin Sculpture Garden with twenty bronzes by Auguste Rodin. To call this a unique feature of a university campus doesn't begin to do it justice. This spot proves particularly popular with families on the weekends. To take in even more nontech history, head over to the Red Barn next to Stanford's golf course. Included on the National Register of Historic Places, this 1879 building predates the university. It once housed some of the 550 horses of founders Leland and Jane Stanford; today it's used for equestrian classes. (Locals and students often refer to Stanford as The Farm to this day.)

A trip around the campus core proves easy enough, but visitors planning to hit up some of the more exotic Stanford locations will want to pick up a map from the school or online. Those heading to the university for functions during the week will likely have to pay for parking, while families and others on campus for a weekend stroll can park for free.

BIRTH OF AN ACADEMIC POWERHOUSE

Stanford University dates back to 1884, when California railroad magnate and former governor Leland Stanford set out to build a school in honor of his fallen fifteen-year-old son. The youngster's unexpected death from typhoid fever prompted Stanford and his wife to form the belief that "the children of California shall be our children." The couple started with close to 650 acres used primarily for a country home and the Palo Alto Stock Farm. Over time, the school consumed more than 8,000 acres of the surrounding area, which has since turned into the vast Stanford University campus.

Stanford University's main entrance is at the corner of El Camino Real and University Avenue. There's plenty more information on Stanford's attractions at www.stanford.edu; click on About Stanford. The school offers a wide variety of tours for prospective students as well as tourists and locals. For more information, see Visitor Information on the same Web site.

The school officially opened its doors in 1891. Unlike more traditional establishments, it welcomed male and female students and declined to form ties with a religious organization. A total of 559 men and women in the first class were taught by fifteen faculty members.

Stanford, like the entire Bay Area at the time, struggled to attract and keep gifted minds. Palo Alto itself wasn't much to speak of, and an economy based on growing fruits and nuts did little to enthuse budding scientists or businessmen. Over time, however, both school and region benefited from a collection of radio and electronics hobbyists who tried to do the unthinkable and set up businesses that could thrive in niches outside the clutches of large eastern corporations.

It took a solid fifty years and much creativity from numerous parties to make learning and working in Santa Clara County an attractive long-term option for bright youngsters. With the help of its ample resources and some good luck, Stanford became an engineering and science powerhouse. It has extended this strength to many fields of study over the subsequent decades.

From its early days Stanford has also functioned as the lifeblood of Silicon Valley, encouraging students to pursue their own business ventures while maintaining tight associations with both former professors and new crops of youngsters. This untraditional, adventurous approach to academics has certainly paid off: Stanford has an astonishing track record of producing some of the most successful young businesspeople on the planet. Sun, Silicon Graphics, Cisco Systems, Yahoo!, and Google all sprang from work done here. No other school has such deep ties to Silicon Valley.

▶ STANFORD RESEARCH PARK

THE STANFORD RESEARCH PARK MAY BE ONE OF THE university's more unusual efforts to raise extra crash and bolster its ties to industry. Frederick Terman, dean of engineering, spearheaded the development of this facility in the late 1940s at a time when the land-rich, cash-hungry university needed a way to fund its postwar growth and continue attracting talent. The school's charter forbade the sale of its vast grounds but did allow for leasing of the property. So Terman encouraged the school to dole out parcels of land to budding technology companies. In so doing, the university could develop closer links to industry and create an exchange of bright minds and resources.

The Stanford Research Park is located next door to the main campus in the area around Page Mill Road. For more information, visit www.stanford.edu; click on Introduction to Stanford.

CARL DJERASSI
Father of the Pill

IN THE MID-1950S STANFORD UNIVER-SITY professor Fred Terman worked his magic once again. The same fellow who convinced Hewlett and Packard and countless other Stanford graduates to conduct their business in Silicon Valley helped woo birth control pill co-inventor Carl Djerassi to Palo Alto.

Terman had already polished up the image of Stanford's Electrical Engineering Department and wanted to do the same for the school's Chemistry Department. He saw Djerassi as a great name to add to the rolls of Stanford's faculty. His persistence paid off in 1959, when Djerassi signed on. At the time, he was still working with Syntex, the Mexico-based company that had facilitated his contraceptives work. At both Djerassi's and Terman's urging, Syntex agreed to set up a research center in the Stanford Industrial Park.

Eventually the presence of high-profile Djerassi and Syntex led to a new crop of companies focused on biology and medicine. Such companies complemented the area's computing firms and helped expand Silicon Valley's industrial base into new realms.

Syntex—now dubbed Roche Palo Alto—operates on a large research site in the Stanford Research Park at 3431 Hillview Avenue. Djerassi is still a Stanford professor. You can find his Web page at www.stanford.edu/dept/chemistry/faculty/djerassi.

Varian Associates set up shop at the Stanford Industrial Park in the early 1950s, and other prominent firms soon followed. By 1977 close to seventy-five companies had located in the area, bringing with them some 26,000 staff. (Stanford Industrial Park was renamed Stanford Research Park in the 1970s.) The facility served as a model for other universities, which have worked hard to mimic its symbiotic relationship between academia and business. Today HP has its headquarters in the research park, as do numerous Silicon Valley heavyweights. Even *The Wall Street Journal* maintains an office here to keep an eye on the companies it covers.

Close to 150 firms (in about 160 buildings) operate in the research park, spanning the electronics, software, and biotechnology fields. In addition, law firms, venture capital companies, and financial services firms call the area home.

▶ THE STANFORD DISH

A FAVORITE FOR THE SILICON VALLEY OUTDOORSY SET IS the Stanford Dish. The actual 300,000-pound Dish—a radio telescope—spans 150 feet and sits atop a hill with Interstate 280 on one side and Stanford University proper on the other. But when locals talk about "the Dish," they're referring to a site that extends across several hundred acres below the 'scope itself. After spotting even a hint of sunlight, hundreds of residents head out to this area for a walk or jog. Folks in Palo Alto, Mountain View, and other nearby suburbs can reach the Dish in about ten or fifteen minutes, then set out on a 5-mile trek on a trail that weaves through grassy, tree-covered valleys before climbing to the telescope. If you take the hike, you'll enjoy tremendous views of the towns that make up Silicon Valley. You're likely to run into some wildlife, too, including myriad birds, squirrels, and cows. All told, the walk will last a little under two hours. You won't be disappointed.

In the good old days, the Dish never closed, and visitors were free to roam as they pleased across the expanse donated by Stanford. Now, however, Stanford has put policies in place that it believes will help preserve the land and keep wildlife happy. You can access the site for free from about sunup to 7 p.m., depending on the season.

> Finding the Dish can be a bit tricky for tourists. Your best bet is to head up Stanford Avenue to Junipero Serra and park on the side of the road; the entrance to the Dish will be visible. Another entrance can be found near Junipero Serra and Campus Drive East. Neither dogs nor bikes are permitted. For more information, see http://dish.stanford.edu.

PROFESSOR FREDERICK TERMAN
Father of Silicon Valley

SILICON VALLEY MAY WELL HAVE popped up somewhere else were it not for the guiding hand of ultimate Stanford man Frederick Terman. During the first half of the twentieth century, bright minds generally furthered their education on the East Coast, with its stellar universities and vibrant business community. Terman's goal was to end this exodus of talent from his beloved alma mater.

Terman—son of a prominent Stanford professor—had virtually grown up on the Stanford campus. He did his undergraduate work here then headed off to MIT to obtain a doctorate in electrical engineering. He may well have stayed on the East Coast were it not for his battle with tuberculosis, which made the warmer California climate desirable.

MIT degree in hand, Terman took up an assistant teaching post at Stanford and quickly carved out a niche for himself in the fields of radio and electronic technology. He loved to take students on field trips to visit technology-based companies in the Bay Area. The collegians would meet the likes of TV entrepreneur Philo Farnsworth and electronics gurus Charles Litton and the Varian brothers.

Two students—Bill Hewlett and Dave Packard—were inspired by these trips and made it clear to Terman that they would like to pursue a business venture of their own someday. The teacher nudged them to go after this idea, providing suggestions on products ripe for improvement and introducing them to people in the industry. He would go on to encourage numerous others as well. The notion of professors helping students start businesses was not a common one at the time. In fact, many credit Terman with pioneering the practice, which ultimately gave Stanford an attractive edge over East Coast institutions that wanted to keep their talent in-house.

The professor was also instrumental in the 1951 establishment of the Stanford Industrial Park, and in convincing the legendary William Shockley to set up his transistor laboratory in nearby Mountain View. Terman—along with Shockley and Intel co-founder Robert Noyce—truly earned the title "Father of Silicon Valley." He would go on to become the Stanford provost and have a tremendous impact on both the Engineering and Chemistry Departments. Most of all, the ideal of the academic entrepreneur that he pursued so vigorously lives on to this day in both Stanford and Silicon Valley.

The radio telescope was built in the 1960s and is owned and maintained by the SRI International research lab once affiliated with Stanford. It has been used for a wide variety of functions, including monitoring signals from GPS satellites, searching for signals from Mars-bound spacecraft, and helping calibrate space instruments.

▶ THE SILICON VALLEY ARCHIVES

IF YOU'RE A TRUE TECHNOPHILE, A HIDDEN TREASURE lurks within the vast Stanford University archival stores. Since 1986 technology researchers have been able to peruse the Silicon Valley Archives. This collection-within-Stanford's-Special-Collection is an amazing repository of documents, photos, interview transcripts, audiotapes, and videos from numerous prominent figures and organizations that have contributed to Silicon Valley's history. You'll find information on Apple Computer, Fairchild Semiconductor, the Homebrew Computer Club, Varian Instruments, and Frederick Terman, among others.

According to project historian Leslie Berlin, "We get to use all the resources of the Special Collection—all of the staff, the security systems and the beautiful, beautiful reading room" in the Cecil H. Green Library. In recent years Berlin and other historians have made a concerted effort to gather as many documents as possible from computing pioneers, many of whom had long since planted their papers in a closet and forgotten about them.

> You can find the Silicon Valley Archives home page at http://svarchive.stanford.edu. You can also search the material at http://oac.cdlib.org.

"I was in the process of interviewing people, and they would show me these documents in their basement where the edges of papers were being chewed off by mice or they were covered in mildew," Berlin said. "Most of these guys had no idea what to do with their stuff. They hadn't given it any thought. They had no idea this resource was right there."

Stanley the Robot Car

IF ALL THE ROBOT CARS IN THE WORLD were to hold a vote, they would elect Stanley their king.

Produced by Stanford's storied Artificial Intelligence Lab (SAIL), Stanley captured the $2 million Grand Challenge in October 2005. This government-sponsored event required an autonomous vehicle to cross 132 miles of Nevada desert packed with obstacles, diversions, and other racers. Stanley completed the event in style, cruising past rivals to finish the course in six hours and fifty-four minutes at an average speed of 19 miles per hour.

Few expected such a stellar run after the first Grand Challenge, held in March 2004. DARPA (Defense Advanced Research Projects Agency)—the ambitious research and development arm of the Defense Department—organized the contest in hopes of advancing robot technology. For the 2004 run, DARPA offered $1 million and called on universities, corporations, inventors, and entrepreneurs to try their hand at crafting robotic vehicles. It was, however, unprepared for the interest such a contest would generate. Proposed entrants included a motorcycle, sport utility vehicles, Hummers, all-terrain vehicles, and cars. Many relied on custom software, GPS devices, radar, laser radar, and tons of processing power for navigation. These robot cars could sense rocks, cliffs, and dips in the road.

Yet in the event, the vehicles failed to impress. Only two teams went any distance at all before breaking down.

Still, DARPA and the hungry robotics aficionados soldiered on, believing they could do much better in a second run. DARPA doubled the cash prize and crossed its fingers. And in the nail-biter of a race, Stanford's Stanley overtook the favorite Carnegie Mellon team and zoomed to the finish line, winning by eleven minutes.

The victory stood as a major accomplishment not only for Stanford but for robotics in general. Prior to the event, robotic cars could only go short distances at very slow speeds before hitting barriers or running amok. Yet five teams completed the course in 2005—a stunning total considering the disastrous first race just eighteen months earlier. Stanley, a modified Volkswagen Touareg, now appears at numerous conferences and technology gatherings and garners tremendous applause.

For more information about Stanley, see Stanford's Artificial Intelligence Lab located in the Gates Computer Science Building or visit http://ai.stanford.edu.

The Silicon Valley Archives have hit a couple of jackpots. When Apple Computer closed a museum at its Cupertino headquarters, it sent box after box of papers, marketing material, and other paraphernalia to the collection. In addition, Berlin managed to secure some prized possessions from William Shockley and Robert Noyce as a result of her research for The Man Behind the Microchip: Robert Noyce and the Invention of Silicon Valley.

Stanford has done a marvelous job of providing rich descriptions for all the items stored in its collections. Once researchers locate a particular item of interest via an online search, they put in a request, wait a couple of days, and then go visit the archives to dig through the materials.

UNIVERSITY AVENUE AND THE STANFORD SHOPPING CENTER

COMBINE THOUSANDS OF WELL-SUPPORTED COLLEGE students with tens of thousands of well-funded adults and what do you end up with? A shoppers' paradise. The main Stanford campus is surrounded by stores and restaurants, giving students and Palo Alto residents plenty of chances to spend their cash.

Central to the shopping experience is University Avenue—an extension of Palm Avenue that runs through Palo Alto and pulses with a lively collegiate feel. You can find a Stanford store full of T-shirts, hats, and sweaters; a pizza place; and a health food shop. There are also plenty of midrange to high-end restaurants along with clothing, antiques, and crafts stores. It's a great excuse for a weekend walk coupled with some window-shopping. Stroll a block or two away from University Avenue in any direction and you'll discover posh neighborhoods decked out with manicured lawns and sculpted trees.

More serious buyers will head to the Stanford Shopping Center.

JOHN HENNESSY
President of Stanford

HEADING UP AN INSTITUTION AS prestigious as Stanford University carries with it a certain amount of power. In true Silicon Valley fashion, John Hennessy complements this authority with board positions at technology giants and start-ups, as well as a penchant for investment.

Hennessy became Stanford's tenth president in 2000 after serving in a variety of roles at the university, including chair of computer science, dean of the School of Engineering, and provost. Before assuming the top post, he was perhaps best known for organizing a group of researchers to work on RISC (Reduced Instruction Set Computer) processor designs in 1981. This work became the foundation for MIPS Computer Systems—a company Hennessy co-founded during a sabbatical in 1984. (SGI bought the company in 1998, then spun it off.)

In addition to his work as an entrepreneur, Hennessy contributes his expertise to the boards of networking giant Cisco Systems and wireless semiconductor start-up Atheros Communications . . . not to mention a little firm called Google. He received a tidy 65,000 shares in Google for joining the board, then watched those shares turn into millions following the company's initial public offering.

This open-air mall makes use of the near-perfect weather to give shoppers a relaxing experience. You have to pay for such luxury, though: The Stanford Shopping Center boasts one high-end store after another and will take a toll on any credit card.

Those looking to avoid the crowds can head to a less dense strip on California Avenue with a number of shops and eateries. La Bodeguita—a Cuban restaurant and cigar lounge—proves a popular lunchtime spot with the Silicon Valley workers. It's at 463 South California.

▶ THE STANFORD THEATRE

IT MAY SEEM AN UNLIKELY SPOT FOR OLD HOLLYWOOD TO reside, but Palo Alto owns the market for movie classics in Northern California.

The Stanford Theatre has enjoyed a prime location on University Avenue since 1925. Over the decades the elegant, one-screen theater has entertained Stanford University students, Palo Alto residents, and other Bay Area denizens willing to travel out and catch one of their old favorites. Owned since 1987 by the David and Lucile Packard Foundation, the renovated facility features Greek and Assyrian ornamentation, chandeliers, a balcony, and a crimson velour curtain in addition to the spacious foyer. A "Mighty" Wurlitzer organ is played before shows start, during intermissions, and as patrons exit.

The theater is located at 221 University Avenue, Palo Alto, and can't be missed thanks to a glowing neon marquee. More information on the movies and showtimes is available at www.stanfordtheatre.org.

Typical weeks will have the Stanford Theatre showing six different films, most of them classics—*Gentlemen Prefer Blondes, How to Marry a Millionaire, It's a Wonderful Life* (shown every Christmas Eve). Come early to grab one of the 1,200 seats.

HEWLETT-PACKARD

SOME SILICON VALLEY COMPANIES BOOM AND BUST IN THE span of a few months. Others impress by hanging around for ten or twenty years. Hewlett-Packard has put every other success story to shame by thriving for decades and decades.

Many hold up HP as the first major technology player in the region. That, however, isn't exactly true. HP grew out of a vibrant electronics tradition that stretched from San Francisco to San Jose and included companies such as Federal Telegraph, Varian Associates, and Litton Engineering Laboratories. HP happened to emerge as the most successful and enduring member of this bunch.

BILL & DAVE'S EXCELLENT ADVENTURE

Bill Hewlett and Dave Packard both arrived at Stanford University in 1930 with a passion for electronics and a history of homemade gadget construction. Their interests were nurtured in college by Professor Fred Terman, who served as a type of conductor in Hewlett's and Packard's lives. He was the one who encouraged the two to start a business together, helping them with everything from suggesting products to introducing them to potential customers.

Hewlett and Packard graduated in 1934, the heart of the Great Depression. Times were tough in Palo Alto and elsewhere. So Packard accepted a job in New York working for GE, while Hewlett rounded out his education via some work at MIT and a research program back in Palo Alto.

In 1938 the two men were back in the area, where they officially kicked off a Silicon Valley tradition by founding a new company from their garage—the iconic HP Garage at 367 Addison Avenue, Palo Alto.

The pair dabbled with a variety of projects, making motors for telescopes, foul-line alert systems for bowling alleys, and even pulsating exercise machines. Eventually they made two crucial decisions: A coin flip decided that their new company would be called Hewlett-Packard, while an audio oscillator that Hewlett had designed at Terman's lab became their first product. Hewlett and Packard named the device the Model 200A, hoping the name would imply that they were on at least their second-generation of gear.

As it turned out, the Model 200A was cheaper and worked better than competing systems—the Silicon Valley recipe for success—and caught the eye of numerous customers, including Disney. Much has been made of this Disney deal. Some writers have described it as a huge project that ultimately made *Fantasia* a much better movie while also solidifying Hewlett-Packard's fortunes. Not so, according to Dave Packard. In his book *The HP Way,* he notes that HP "did not make a technical contribution" to the movie. Rather, Disney pushed HP to tweak its product all the way into the Model 200B. The company sold eight of these units to Disney for $71.50 each.

HP started to grow relatively quickly, expanding its product line and offices. The pair moved out of the garage in 1940, opening a new office at the corner of Page Mill Road and El Camino Real. Thanks to World War II, an influx of US government contracts pushed revenue from $5,000 to $34,000 by the end of the year.

THE HP WAY

When Bill Hewlett left to join the army, Dave Packard kept running the show. Revenue neared $1 million by 1943 with a product line of testing and electronics devices. By the 1950s HP was really soaring. Famously, the founders put some of their business objectives into writing in what would become known as the "HP Way."

The HP Way can seem a bit abstract to outsiders, but it's basically just a management philosophy that reflected how Hewlett and Packard thought a decent, innovative, and profitable company should function. It includes profit-sharing for almost all workers, the practice of leaving equipment unlocked so workers could run their own experiments, and the notion of everyone sharing the financial burden during lean times by reducing their hours rather than laying off staff.

HP headquarters are located in the Stanford Research Park at 3000 Hanover Street; (650) 857-1501. The headquarters of its well-known spin-off, Agilent, are at 395 Page Mill Road, which was the first HP-owned building and constructed in 1942. Neither company offers tours.

In the good old days, HP gave a wedding present or baby blanket to every employee who got married or had a child. It held barbecues at which Bill and Dave themselves would grill up steaks and serve them to the staff. Alas, these practices died out as the company grew.

There was more to the philosophy, including a total focus on the customer, an open invitation for workers to voice their opinions to executives, and a decentralized style of management. The goal is for workers to figure out their own unique way to get their jobs done rather than being governed by a rigid set of corporate guidelines. Taken as a whole, the HP Way helped turn the company into one of best places to work in Silicon Valley.

GROWING PAINS

HP continued to thrive over the next couple of decades and built out its product lineup in a couple of key areas. The company designed its first computer—the HP 2116A—as a tool for controlling its other test measurement products. It also started to move into the scientific calculator business. By the 1970s HP founders Hewlett and Packard began to scale back their day-to-day duties. Company veterans John Young and, later, Lew Platt, were tapped as CEOs.

Platt in particular enjoyed great success during the early part of his tenure—almost doubling company revenues. He also initiated the spin-off of test and measurement company Agilent in the 1990s. In so doing, of course, HP got rid of a huge chunk of its history.

But on the whole, Platt did not have an image or demeanor suited to the dot-com gold rush. He was once described as a "chess guy in a video game world," and this characterization could have carried over to HP as a whole by the time of his tenure. The company prided itself on a methodical decision-making process and a teamwork-friendly culture. Meanwhile the Internet boom often demanded rapid shifts in thinking to capitalize on "the next big thing" and to keep up with changes in technology.

Not shy about confronting the realities of HP's situation, Platt surveyed workers and other executives about the state of the company. The feedback they provided proved painful: HP, they said, had become a bloated, slow-moving force ill equipped to deal with the frenetic Internet age. Many saw a leadership change as necessary. After some urging, Platt agreed to step aside and kick off a new era at HP.

So for the first time in its history, HP hired an outsider as CEO. Carly Fiorina arrived from Lucent Technologies with the goal of turning HP into a faster-moving creature. With her, HP's board hoped to secure both substance and style.

MY BIG **FAT** GEEK **MERGER**

Fiorina's flair for the dramatic helped HP to a degree. The Internet boom had created a climate that rewarded a well-told story as much as actual results. Fiorina presented HP as a type of one-stop shop for everything from printers and PDAs to supercomputers. An impressive, smooth speaker, she was able to sell this vision to investors and analysts—many of whom believed HP was making a move away from dependence on its printing business and toward the nimbleness that would allow it to compete with the likes of Dell and Sun.

On the internal front, Fiorina set very ambitious revenue targets and shifted from a profit-sharing plan to one where employees would receive large bonuses for market share gains. Every move was accompanied by slick advertising campaigns, highlighting Fiorina's passion for marketing.

Even in the early days of her tenure, Fiorina became a polarizing figure at HP. Many employees were inspired by HP's new vigor, while others felt Fiorina was killing the best elements of the collegial HP Way. This situation came to a head in 2001 when HP announced its mega acquisition of Compaq. The contentious $18 billion deal—the largest ever in technology history—dominated Silicon Valley headlines for eight months. A proxy battle of fantastic proportions pitted Fiorina against major HP shareholder and former board member Walter Hewlett, the eldest son of company co-founder William Hewlett. Ultimately, Fiorina's

KEN KESEY AND THE ACID TESTS
Pushing pharmacological research to its limits

WELL BEFORE SILICON VALLEY ESTABLISHED itself as a biotech giant, a young Stanford student did his best to push the boundaries of pharmacological research. Author Ken Kesey attended Stanford's Creative Writing Program on a Woodrow Wilson scholarship in the early 1960s. While enrolled, he found his way into an army-sponsored experiment into the nature of hallucinogenic drugs. The government paid students such as Kesey to dabble with LSD and other mind-altering substances. He received $75 per session for his hard work, which took place under the watch of Stanford scientists at the Menlo Park Veterans Administration (VA) hospital.

The writer took a liking to the experiments and found a job as a night aide at the hospital, serving in its psychiatric ward. This work would provide the core material for Kesey's most famous novel, *One Flew Over the Cuckoo's Nest,* considered a classic of American literature.

During this time, Kesey and his wife lived in a cottage along the bohemian Perry Lane strip next door to the Stanford golf course. The drugs Kesey researched started to make their way back to the parties thrown as this house. This scene led to the famous Acid Tests in which Bay Area members of the counterculture ranging from Kesey and the Grateful Dead to the Hell's Angels all partied together in a scene made even more famous by Tom Wolfe's 1968 book *The Electric Kool-Aid Test.* Eventually Kesey moved to a wooden cabin, in nearby La Honda.

Those interested in Kesey won't want to go looking for the Perry Lane cottages. As it turns out, Wolfe didn't get the name of Kesey's street quite right in his novel. You'll need to look for Perry Avenue if you're in the area today. This is a spot you'll want to visit sooner rather than later. The tiny avenue can barely accommodate two cars driving by each other and holds only about a dozen houses on either side. You can still find about six of the humble cottages that existed when Kesey lived on the street—now decaying wooden shacks roofed by metal and plastic tarps. Much more elegant residences are popping up, however, and it won't be long before all the old cottages have been replaced.

Perry Avenue is now part of Menlo Park. Just off Sand Hill Road it runs between Leland and Vine. An easy way to find the small street is to perform an Internet map search for 11 Perry Avenue in Menlo Park. That will put you near the Leland end of the street.

stumping led to HP barely winning the proxy fight and closing the deal. HP's workforce expanded from 88,000 to 141,000 people overnight.

In 2005, HP's board decided to change directions once again and ousted Fiorina behind her back. It then hired former NCR CEO Mark Hurd—portrayed as a conservative, no-nonsense executive—as its new chief.

For all its ups and downs, HP remains one of the few constants in Silicon Valley and is respected the world over for treating employees and customers well. In a region where people rarely admire the past, it is a cherished throwback. Silicon Valley considers the company one of its treasures.

THE HP GARAGE

THE FAST-PACED, BOOM-AND-BUST NATURE OF THE technology industry tends to undermine the work of historians. Scholars go searching for old corporate headquarters or the former residences of luminaries and find that they've been torn down and rebuilt many times over. That's what makes the HP Garage such a rarity.

One of Silicon Valley's best-preserved links to its past, this humble 12-by-18-foot structure marks the spot where Bill Hewlett and Dave Packard started work on their first products. From here Hewlett-Packard would evolve into one of Silicon Valley's biggest and most innovative employers.

Unfortunately, tourists cannot see into the garage—or the house and shed also part of the property. The site remains zoned for residential use in an effort by HP to placate neighbors in the quaint, tree-lined Palo Alto neighborhood. The firm does, however, hold business meetings at the house, and periodically hosts corporate events where visitors can see the site.

Those lucky enough to enter will be transported back in time. The garage itself has been re-created to model what it might have looked like when Hewlett and Packard were working there. HP has put up workbenches, tools, and early products inside the garage. The cramped shed next-door where Bill lived in 1938 has been outfitted with a bed, a desk, and a sink, just as he experienced it. In the house— which Dave occupied with his wife, Lucile—efforts have been made to replicate their living room and kitchen, while the dining room has been turned into a makeshift boardroom. An HP employee lives in the upstairs flat, helping HP stay in line with city codes and making nice with the neighbors.

Thousands of people a year come by the property and try to peek in the windows of the main residence or take photos of the garage, which is clearly visible from the street. A marker outside the house designates it the BIRTHPLACE OF SILION VALLEY and recounts a brief portion of the HP story.

"THE ROASTS NEVER QUITE TASTED THE SAME"

The story of the HP Garage property began in the early 1900s, when a house and small shed were constructed. Well-known physician Dr. John Spencer and his wife took up residence in the house; a couple of years later Spencer was tapped as the first mayor of Palo Alto. By 1918 the property owner decided to split the house into two separate apartments—a configuration that has continued throughout its history. And around 1924 a garage popped up on the lot.

Both Hewlett and Packard graduated from nearby Stanford in 1934. The pair had decided to follow the advice of their professor Fred Terman and start a business together but figured they could use some more experience first. Packard headed east to work for GE, while Hewlett did graduate work at MIT and then returned to Stanford to conduct more research. By 1938 the pair were ready to become businessmen, although they still weren't exactly clear about what they would make.

In this Addison Avenue home, they discovered an almost perfect property. Dave and Lucile Packard took up the first-floor apartment, while Bill Hewlett lived in the humble shed out back. The landlady then let the pair set up a workshop in the garage. There they hammered away on projects such as a motor controller helping the telescope at Lick Observatory track objects better and a bowling alley device that chirped when someone crossed the foul line. During these experimental times the house, too, became part of the manufacturing process. Hewlett and Packard would often spray-paint some of their products and then cart them into the home's oven to make the markings permanent. Health inspectors have since marveled at the idea of cooking what was probably lead-based paint inside the house. Lucile Packard is said to have remarked, "The roasts never quite tasted the same after that."

You'll find the HP Garage—a model for countless similar makeshift workshops in Silicon Valley—at 367 Addison Avenue, Palo Alto. More information on the garage is available at www.hp.com/hpinfo/abouthp/histnfacts/garage/.

Eventually the inventors came up with their first real success—an audio oscillator that proved attractive to Disney and others. Hewlett and Packard closed out 1939 with $5,369 in sales and needed to find a new location for their growing business. In addition, Hewlett left his wee shack and moved into a proper house with his new wife, Flora. In 1940 HP started working out of a shop on 481 Page Mill Road, and Packard and his wife moved to Barron Park in Palo Alto.

While HP had but a short run in the garage, the city has happily grabbed on to the site as the "Birthplace of Silicon Valley." (The proud citizens of Mountain View dispute this claim, calling for the original site of William Shockley's transistor lab on San Antonio Road to hold the birthplace title.)

Rather remarkably, the garage has remained standing throughout the history of the Addison property. In fact, when HP purchased the property in 2000, it found the original garage roof still intact, along with the original foundation slab and the original, unpainted inside of the wooden building. The firm paid for a restoration of the garage, the main house, and the shed. It rededicated the site, which is a California landmark, in 2005.

STANFORD LINEAR ACCELERATOR CENTER

FEW PEOPLE EQUATE BRUSHING UP ON THEIR HIGH-ENERGY physics knowledge with a good time. For that reason, the Stanford Linear Accelerator Center (SLAC, pronounced slack) can seem more than daunting. It can seem downright boring. And that's the very image the scientists at SLAC have been trying to fight for decades.

SLAC (tours available) stretches over 460 acres of prime real estate owned by Stanford University and provides scientists around the globe with one of the top centers for studying high-energy physics. Perhaps its most stunning piece of gear is the 2-mile-long Stanford Linear Collider. Here you can see an aboveground portion of the collider year-round, as well as peeking at underground caverns that hold more equipment, during select periods when experiments aren't under way. (The best time to catch the underground area is between July and September, although there are no guarantees during this stretch, either.) You can't help but marvel at the structure: One can see from one end to the other with ease as the facility divides the hilly SLAC land and cruises right beneath Interstate 280.

SLAC provides tours almost every day and plays host to thousands of visitors each year. Upon arriving at the scenic facility, you're escorted to a mini museum packed full of information about the center. From there, you're driven to the visitor portion of the collider and given the technology basics. Besides the collider, you'll learn about

CARLY FIORINA
The most powerful businesswoman on the planet

BY THE LATE 1990S, VENERABLE Hewlett-Packard realized that its glow had faded. Looking for pizzazz, the company hired new CEO Carleton (Carly) Fiorina in 1999. With this stroke she became the most powerful businesswoman on the planet.

Fiorina's background might seem unlikely to create a hard-charging, super-ambitious executive. The daughter of a University of Texas law school professor, she received undergraduate degrees in medieval history and philosophy from Stanford. People who knew her in her college days have described her as showing no inclination toward business whatsoever. Still, she decided to pursue an MBA at the University of Maryland with little more than an inkling that this might be the right direction for her. In no time Fiorina became enthralled by the business curriculum and rose to the top of the school's ranks.

Fiorina then snagged a coveted position as a mid-ranking sales manager at AT&T. A young, attractive female, she stood out in a department dominated by AT&T's old-boy network. Indeed, Fiorina would prove adept at besting the old guard and establishing herself as a vital contributor.

In 1995 AT&T tasked Fiorina with spinning off its telecommunications and research business. This work included everything from picking the new company's name to selling the spin-off to Wall Street. On April 4, 1996, Fiorina rang the closing bell at the New York Stock Exchange, having watched the $3 billion IPO of her new firm—Lucent—become the biggest in history. Fiorina continued to earn accolades in her new post.

This high profile executive attracted HP when it went looking for a plucky outsider to take control of the company. Not only was HP gaining a technology-savvy executive, but it was also pulling in a marketing and sales standout.

Fiorina's tenure at HP was defined by controversy. She did deliver a polished, slick image to HP and turned in decent results during a difficult economic period. Still, the company oscillated between profits and losses. Most of all, Fiorina will be remembered for the decision to acquire Compaq Computer in the largest technology merger in history. It was this decision (and the firm's subsequent struggles) that led to her 2005 ouster.

the Stanford Positron Electron Asymmetric Ring (SPEAR) and the Stanford Synchrotron Radiation Laboratory (SSRL)—lovely stuff if you're into those kinds of things. And you'll hear about the Gamma-ray Large Area Space Telescope.

INSIDE SLAC

SLAC's famous particle shooters lie 25 feet below the ground and fire off both electrons and positrons, which travel 2 very straight miles and then curve through a tube before colliding. SLAC runs a number of experiments with the collider, and scientists located around the facility collect data day and night. In fact, SLAC boasts the world's largest database, which is needed to sort through the immense amount of information that this facility produces.

To get a sense of the collider's speed, imagine a rifle firing a bullet at the same time as a particle leaves the electron gun. By the time the electron has traveled 3 miles, the bullet will have only gone 4 inches—not even exiting the rifle's barrel.

Since work on the linear accelerator started in 1962, SLAC has secured a number of scientific firsts. It pioneered work on quarks and has claimed three Nobel Prizes for various achievements in the field. It also set up the first World Wide Web page in North America.

For more information on SLAC (and to book tours), visit www.slac.stanford.edu. The center is located at 2575 Sand Hill Road in Menlo Park and can be reached at (650) 926-3000.

Overall, SLAC—pumped with funding from the Department of Energy and staffed with graduate students from across the globe—ponders some of the most fundamental questions in science, from how matter behaves over time to how proteins operate. It's been at the forefront of physics research for decades and doesn't appear to be slowing down . . . God willing.

You wouldn't think that one of the most delicate scientific instruments on the planet would be located next to the San Andreas fault, but it is. Still, SLAC has operated relatively unaffected by earthquakes over the years—though it did have to make some repairs after the 1989 temblor. It must also make constant adjustments for the minute effects that the moon and Pacific tide have on particles and its machinery.

OVER THE YEARS, BASHING XEROX'S PALO ALTO RESEARCH Center (PARC) has turned into an art form. Business types huddle together and giggle over how inept PARC—or rather Xerox—was at turning cutting-edge inventions into profitable franchises. Entrepreneurs marvel at out how easily PARC let its research and development work fall into the hands of companies such as Apple and Sun Microsystems. The center seems almost an archetype of the way big businesses can miss out on capitalizing on their own research. (No public tours available, although visitors can attend weekly speeches at PARC.)

In reality Xerox wasn't as hapless at making good on its research as many modern-day observers would have you believe. In fact, PARC was quite exceptional not only at creating an amazing range of inventions but also at helping Xerox's bottom line.

PARC's campus is located on a beautiful, hilly bit of land in Palo Alto. The lab doesn't offer any tours, although you can attend the PARC Forum speaker events held just about every Thursday at the George E. Pake Auditorium. Most of the talks are open to the public and cover a wide range of topics on cutting-edge research being done by folks around the globe. The forums aren't usually crowded, and they provide a nice excuse to take in the lush PARC campus.

A HISTORY OF FUTURISM

PARC officially came to life at 3180 Porter Drive in Palo Alto in July 1970; in 1975 Xerox opened a larger facility for researchers at the current Coyote Hill Road location. By 1973 the lab had the first laser printer

PAUL KUNZ
World Wide Webicist

IT'S NOT ALL PARTICLE ACCELERATION and energy collisions at SLAC. Well, okay, it's *almost* all particle acceleration and energy collisions. Every now and then, though, the physicists' unrelenting quest for knowledge pushes them in some unexpected directions.

Take Paul Kunz. His business card outs him as an experimental physicist at SLAC and, in fact, he spends most of his days in that role. Back in 1991, however, he enjoyed a run as an Internet pioneer.

He had been in communication with a chap named Tim Berners-Lee from CERN, the European Particle Physics Laboratory in Geneva, Switzerland. Berners-Lee developed something called the World Wide Web—you've probably heard of this—in 1989 and thought it might be useful for swapping information among scientists. Along with the Web, Berners-Lee developed tools for displaying information on what would become Web sites and a protocol for sending the data.

Kunz heard about the World Wide Web but didn't pay much attention. Then in September 1991 he visited Berners-Lee at CERN. There Kunz became interested in Berners-Lee's Web interface to CERN's IBM mainframe. He vowed to create something similar back at SLAC and see if the two could swap information.

So on December 12, 1991, Kunz set up the first Web server in North America. Really, it was the first outside Europe. Almost overnight, word of SLAC's new system—which suddenly let scientists search its valuable database with relative ease—spread throughout the scientific community. Many other labs started to look at the World Wide Web for the first time.

"It was the first page people wanted to use," Kunz said. "And it's not an accident that the World Wide Web developed at a high-energy physics lab." Early writings by Berners-Lee explained: "In few disciplines is the need for wide-area hypertext so apparent and at the same time so soluble as in particle physics. The need arises from the geographical dispersion of large collaborations, and the fast turnover of fellows, students, and visiting scientists. . . . Fortunately, the community necessarily has a good computing and network infrastructure."

Should you happen to stop by Paul Kunz's office at SLAC, you'll see the original SLAC Web pages up and running. Or check them out at www.slacstanford.edu/history earlyweb/firstpages.shtml.

running, churning out documents at one page per second. This invention would go on to serve as the basis for Xerox's hugely profitable printing business. PARC also put out a patent memo describing new networking technology called "Ethernet" that would become the standard for linking computers. It developed the Superpaint frame buffer, which made it easier to process bulky animation and graphics data—technology that would win an Emmy. And it fired up the Alto personal computer—the first genuine personal computer, complete with a mouse, a graphical user interface (GUI), and the menus and icons so familiar today.

Such a flood of innovation was made possible by Xerox's attitude toward the research and development group. It hired some of the most talented researchers on the planet and let them beaver away in an unstructured environment. Most importantly, Xerox gave the researchers ample funding for their work at a time when venture capitalism was immature.

Core to Xerox's mission with PARC was the development of "the office of the future." The company didn't know exactly what such an office would look like, but it did know it wanted to own the technology ahead of the competition—namely IBM.

The Alto computer emerged as PARC's most obvious tool for future office workers. It sits at the heart of where PARC succeeded and Xerox failed. You can argue that today's PCs differ little from this first attempt at a device that could fit under someone's desk and function as a personal workstation. A team of Xerox researchers had developed a relatively powerful computer that had a user-friendly graphical interface and that could be linked to other Altos via Ethernet. Anyone who saw an Alto wanted one, and workers both in and out of PARC were fascinated with the system.

To call such a product ahead of its time hardly does it justice, especially when you consider that back then, most computer users had to fight for space on large, bulky systems. Many stories have been written about Apple's Steve Jobs taking a tour of PARC and then "borrowing" the

Alto's innovations for Apple's Macintosh. Exactly how much inspiration Apple took from PARC and how much similar work was already under way at Apple remains up for debate, although Jobs certainly found the graphical interface software an inspiration and used the Alto to refine his concept of what personal computers should look like.

The Alto also inspired Sun co-founder Andy Bechtolsheim to design a workstation that could be used by individual researchers, freeing them from sharing larger, more expensive machines. "The Alto computer was really the only personal computer or workstation on the planet," Bechtolsheim said in an interview. "There was no such thing anywhere else. If you hadn't seen the Alto, it was hard to imagine it. . . . The main thing was they didn't want to turn this into a commercial product. I kept struggling to figure out why they wouldn't want to sell this."

Stories abound about PARC researchers trying to sell their work to Xerox management. The old-line company, however, struggled to see how things like personal computers or Ethernet networking could do much to improve its fortunes in the near term. Still, as some PARC historians—most notably Michael Hiltzik in his book *Dealers of Lightning*—have pointed out, it would have been difficult for the large printing-focused Xerox to change gears and begin hawking such products as PCs and net-working protocols. Alas, it seems Xerox PARC will forever be linked to the notion of unfulfilled business promise.

You'll find the campus at 3333 Coyote Hill Road, Palo Alto For a calendar of events and talks, visit www.parc.xerox.com/events or call (650) 812-4000.

Many of the PARC researchers would scamper off to Silicon Valley start-ups over the years. Meanwhile, the lab continued to pump out a steady stream of new ideas and inventions. In 2002 Xerox PARC turned into PARC Inc.—a subsidiary of Xerox. It now has the freedom to work on pushing technology forward with other companies via research and development projects, although Xerox remains its largest customer.

HOPES, DREAMS, INNOVATION, AMBITION, GREED, AND impetuousness—they're all found in abundance on Sand Hill Road. As, quite often, are massive profits. Those souls who think they've come up with the greatest idea since instantpeanutbutter.com all seem to make their pilgrimage to this stretch of pavement and start pitching.

Sand Hill Road makes life relatively easy on cash-hungry start-ups. The road itself links the scenic 280 freeway with Stanford University and prominent Silicon Valley artery El Camino Real. Myriad venture capital firms have set up shop here. It's really the West Coast's take on Wall Street.

If you head to Sand Hill Road, make sure to turn off into one or two of the business parks. Elegant, sculptured gardens surround many of the offices. And you owe it to yourself to see what $144 per square foot in rent (that was the price at the dot-com peak, 2000) looks like.

Once you're done with the venture capital bit, you can cruise down the road to Stanford and the Stanford Shopping Center or come to grips with particles at the Stanford Linear Accelerator that sits across the street.

► 3000 SAND HILL ROAD

PROPERTY MAGNATE TOM FORD DEVELOPED THE IDEA FOR 3000 SAND Hill Road in the late 1960s, hoping to create a vibrant spot for business types. Few would fault his thinking. That era saw a dramatic rise in the numbers of electronics and semiconductor companies in the area; this in turn created a demand for a new type of funding that could move with the speed so crucial to these rapidly advancing fields.

The Menlo Park location that Ford selected for his facility put venture capitalists within striking distance of the San Jose and San Fran-

HP's Infamous Mole Hunt

IN 2006 HP'S BRASS HAD ONLY themselves to blame for battering the company's once sparkling image. Executives including CEO Mark Hurd and then chair Patricia Dunn confessed to participating in an internal probe meant to flush out a board member who had leaked information to reporters. Ultimately, HP did find its leaker—but in so doing it also found a gushing fountain of negative ink.

HP's concerns over leaks to the media arose in 2005 when reporters from *BusinessWeek* and *The Wall Street Journal* exposed parts of the company's boardroom discussions—including intense squabbles—that took place during former CEO Carly Fiorina's tenure and later under CEO Mark Hurd. It was clear that at least one member of HP's board of directors had been talking to reporters. So the company started a formal investigation to find the leaker. When, in January 2006, details of yet another executive planning session hit the press, HP escalated its investigation. That's when the real trouble began.

Aided by outside investigative firms, HP secured the personal phone records of its directors, some employees, reporters, and family members of these people. The phone records were obtained via a dubious technique euphemistically called "pretexting." This form of fraud has an impersonator contact a phone company to obtain the phone records of an individual and supply information such as someone's date of birth and Social Security number to convince the phone company to release the records.

HP's investigators also followed some suspects and tried to trick one reporter by embedding tracking software in a fake e-mail to see where she sent the information.

All told, HP was found to have conducted one of the most questionable corporate investigations in recent history, prompting probes by the California attorney general, the SEC, and Congress. In September 2006 HP pushed out Dunn and promoted Hurd to the chairmanship in an effort—itself controversial—to deal with the crisis. Other board members, too, left the company.

The scandal proved a huge blow to HP's image and distracted the company at a time when it was finally showing consistent financial performance after numerous rocky quarters. And ironically, HP's probe into its leak ended up disclosing many more juicy details about boardroom disarray than the leak itself ever had.

cisco airports. It kept them close to Stanford and many of the Valley's most prominent companies. In addition, it offered relaxing surroundings such as rolling hills and the prime residential enclaves of Woodside and Atherton. Lastly, both the venture capitalists and their business partners could take in all San Francisco has to offer when their work was done.

For all these reasons, Ford's facility remains today the prime venture capital location. Companies such as Sequoia Capital, Leapfrog Ventures, and Menlo Ventures share buildings and courtyards and can see which start-ups have visited rivals to make their sales pitch from their office windows.

> This famed venture capitalist facility sits at, well, 3000 Sand Hill Road. More information on Sand Hill Road can be found at the companion web site for this book— www.theduckrabbit.com/siliconvalley.

THE CAPITALISTS AND THE CRASH

Plenty of stories have been penned about the number of sales pitches that venture capitalists bought during the heady days of the Internet boom. Just about any company looking to sell anything online, it seemed, could secure a few million dollars in those glory days. Looking back, this period didn't do much for the reputation of the venture capital craft. Many grew to view the firms as greedy and not terribly savvy. Professional investors, it was felt, are meant to see things a bit more clearly than the Average Joe and should have known the bubble would explode.

Which it did, and many of the so-called vulture capitalists went out of business. The firms that had started up with hopes of cashing in on the dot-com frenzy had no staying power. The old guard remained but in a weakened state.

Today entrepreneurs view venture capitalists with a wary eye. Plenty of start-ups still want and need the cash. Their top executives, however, often feel that venture capitalists try to exert too much control over their young concerns, and fear that they will be pushed

ARTHUR ROCK
The first major Silicon Valley venture capitalist

AFTER GRADUATING FROM HARVARD Business School in 1951, Arthur Rock ended up at New York investment banking firm Hayden Stone. At that time, formal venture capital firms didn't exist, but young companies could turn to wealthy family institutions such as the Rockefellers or Whitneys for funds.

In 1957, however, something unusual happened. A group of eight scientists working for Nobel Prize winner William Shockley decided to break away from his Mountain View–based transistor lab. They hoped to be hired as a group by a large company or, even better, to start their own venture together, though they figured the latter option was a long shot.

One of the eight—Eugene Kleiner—knew of Hayden Stone because his father had a brokerage account there. So he sent the group's request for help finding a corporate patron to the firm, and it landed on Rock's desk.

Intrigued, Rock and co-worker Arthur Coyle flew out to San Francisco and met with the scientists. They became convinced that the best possible course of action would be to help the group find a larger company to fund their efforts as a new venture. After thirty-five companies passed on the idea, Sherman Fairchild—the head of Fairchild Camera and Instrument and the largest stockholder in IBM—bit.

The success of Fairchild Semiconductor solidified Silicon Valley's place as the hub of semiconductor development. Rock, like others, has looked back at Fairchild's founding as the key reason that this area came to dominate the rise of the computing industry.

When two of Fairchild's founders, Robert Noyce and Gordon Moore, looked to break out and start their own company, Rock stepped in once again with guidance. He had moved out to Silicon Valley in 1961 and created Davis and Rock with partner Tommy Davis to invest in budding technology firms. The firm was a huge success, investing in the likes of Teledyne and Scientific Data Systems—a company later acquired by Xerox for close to $1 billion.

Rock eventually broke off from Davis and in 1968 helped Noyce and Moore organize the financial structure around their new company, Intel. Rock took the position of chairman at the company and has said that Intel was the only one of all his investments that he knew would be a success, thanks to Noyce's and Moore's talents.

A few years later, Rock also put some of the initial money into Apple Computer.

The example that Fairchild and Rock set fueled a new era in Silicon Valley where it became an accepted practice for employees to break off from their parent company, seek funding, and go it alone.

out in favor of more seasoned executives. Still, even those most critical of the venture capital game admit that some top-class firms do have the best interests of their young clients, investment partners, and the technology scene at heart.

▶ IN-Q-TEL, MENLO PARK

ONE SAND HILL ROAD COMPANY WINS THE TITLE OF THE spookiest venture capitalist in Silicon Valley.

In-Q-Tel fired up operations in 1999 as the venture capital arm of the Central Intelligence Agency (CIA). The not-for-profit organization, named for the gadget-happy character from the James Bond movies, builds on a long history of direct and indirect government funding of Silicon Valley technology. In this particular case, In-Q-Tel puts funds behind companies that it believes can aid US intelligence-gathering operations.

"By the 1990s, the blistering pace of commercial IT innovation was outstripping the ability of government agencies—including the CIA—to access and incorporate the latest information technology," In-Q-Tel says on its Web site. "This commercial innovation was driven by private sector research and development investment which placed billions of dollars, and the nation's top talent, behind commercial technology development. For the CIA's Directorate of Science and Technology, the information revolution was creating a new and widening gap."

> In-Q-Tel refuses to publicize the exact location of its offices, but you can have a snoop around the snoops by visiting 2440 Sand Hill Road. Or so said a couple of guys in black trench coats.

So the firm began investing between $1 million and $3 million in promising start-ups. Any money made from the investments goes back into In-Q-Tel's coffers and is put toward future funding.

With headquarters in Arlington, Virginia, In-Q-Tel also has an office located on the high-profile venture capital hub of Sand Hill

Road. And from the outside it looks like any other venture capital operation—until you notice the cameras monitoring visitors and the fingerprint scanners used to govern access to the offices. It backs a wide variety of start-ups dabbling in the storage, nanotechnology, sensor, and networking markets. Of course it also funds some more controversial ventures, such as those working on facial recognition and database monitoring technology.

The success of In-Q-Tel has inspired the government to consider other, similar operations. The army, for example, started its own venture capital arm called OnPoint Technologies in 2002.

⏻ SRI INTERNATIONAL

MORE THAN A DECADE BEFORE AN ACTUAL PERSONAL computer would arrive, Douglas Engelbart demonstrated much of the technology that would come to define the device. Engelbart and a team of researchers put on what many consider the most impressive display in computing history when they unveiled the NLS online system in front of 1,000 computer geeks at the Convention Center in San Francisco.

You can find SRI at 333 Ravenswood Avenue just a couple of miles from Stanford's campus. The video from Engelbart's 1968 demo is available at http://sloan.stanford.edu/mousesite/1968Demo.html.

The year was 1968, and most people's relationship with computers consisted of feeding thousands of punched cards through massive mainframes. Engelbart and his team at the Stanford Research Institute (SRI) in Menlo Park obliterated this paradigm. The SRI team set up a network that allowed Engelbart to sit in front of a computing console in San Francisco and then tap into systems back in Menlo Park.

That sixty-three-acre headquarters today hosts an impressive array of gear, including robotics, laser, sensor, drug and networking labs. The SRI campus appears to come straight out of the 1950s—its drab beige buildings sticking out among the Menlo Park homes and manicured gardens. The retro look should give SRI away, but, if you're struggling to find it, just search for the building with a guardhouse.

THE MOTHER OF ALL DEMOS

The basics of Engelbart's computing console were impressive enough. The audience, for the first time, saw Engelbart's invention of the computer mouse. In addition, they watched as he demonstrated a graphical display that allowed him to enter text and then manipulate it by cutting and pasting. If he clicked on a term such as "Grocery List," they looked on as he was brought to a full list of all the products his wife wanted him to buy at the store. Engelbart could group the items using his mouse and move through different categories via the linking system—a precursor to today's hyperlinking that allows us to move around the World Wide Web. Engelbart even showed them a graphical map of all the places he had to go in a given day while running errands. He could click on a location and receive information about an appointment, for example, or what he needed to purchase at a given spot.

But as the man says on TV, that's not all.

During the presentation, Engelbart communicated with his team back at headquarters via a telecommunications headset. Even more impressive, the Menlo Park researchers appeared on a video screen along with Engelbart. Audience members in San Francisco were able to see the Menlo Park crew and their equipment. It was the first-ever videoconference.

At the end of the ninety-minute presentation—now known as "the Mother of All Demos"—the audience gave Engelbart and his team a standing ovation. They had never seen anything like this and would never forget it.

INNOVATING SINCE 1946

Astoundingly, Engelbart had actually envisioned almost all of this technology in 1950 and spent eighteen years turning his dream into reality. Plenty of people called him crazy along the way, but Engelbart managed to convince SRI to let him set up the Augmentation Research Center and pursue the technology. Years later, researchers at Xerox PARC would create a type of personal computer that brought much of Engelbart's work to individuals. Then companies such as Apple and IBM would refine the technology in the early 1980s.

While the most dramatic, the Engelbart breakthrough was just one in a long line of innovations to come out of SRI.

GEORGES DORIOT
The Venture Capital General

THE FATHER OF US VENTURE CAPITALISM?
Who is General Georges Doriot, Alex?

Yes, it took a French-born, US Army general to get the venture capital machinations flowing. An odd combination perhaps, but the right one.

Born in France in 1899, Doriot served as an artillery officer in the French army during the First World War and later graduated from the University of Paris. In 1921 he took off for the United States and ended up at Harvard Business School. Just five years later Doriot was tapped as assistant dean and associate professor of industrial management at that school.

Over the next few years, he became a naturalized citizen and started working with the US military. In particular, he helped create the Army Industrial College for the US War Department. In his role as chief of the Military Planning Division, Doriot would recruit talented researchers, scientists, and industrial planners for the United States during World War II. Under his direction, the US military made better use of plastics and fine-tuned its gear for different climates and conditions. In short, Doriot helped add a new appreciation for technology in some unique areas.

At the end of the war, Doriot went back to Harvard and stayed on as a teacher until 1966. In 1946, however, he also started the American Research and Development Corporation—the first publicly owned venture capital firm. Close to half of ARD's shares were in the hands of insurers and educational bodies. ARD put its $5 million bankroll behind young companies in exchange for a piece of their ventures.

One of Doriot's best-known investments was a $70,000 gamble on a company called Digital Equipment Corporation in 1959. DEC would go on to be one of the first major hardware success stories, paving the way for the likes of Sun Microsystems and Silicon Graphics Inc. (DEC would later be acquired by Compaq, which was then bought by Hewlett-Packard.) When it went public in 1968, DEC has a reported market value of $37 million.

In more than twenty years at the helm of ARD, Doriot is credited with a 15 percent average return on his investments in more than 150 companies. He died in 1987.

Since the 1920s, Stanford leaders had pursued the idea of setting up a research institute that would allow the university and students to charge after new ideas. The Great Depression and then World War II delayed the development of such a research center. But in 1946 Stanford got its act together and set up SRI as a nonprofit organization. A year later the venture moved to a new campus in Menlo Park. Even in these early days, a staff of about 200 dabbled in areas ranging from the study of rubber-producing plants to air pollution. This broad work fit in well with SRI's charter, which is the same today as in 1946:

> SRI, A NONPROFIT CORPORATION, IS COMMITTED TO DISCOVERY AND TO THE APPLICATION OF SCIENCE AND TECHNOLOGY FOR KNOWLEDGE, COMMERCE, PROSPERITY, AND PEACE. SRI HAS A BROAD CHARTER THAT ENCOURAGES US TO MAKE A DIFFERENCE IN THE WORLD THROUGH BASIC AND APPLIED RESEARCH, RESEARCH SERVICES, TECHNOLOGY DEVELOPMENT, AND COMMERCIALIZATION OF OUR INNOVATIONS.

Over the years SRI has mixed it up, working for the private sector as well as government customers. In the 1950s, for example, it assisted Disney in picking the site for Disneyland. Later it built an airline reservation and check-in system for Scandinavian Airline System that IBM would tweak for other airlines, banks, and stores. SRI also teamed with the Defense Department's Advanced Research Projects Agency on the creation of the ARPAnet—the precursor to the Internet. The first ARPAnet transmission traveled from UCLA to SRI in October 1969. SRI has since aided government research on numerous fronts.

In 1970 the institute broke off from Stanford; it was renamed SRI International in 1977. The break with Stanford was due, in large part, to student protests against the lab's military ties. Like many research institutions, SRI relied on government contracts to fund much of its cutting-edge work.

Today SRI employs close to 1,400 people and brings in about $300 million a year in revenue. The research center has given birth to dozens of start-ups in Silicon Valley.

PALO ALTO'S STRONGEST CLAIM AS THE "BIRTHPLACE OF Silicon Valley" remains the HP Garage. Still, a decent case can be made that the real spark happened at the original Fairchild Semiconductor office. Although the company is no longer based there, Fairchild's story must be told to explain how the region rose to the forefront of the computing industry and helped create the silicon age.

True technology aficionados will have heard the oft-repeated story of the "traitorous eight." This group of employees broke off from famed physicist William Shockley and his fledgling Shockley Semiconductor Laboratories without knowing exactly what they would do next. They simply knew they couldn't tolerate the man's harrowing management style any longer. Eventually they founded Fairchild Semiconductor.

THE FOUNDING OF FAIRCHILD

William Shockley has received credit, along with two other Bell Labs staffers, for creating the first transistor in 1947. This tiny switch promised to replace myriad more cumbersome and less reliable products dominating the electronics industry, and Shockley decided to pursue the technology at his own lab. So he headed back to California—his boyhood home—and in 1956 set up a lab in Mountain View. There he handpicked a cadre of talented scientists. While few of them knew anything about transistors or semiconductor technology, they joined based on Shockley's reputation. Most would come to regret their decision.

While renowned for his stunning intellect, Shockley struggled to display any of the core skills needed to run a successful business. He kept workers isolated, showed a distrust of his staff, and failed to provide a focused, achievable goal. Most importantly, Shockley insisted on pursuing experimental new semiconductor designs when the brightest members of his staff recommended that the lab concentrate first on building reliable transistors with existing methods in hopes of actually attracting customers.

A group of seven employees eventually decided to mount a coup and tasked Gordon Moore with calling Shockley's financial backer, Arnold Beckman, to suggest that Shockley be removed from managerial duties and placed in a consulting role. This rebellion didn't go well: Beckman refused to take action and Shockley reeled in horror over the defection.

You can visit the original Fairchild headquarters (historical marker only) at 844 East Charleston Road. The rather run-down two-story building is currently occupied by a design firm and sits next to a car repair shop.

Figuring that their time at Shockley's lab had come to end, the seven workers (Julius Blank, Victor Grinich, Jean Hoerni, Eugene Kleiner, Jay Last, Gordon Moore, and Sheldon Roberts), plus late recruit Robert Noyce, decided to leave the start-up and see if they could be hired en masse by a larger company. Fortune smiled on the group when millionaire inventor Sherman Fairchild caught wind of their plan to produce a steady stream of transistors for commercial use—the plan Shockley would never embrace. In an unusual move, Fairchild agreed to hire the whole team and place their new company, Fairchild Semiconductor, under the aegis of Fairchild Camera and Instrument.

Two savvy financial gurus, Arthur Rock and Bud Coyle, had helped make the contacts behind this deal and set it up. The men provided invaluable guidance to the Fairchild Semiconductor staff and paved the way for many practices that would one day be core to the venture capital business.

The Fairchild crew set up shop about 1.4 miles from the Shockley lab in 1957. Just as he had under Shockley, Noyce enjoyed a position of prominence at Fairchild. He came into the industry knowing far more about transistors and semiconductor technology than the other staffers and possessed the sharp wit, scientific drive, competitiveness, and charisma so essential to a business leader. On paper an

The Dutch Goose, Menlo Park

THROUGH BOOM OR BUST YOU CAN COUNT on the proprietors of the Dutch Goose for a solid meal and a friendly face. This brewpub has been flipping burgers for the past forty years. And you're just as likely to find a local teenager as a seasoned venture capitalist grabbing lunch at the Silicon Valley institution.

The food ranges from top-notch burgers and hot dogs to piled-high pastrami or smoked brisket sandwiches. If you're a fan, that brisket is a special treat. It's smoked for twelve hours at the restaurant. Patrons also rave about the spicy deviled eggs and homemade chili.

Despite its location near the heart of venture capital country, the Dutch Goose is a no-frills joint. Pop in, grab a beer, and then pick from booths inside or outdoor tables. With peanut shells littering the floor, names carved into tables, a pool table, and a jukebox, the laid-back ambience can't be beat. The Dutch Goose caters to a broad lunch crowd and serves up plenty of beers at night to locals catching a game on one of the restaurant's seven plasma TVs. "At the Goose we will call you by your first name and not a number," the restaurant boasts.

You can find the Dutch Goose at 3567 Alameda de las Pulgas, Menlo Park; or on the Web at www.dutch goose.net. The restaurant is open from 11 a.m. to 2 a.m. and can be reached at (650) 854-3245.

equal partner in the enterprise, Noyce nevertheless stood out from the other founders, particularly in the eyes of officials at the corporate parent. While he rebuffed a push to make him manager of the new venture, he did become the technical head of Fairchild's lab.

A SINGLE PIECE OF SILICON

From the start, Fairchild enjoyed fortuitous circumstances. The military and large technology companies had started searching for something like the transistor that could replace unreliable vacuum tubes and other clunky components in electronics. IBM, in fact, placed the first major order for Fairchild's silicon transistors before the company even knew whether it could deliver them. Nonetheless, the product Fairchild managed to ship in 1958 outclassed anything else on the market, and basically handed the young company a short-lived monopoly.

Fairchild's major breakthrough came in 1959 when Hoerni developed something known as the planar process. Simply put, this new manufacturing process allowed Fairchild to create more

reliable products, more easily. The planar process made it possible for Noyce to pursue the idea of an integrated circuit (IC) that would combine numerous components on a single piece of silicon. Several accounts show that Noyce came up with the idea of an IC well before he publicized the discovery. Officially, however, Noyce and Texas Instruments researcher Jack Kilby are credited with originating similar concepts for an integrated circuit at about the same time.

Regardless of who came up with the concept first, Noyce produced a more practical IC design that Fairchild could actually use. A team led by Jay Last—often described by his peers as one of the brightest Fairchild staffers—would turn Noyce's vision into a reality. The company again exploited its technology to gain an advantage over rivals, and the IC truly ignited the computing industry's fascination with silicon devices.

Today a marker outside Fairchild's original headquarters building reads,

SITE OF INVENTION OF THE FIRST COMMERCIALLY PRACTICABLE INTEGRATED CIRCUIT—AT THIS SITE IN 1959, DR. ROBERT NOYCE OF FAIRCHILD SEMICONDUCTOR CORPORATION INVENTED THE FIRST INTEGRATED CIRCUIT THAT COULD BE PRODUCED COMMERCIALLY. BASED ON "PLANAR" TECHNOLOGY, AN EARLIER FAIRCHILD BREAKTHROUGH, NOYCE'S INVENTION CONSISTED OF A COMPLETE ELECTRONIC CIRCUIT INSIDE A SMALL SILICON CHIP. HIS INNOVA-

TION HELPED REVOLUTIONIZE "SILICON VALLEY'S" SEMICONDUC-
TOR ELECTRONICS INDUSTRY, AND BROUGHT PROFOUND CHANGE
TO THE LIVES OF PEOPLE EVERYWHERE.

■ ■ ■

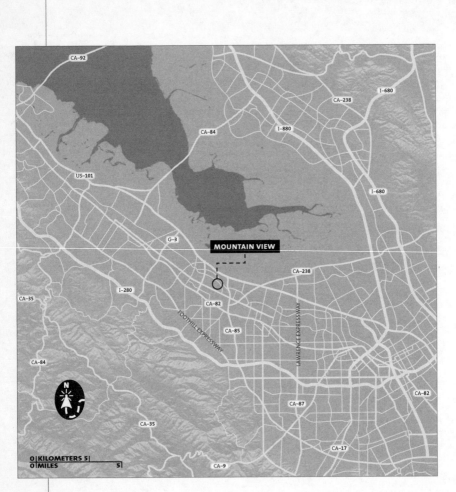

CA-92

CA-238

I-680

CA-84

I-880

US-101

I-680

G-3

MOUNTAIN VIEW

CA-238

CA-35

I-280

CA-82

FOOTHILL EXPRESSWAY

CA-85

LAWRENCE EXPRESSWAY

CA-84

N

CA-82

CA-35

CA-87

0 | KILOMETERS 5 |
0 | MILES   5 |

CA-17

CA-9

OU CAN EASILY MAKE A CASE FOR Mountain View as both the historic birthplace of Silicon Valley and the contemporary epicenter of the region's next technology wave.

William Shockley put the silicon in Silicon Valley when he opened Shockley Semiconductor Laboratory in 1956. From Shockley's Mountain View lab sprang Fairchild Semiconductor and then Intel, which both pushed computing power to new levels. Just about every company in Silicon Valley can trace its lineage back to these companies—or at the least thank the firms for developing a competitive environment that let them thrive.

Over the years numerous other companies have set up shop in Mountain View as well, lured by the city's proximity to San Francisco, Stanford, and San Jose. Google, for example, moved into a massive Mountain View facility in 1999, making the city one of the hottest areas in Silicon Valley once again. Houses, apartments, and shops have sprung up just to deal with the influx of Google personnel—many of whom became paper millionaires overnight when Google went public in 2004.

Mountain View does indeed offer a nice mix of green spaces, prosperous businesses, solid schools, and a vibrant downtown, making it a prime destination for myriad Silicon Valley types. And outside San Francisco you will struggle to find a more concentrated collection of eclectic restaurants, bookstores, and shops than Mountain View's main drag—Castro Street.

CHAPTER 2

☕ CASTRO STREET

IT TAKES ALL OF ABOUT TWENTY-FIVE MINUTES TO TREK FROM ONE end of Castro to the other. But on that short route lie a host of Italian, Thai, Chinese, Indian, Mediterranean, Japanese, seafood, Mexican, and pub-style restaurants. The selection and quality of food in such a small area give Mountain View a gourmet edge over neighboring towns and provide both comfort and adventure for locals. Complementing the eateries are local coffee shops willing to duke it out with Starbucks and a mix of trendy bars and relaxed watering holes. In addition, residents can cap off a night of vigorous dining and drinking with some homemade Italian ice cream at Gelato Classico or a mango ice treat at one of the Asian dessert cafes.

> More information on Mountain View is available at the city's Web site www.ci.mtnview.ca.us/.

All of it is a welcome respite from the strip malls and chain restaurants that dominate much of Silicon Valley. Like anywhere in these parts, though, the market remains competitive, and your favorite restaurant might not be around for long. Expect to see one or two establishments undergoing a renovation when you walk down Castro Street.

A collection of booksellers give Mountain View a hint of intellectualism. Books Inc., in particular, pulls in some top names for speaking engagements: Recent appearances have included the likes of Alan Alda and Salman Rushdie, as well as local romance novelist Molly Madigan. When not eating or drinking, locals can check out sophisticated furniture stores, arts and crafts shops, and a couple of clothing outfits—though the shopping arguably doesn't quite match up to Castro Street's digestible treasures.

THE MOUNTAIN VIEW ART AND WINE FESTIVAL

Every year the folks in Mountain View and tens of thousands of their closest friends celebrate the culinary and artistic traditions of the area at the Art and Wine Festival. This party has run for more than thirty years and usually takes place the second week of September. Close to 200,000 people flood Mountain View to consume all different types of barbecue, pizza, seafood, and Asian delights. Vendors line Castro Street, and—as the festival's name suggests—there's plenty of drink on hand. The local Tied House Café and Brewery conjures up a one-of-a-kind brew every year, while winemakers from the likes of Beringer, Mondavi, and Echelon strut their grapes. The free event also draws hundreds of artists who hawk their goods and brings in tons of musicians to keep the crowds entertained. The festival is considered one of the most popular events of its kind in California and should not be missed.

A HISTORIC **THOROUGHFARE**

Mountain View officials have welcomed Castro Street's economic and cultural revival. The city has centered itself on the path marked out by Castro's run from the local train station on up to El Camino Real for more than a hundred years. In fact, during its first fifty years or so Castro Street served much the same function as it does now, hosting a variety of businesses such as hotels, restaurants, and grocers along with providing ample space for houses. (Many of the buildings from the 1920s and later still stand today.)

After about 1950, however, the street could no longer compete with shopping centers opening up in the surrounding area. Chain stores that once called Castro Street home took off, and other businesses followed. But while downtown traffic dwindled, it never died out, and civic leaders were able to revive Mountain View's central thoroughfare in the 1980s. Instead of tearing down old buildings in favor of the strip-mall designs adopted by nearby towns, Mountain View made the most of what it had. It turned Castro Street into a pleasant venue for pedestrians and encouraged small-business owners to give the area a go. Over time Mountain View's downtown grew back to life. It also managed to attract large businesses such as the prestigious law firm Fenwick and West and online payment specialist PayPal—before it was acquired by eBay.

Today you'll found a thoroughfare surrounded by well-groomed, cozy houses that cost well over $1 million each. Many are filled with young couples who have picked the relative ease and convenience of Mountain View over San Francisco or San Jose. Almost everyone appreciates all Castro Street has to offer. It really is one of the keys to making Mountain View stand out from the other Silicon Valley suburbs.

SHOCKLEY SEMICONDUCTOR LABORATORY

YOU'LL GET A DIFFERENT ANSWER IN PALO ALTO. BUT ASK any Mountain View city official for directions to the birthplace of Silicon Valley and he or she will point you to San Antonio Road. That's where William Shockley took over a former fruit-packing shed in 1956 and set up Shockley Semiconductor Laboratory.

Look for the former Shockley labs at 391 San Antonio Road, Mountain View.

Ironically, that former fruit-packing shed has most recently operated as a fruit store. As of this writing, the remains of the International Produce Market can be found within a nondescript gray building that used to contain a tribute to Shockley sitting above some produce. The fruit market closed in 2007 and is expected to be replaced by a grocery story. Outside the store a sidewalk plaque commemorates the site.

SHOCKLEY AND THE TRANSISTOR

A difficult genius, Shockley pioneered research into solid-state electronics. After being educated at the California Institute of Technology and MIT, he pursued his work at Bell Labs in Murray Hill, New Jersey. It was there in 1947 that John Bardeen and Walter Brattain created the first transistor device while working under him.

Shockley did not directly assist Bardeen and Brattain with their invention, although Bell Labs demanded that he, too, receive credit for developing the transistor. Distraught by his colleagues' success, Shockley looked to make his own contribution to transistor technology and soon invented a device known as the junction transistor. It was this product that ultimately proved useful to the electronics industry and restored Shockley's place in transistor history.

His obvious brilliance aside, Shockley frustrated co-workers with his grating personality. His behavior started to make life intolerable for everyone at Bell Labs, and Shockley decided to pursue a fresh start in California, looking to set up his own transistor company. Toward this end he made contact with scientific device maker Beckman Instruments and its chief Arnold Beckman, who agreed to fund the new venture in 1955. While Beckman preferred to see the semiconductor shop open near Los Angeles, Shockley insisted that the lab sit close to his boyhood home of Palo Alto, where his mother still lived. The town and its surroundings had already started a transition from a rural area to a small center of commerce. In the coming years, Shockley would directly and indirectly speed up this shift.

In addition to personal reasons, Shockley liked what Palo Alto could offer from a professional standpoint. Frederick Terman, a Stanford University professor, gave Shockley a sales pitch similar to what he had dished out years earlier to Bill Hewlett, Dave Packard, and Russell and Sigurd Varian. He promised that Stanford's budding semiconductor research efforts could aid Shockley, providing talented youngsters to recruit and a place to conduct additional research. The latter idea no doubt proved attractive to Shockley, who took his academic reputation very seriously.

Shockley used his stellar reputation as a scientist and the attractive Santa Clara County climate to lure many of the brightest young minds available across the country. On most occasions he forced recruits to endure a series of unusual psychological tests—machinations the employees were only willing to go through because of the thrilling prospect of working with a true giant.

"I was immediately struck with what a bright mind he had," recalled Jay Last, one of the first Shockley hires. "I was startled at how bright he was and how quickly he picked up on things." Many former employees have expressed similar feelings. Shockley could digest complex subjects at speed and dish out simplified, refined ways for others to understand them. But where Shockley succeeded as a teacher, he failed as a businessman.

Robert Noyce—future co-founder of Fairchild Semiconductor and Intel—was the only Shockley employee with any significant semiconductor experience. The rest of the talented group had to learn on the job. "A group of us held study sessions, working together to learn about transistor theory," Last said. After coming to terms with the technology, many of the workers decided the best idea from a business perspective would be to produce transistors via a consistent, reliable process. Shockley, however, had become more enamored with one of his own inventions—the complex four-layer diode.

The conflict over the lab's future direction dissipated for a moment on November 1, 1956. Word arrived that Shockley and his Bell Labs co-workers Bardeen and Brattain had received the Nobel Prize for physics. It was remarkable news given that the group had invented the transistor just nine years earlier. The employees celebrated the win at a local restaurant, and the event assured the staffers that Shockley—while difficult—had thrust them to the forefront of a scientific revolution.

THE TRAITOROUS EIGHT

The grand feelings did not last long. Soon a group of employees began searching for a way to push Shockley out of the day-to-day operations of the lab. The workers feared Shockley's ever-changing moods and did not appreciate the way he isolated each person, sharing just bits and pieces of information as needed. The staff wanted to work as a cohesive group in the pursuit of building better transistors. Meanwhile, Shockley cared little for producing products that could actually be sold, preferring instead to charge after more semiconductor innovations that would add shine to his already sparkling name.

"He had some real peculiar management ideas," said Gordon Moore, Shockley employee and future co-founder of Fairchild Semiconductor and Intel. "This drove a lot of dissension in the group." Eventually eight scientists decided to leave the lab. "We became convinced," explained Moore, "that our best course was to set up our own company to complete Shockley's original goal—which he had abandoned by this time in favor of another semiconductor device he had also invented—to make a commercial silicon transistor." According to semiconductor pioneer Carver Mead:

> HE WAS ABSOLUTELY, TOTALLY BLIND TO THE INFORMATION REVOLUTION. HE SAW THE POWER REVOLUTION, AND HE DIDN'T REALIZE THE INFORMATION REVOLUTION WAS GOING TO COME BEFORE THE POWER REVOLUTION. HE JUST DIDN'T GET THAT LOGIC TRANSISTORS WERE GOING TO OUTNUMBER POWER TRANSISTORS BY 100,000 TO 1 OR SOMETHING ON THAT SCALE.

> SO THE BIG DISCONNECT WAS WHEN PEOPLE LIKE NOYCE AND HIS COHORTS REALIZED THERE WAS A MARKET FOR LOGIC STUFF, AND THIS INFORMATION STUFF THAT WAS HAPPENING, AND THERE WAS A LOT OF UNIT VOLUME THERE. SHOCKLEY DIDN'T SEE THAT.

> IN FACT, THOUGH, YOU CAN SEE TODAY THAT WHAT HE SAID WAS TRUE. HE WAS SEEING FURTHER AHEAD THAN THE OTHER GUYS SAW. I HAVE NEVER HEARD ANYONE GIVE SHOCKLEY CREDIT ON THAT BECAUSE HE WAS UNBEARABLE ON OTHER STUFF. BUT HE DESERVES THAT IN A WAY THAT HAS NEVER BEEN GIVEN HIM. IF HE LOOKED AT THE WORLD TODAY, HE WOULD SEE A LOT OF THINGS AND SMILE.

The eight defectors founded Fairchild Semiconductor about a mile and a half away from Shockley. In a diary entry from September 18, 1957, Shockley noted quite simply, "Group resigns." By focusing on transistors, the new company would move into the black during its first year of operations.

THE END OF AN ERA

Shockley's entrepreneurial adventure, on the other hand, faded fast
after the "traitorous eight" left. He suffered through a major car accident in 1961 and then accepted a professorship at Stanford in 1963.
(He would retire in 1972.) Shockley Labs was eventually sold off—first
to Clevite and then ITT—and closed down in 1968.

Rather sadly, Shockley's personal life was also tarnished in his
later years. He linked up with a program to have Nobel Prize win-

CLICK HERE **Firing Up Google's Free Wi-Fi**

GOOGLE HAS MADE FINDING A WIRELESS
connection in its hometown of Mountain View about as easy as it gets. Anyone willing to sign up for a free Google
account can also receive free wireless
throughout much of the city.

Google teamed with Mountain
View officials to mount wireless devices
on lampposts and other structures at
its own cost. After working for about a
year, Google managed to erect close to
350 of the so-called wireless access
points, covering 12 square miles and
70,000 Mountain View residents. The
service works best outdoors and inside
the public library, where the firm placed
additional wireless devices.

The access has been pitched as
type of community service by Google—
although some stores might disagree.
Smaller coffee shops, for example, have
offered free wireless access in a bid to
compete against Starbucks, which
charges for its service. Meanwhile, all
customers in Starbucks now get free
wireless access via Google, which must
make those shelling out for Starbucks'
wireless cringe a bit.

By most accounts, the service
works well, pumping out data at one
megabit per second. That's not terribly fast, but it's pretty good when you
consider the cost. At this writing there
are still some areas that Google hasn't
reached, either because public spots
are not available from which to hang
wireless access points or because
Google's presence is not welcome,
such as on Microsoft's Mountain View
campus.

You can find a coverage map at
http://wifi.google.com/city/mv/
apmap.html. Those in the dark can
propose to host a wireless access
point; Google has vowed to consider
such requests on a one-off basis.

ners contribute their, er, genetic prowess to a sperm bank to improve the lot of humans. Shockley was also rather vocal about the idea that African Americans did not have the same innate intelligence as Caucasians. He went on to urge that individuals with low IQs be compensated if they agreed to voluntary sterilization. Some of Shockley's views led to him being panned in a *Saturday Night Live* skit known as "Dr. Shockley's House of Sperm."

A rather lonely man, Shockley died of prostate cancer in 1989 at the age of seventy-nine.

The rich technology legacy left by Shockley lives on to this day in Silicon Valley. In some ways, of course, his influence was indirect in that he never managed to develop the semiconductor technology that would sit at the heart of all computing devices. "People now say that Shockley is the Moses of Silicon Valley," said one former employee. "He showed the way to the promise of silicon technology, but he didn't reach it himself."

That said, most of the major companies in Silicon Valley can trace their roots back to Fairchild—the direct descendant of the Shockley lab—in one way or another. In addition, it was Shockley who picked silicon as the material for his semiconductor work. While such a decision would seem obvious later, it was a true risk at the time. "It is pretty hard to see how this area would have turned into a big device producing area without [something like the Shockley lab]," Last said. "The valley is called Silicon Valley; it is not called Software Valley. We all owe a great debt of gratitude to Bill Shockley for his pioneering efforts getting things started here."

THE COMPUTER HISTORY MUSEUM

THE NATURAL ASSOCIATION BETWEEN COMPUTERS AND contemporary life might lead you to believe that there's no pressing need to gobble up IT "artifacts." How can you start collecting something that seems a couple of decades old, at most?

The Computer History Museum takes exception to such thinking and has been working for years to collect every possible object that tells the story of technology's rise. While still in its early stages at this writing, the museum plans to become the preeminent location for displaying technology artifacts and honoring computing pioneers.

You can find the museum at 1401 North Shoreline Boulevard, Mountain View, and give it a ring at (650) 810-1010. Much of the collection can be viewed online, and the museum also has a ton of documentation on the Internet. Have a dig at www.computerhistory.org.

In fitting fashion, the museum makes its home in an actual computing relic. The large, space-age-style building that sits just off the 101 freeway used to belong to hardware maker SGI. Remnants of SGI linger throughout the structure: Old cubicle walls display the company's trademark purple color, for instance, and a stunning purple tower shoots up through the body of the building and out its roof. (There is a debate whether or not to keep the purple reminders of SGI's past prominence.)

The museum has close to thirty-five full-time staffers and 200 volunteers. One of these folks will be available to take you through the exhibits on Wednesday and Friday at 1:00 and 2:30 p.m., and Saturday at 11:30 a.m., 1:00 p.m., and 2:30 p.m. The tour can take anywhere from an hour to two hours, depending on how verbose or nostalgic the docent is. You're also free to guide yourself through the museum 1:00 to 4:00 p.m. on Wednesday and Friday, and 11:00 a.m. to 5:00 p.m. on Saturday. The museum is free, although it won't frown upon a donation. Individual memberships, which let you attend special speaker sessions and cocktail hours, start at $40.

BEANTOWN BEGINNINGS

In 1979 legendary Digital Equipment Corporation (DEC) engineer Gordon Bell and his wife, Gwen, were running out of storage space for their collection of historical computing objects. So the Bells worked with DEC to open the Digital Computer Museum in Boston. That facility took off as more pieces of computing history poured in and as technology pioneers held discussions at the Boston facility. In 1983 Digital was axed from the name, and the Computer Museum found a new home in downtown Boston at Museum Wharf. Over the years this museum matured and formed strong ties with the computing and historical communities. It also expanded via a West Coast addition—the Computer Museum History Center in California, which opened in 1996 to help store a growing collection.

In 2001 a forced consolidation of the space in Boston—coupled with a rapidly expanding California collection and a more vibrant Silicon Valley technology scene—led to the creation of the Computer History Museum. After a short run in a NASA Ames warehouse, the museum bought the old SGI facility and laid out the first 4,000 artifacts for visitors in 2003.

Workers will readily admit, "This is a museum in the making." Currently in "Phase I," the museum has just a fraction of its artifacts on display. The majority fall into a category called "Visible Storage" by the curators. That's a rather dramatic description for what is basically the biggest collection of computer hardware you've ever encountered.

SLIDE RULES TO SILICON

The Visible Storage exhibit starts with computing precursors. Think along the lines of an abacus, slide rules, and hand-cranked adding machines. These devices tell the story of the human battle to perform calculations more quickly and more accurately. Strolling the aisles, you'll spot handcrafted machines for discovering prime numbers, looms, and—perhaps most importantly—the census-taking devices of Herman Hollerith.

These machines—which used pin presses and delightful, exposed cups of mercury to form electrical circuits—made it possible for the US government to churn through census data at record speed. Hollerith, however, didn't want to rely on leasing these data-sorting products to a single customer once every decade, so he devised ways to use the gear in the railroad, insurance, and banking industries. In 1924 the company selling Hollerith's census machines would change its name to something more familiar—IBM.

Complementing these early devices, the museum shows off an incredible collection of the earliest computers created in the United States and abroad. We're talking huge, bloated, expensive hardware used to aim and track weapons during the Cold War. For example, the SAGE (Semi Automatic Ground Environment) aircraft warning systems from the mid-1950s cost the US government billions and billions of dollars and took up tons of space with their computing systems, storage, and display consoles. The military required personnel

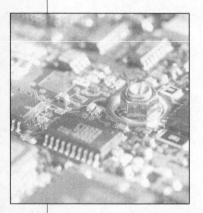

to watch a type of radar screen for hours, looking for any indication of an enemy attack. Thankfully, the SAGE consoles came outfitted with a rotary phone and an ashtray to help pass the time. Ah, the good old days.

There are also plenty of bespoke giants from various universities and companies. Most impressive among this group is the rare Cray 1A supercomputer, complete with multicolored side panels and a cushioned leather base that runs in a C shape around the machine. Museum hands like to call this "the world's most expensive love seat."

You might also run into the rather odd Kitchen Computer sold by Neiman Marcus in 1969. Try to imagine a red-and-white contraption with a broad base and a shaft, topped by a kitchen-counter-like platform outfitted with various buttons. The pricey retailer imagined that tech-savvy cooks could use this Honeywell-computer-powered product to store recipes or to calculate the amount of ingredients needed when cooking for larger crowds. With only eight buttons and no keyboard or screen, the kitchen helper didn't attract many customers. In fact, the weird *Jetsons* and *Leave It to Beaver* combo didn't tempt a single buyer. That's hard to believe given that $10,600 (1969 dollars) sounds like such a bargain.

Aside from these big boxes, the Computer History Museum has collected just about every personal computer, laptop, and handheld device available. You can see the fabled Xerox Alto, the first Sun Microsystems workstation, the first Apple computer, and on and on. To call the hardware cache complete doesn't begin to do it justice. Anyone even approaching the title of computer buff must see these systems.

Overall, the Visible Storage exhibit defines the phrase "no frills." Old SGI cubicle walls still serve as barriers for some of the displays. The exhibits have brief histories on small placards. Visitors will find air-conditioning and other pipes exposed in the ceiling. Simply put, it's row after row of hardware and little more.

Speakers pop in about twice a month to discuss computing topics in a 400-person auditorium located upstairs. Guests have included the likes of Sun Microsystems' four founders, Intel co-founder Gordon Moore, and World Wide Web inventor Tim Berners-Lee. The museum also plays host to conferences and hands out its Fellow awards to computing pioneers at an annual gala.

Future plans are ambitious and include a world-class facility and a research institute for students and scholars. Microsoft co-founder Bill Gates and his wife, Melinda, helped out with this goal in 2005 by donating $15 million.

FENWICK & WEST

FEW LARGE BUSINESSES OPERATE RIGHT OFF THE RESTAURANT-
and bar-rich Castro Street. The exception is quintessential Silicon Valley law firm Fenwick & West, which bucks the trend with its elegant downtown Mountain View spread.

CLICK HERE

The Tied House Café and Brewery

A RELAXED MEAL AND A FINE BEER await you at the Tied House pub just off Mountain View's main artery, Castro Street. This brew house poured its first pint of handcrafted beer back in January 1988. Today it offers up four main beers—Alpine Gold, Cascade Amber, Ironwood, and New World Wheat. It also serves up other seasonal beers and experiments with new recipes now and again.

The Tied House presents a spacious, relaxed atmosphere to enjoy these beers. Customers can pick from standard tables and large, wooden booths or saddle up to the bar. The dining area centers on some hefty beer-making equipment, which serves as a strong reminder of why you ended up in the restaurant. Like any joint worth its hops, the Tied House has a decent beer garden as well. With wooden tables, ferns hanging overhead, and a cobblestone floor, it's definitely one of the more refined beer gardens you'll find.

The food, too, reaches well beyond standard pub grub. The Tied House has put a classy spin on some basic favor-ites. Take, for example, the harvest squash quesadilla or the buffalo tenderloins complemented with a cayenne pepper sauce and cucumber salad. Pricier entrees include the fresh king salmon and the Kahuna-Na-Na pork chops. You can also, of course, grab hold of a monster cheeseburger or scrounge some onion rings. So rest easy, lads.

The Tied House basically gives you a chance to step up the brewpub experience to the next level or, if you prefer, keep it pretty much the same as you're used to. Should you develop a taste for the Tied House ale, you're in luck. Kegs and five-gallon jugs of beer can be had at market price.

You can find the Tied House at 954 Villa Street, Mountain View; (650) 965-2739. A second beer hall beer hall sits at 65 North San Pedro Street, San Jose; (408) 295-2739. Check out the menu online at www.tiedhouse.com.

Fenwick & West has been plugging away in Silicon Valley since 1972. Back then the firm was run by four entrepreneurial attorneys who moved out to the area thinking it could prove lucrative as budding technology businesses expanded. This was clearly the right call, and today Fenwick & West employs hundreds of lawyers, making it one of the largest West Coast law firms.

True to its roots, Fenwick & West specializes in intellectual property matters and mergers and acquisitions—the technology industry basics. The firm has also managed to expand beyond tech clients via a bustling corporate tax practice considered one of the best in the country, representing companies such as Viacom and Chrysler in addition to local giants like Cisco.

You can see the Fenwick & West headquarters at 801 California Street, Mountain View; (650) 988-8500 or on the Web at www.fenwick.com.

Fenwick & West has been a mainstay on the local scene since its early days. The firm, for example, incorporated Apple Computer in 1976 and then took Oracle public ten years later. More recently it guided the $13 billion merger between Symantec and Veritas and Verisign's $21 billion buy of Network Solutions.

The firm often ranks as one of the best companies to work for in the United States and is known for a warm, very California culture. In 2003 it moved its headquarters from Palo Alto to Mountain View, taking up residence in an elegant building on Castro Street.

⏻ MICROSOFT'S SILICON VALLEY CAMPUS

WHILE CONTENT TO CALL REDMOND, WASHINGTON, HOME, Microsoft knows it can ill afford to miss out on the Silicon Valley lifestyle. With that in mind, the big daddy of software set up a sweeping campus in Mountain View adjacent to the NASA Ames site and just behind the Computer History Museum.

You can find Microsoft's shimmering Silicon Valley HQ at 1065 La Avenida; or on the Web at http://research.microsoft.com /aboutmsr/labs/siliconvalley. No tours are available.

Microsoft went for a college-campus theme with its Silicon Valley headquarters and pulled off this goal in style. The site consists of about five contemporary buildings wrapped in a semicircle. Each maintains the same color scheme—slick, overlapping layers of silver, gray, and black.

One of Microsoft's larger research and development teams works out of the Mountain View campus. These folks—a much bigger group than the Microsoft Bay Area Researcher Center crew in San Francisco—focus on a wide variety of projects, including data mining, algorithms, and future software tools. Microsoft also operates its largest Technology Center at this facility, allowing it to show off different types of technology to customers.

CLICK HERE   Shoreline Amphitheatre

IT HAS BEEN CALLED "THE BIGGEST AND most beautiful tent in the world." And while some might squabble over the aesthetic merits of the Shoreline Amphitheatre, few could argue about its size. The two flag-capped points of the white tent can be seen from many spots in Silicon Valley, and the tent itself stretches far enough to cover a massive stage, many rows of seats, and backstage areas of the venue.

Smaller bands will often find themselves at more traditional and ornate San Francisco joints such as the Fillmore, the Great American Music Hall, and the Warfield. But when promoters are really looking to pack in the crowds, they head to Shoreline. Bands such as Coldplay, Phish, and Radiohead have filled up the outdoor venue, which can hold close to 25,000 people. Lucky fans will secure a spot in the 6,500-person fixed-seat area; the masses must fight for their right to get funky on the spacious, sloping grass hill.

The Shoreline tent, while huge, doesn't impress all that much from an architectural point of view. It's just a really big canvas. Still, the tent enjoys aesthetic help from the healthy numbers of trees that surround it and cover much of the sixty-acre area.

Shoreline is easy enough to find. Signs on the 101 freeway tell you where to exit, and if you're not paying attention to those markers, the Shoreline Boulevard exit should serve as a decent reminder.

You'll find the amphitheatre at 1 Amphitheatre Parkway in Mountain View. Check out some of the upcoming events at www.shore lineamp.com/schedule.html.

Having a presence in Mountain View helps soften Microsoft's image as a Silicon Valley outsider. It also gives the company a chance to attract and hire local talent who prefer near-constant sunshine to Redmond's near-constant rainfall.

Microsoft has operated in Silicon Valley since 1981, although the new Mountain View campus has only been up and running since 1999. The site houses more than 1,000 workers.

SILICON GRAPHICS INC.

ONCE UPON A TIME SILICON GRAPHICS INC. (SGI) RULED A grand swath of land stretching from the US 101 freeway to the swampy shore of the San Francisco Bay. It owned a massive head-quarters equipped with the finest hardware imaginable for display-ing huge, complex images. SGI complemented this home base with a series of sprawling office complexes and another ultramodern build-ing. These facilities supported more than 10,000 workers.

The fairy tale, however, started to turn ugly in 2000 as SGI's revenue began to decline, forcing the company to sell off its grand complexes. Today Google, the Computer History Museum, and myr-iad start-ups reside in old SGI offices. Some workers have even main-tained their same SGI cubicles but now work for different companies. Such is life in Silicon Valley. The trademark SGI purple paint coats many of its former buildings to this day, serving as a reminder of how great the company once was.

A SILICON **VALLEY** CAUTIONARY **TALE**

SGI's story line follows that of many hardware companies that once owned their particular market but failed to adjust in time to chang-ing technology trends.

PAUL BARAN
Keeping the Information Flowing

IN 1961 PAUL BARAN DEVELOPED TWO ideas for the Rand Corporation that would eventually serve as key underlying technologies for the Internet. The first was a mesh-like group of distributed communications systems that would allow a network to keep working even if a large number of individual hardware units failed. Up until that point the military and telephone operators had largely relied on more centralized approach to relaying information. If a few key systems went down, the whole network would collapse. Back in those Cold War years, Baran knew that a distributed network would be the only way to keep communications running in the event of a massive Soviet attack.

He pushed the concept of packet switching as well—another technology to strengthen communications networks. With packet switching, an e-mail, for example, is broken up into different parts that make their own way through the network and then reassemble at their destination. Each packet finds the most efficient route through the network; if it runs up against a failed system, it locates another route. This helps keep communications networks pumped full of

SILICON VALLEY IS A VERY INTERESTING PLACE. I LOOK AROUND AND SEE PEOPLE THAT COME FROM MANY, MANY DIFFERENT COUNTRIES. YOU HAVE THE SMARTEST PEOPLE FROM AROUND THE WORLD CONCENTRATED HERE. THAT'S A FANTASTIC RESOURCE.

SILICON VALLEY IS A POTENT PLACE. THERE'S THE ATTITUDE THAT YOU CAN TRY SOMETHING AND FAIL AND THAT'S OKAY. YOU DUST YOURSELF OFF AND TRY AGAIN. ALSO, THE IDEA THAT YOU CAN MOVE FROM COMPANY TO COMPANY. WE DON'T DO THAT BACK EAST.

—NETWORKING PIONEER
PAUL BARAN

data and keeps information flowing even if a number of systems crash.

Scientists familiar with Baran's work would go on to create the distributed, packet-switched networks that would one day form the Internet. Baran also co-founded the Institute for the Future, a Palo Alto think tank.

The company started in 1982 when Stanford University professor James Clark recruited six graduate students to help him pursue a new graphics venture. He had created something called a Geometry Engine that provided a breakthrough in the way computers could process and handle images. In particular, SGI carved out a niche as the master of 3-D images, bringing a new level of display reality to computers. (Clark, a graduate of the stellar University of Utah Computer Science Department, resigned from SGI in 1994 and went on to co-found Netscape.)

Over time a broad range of organizations would come to depend on SGI's hardware for many of their most demanding tasks. The ability of the firm's systems to display complex images and then let customers manipulate them proved attractive to the military, entertainment companies, researchers, and large companies performing modeling operations such as the designs of new cars or airplanes. SGI became the gold standard of the imaging market.

Like Sun Microsystems—also founded in 1982—SGI managed to lower the overall price of technology in its given field. Customers could pay close to $75,000 for a powerful SGI system that would have cost $250,000 or more in the past. Alas, the company did not pursue price reductions with vigor throughout its history. As it realized that customers would pay top dollar for the unique graphics systems, SGI gladly charged them hefty prices.

Having emerged from a bankruptcy, in 2007 SGI abandoned its home at 1500 Crittenden Lane in Mountain View and shifted to a nondescript office complex in Sunnyvale. Still, it's well worth your time to take a drive down Shoreline Boulevard to view SGI's old haunts and gain an appreciation of the onetime hardware powerhouse's influence on the area.

This model, along with a certain cockiness, would come back to haunt the company as the hardware market changed. Like rivals IBM, HP, Sun, and Compaq/DEC, SGI relied on its own processors (MIPS) and Unix operating system (IRIX). During the late 1990s, less expensive processors from Intel—coupled with Microsoft's Windows and the open-source Linux operating systems—began to rival SGI's proprietary goods for some tasks. This trend only increased in the following years. In addition, the dot-com bust and pullback in technology spending hurt demand for SGI's pricey gear.

Just prior to this, SGI had made a costly mistake. It acquired Cray Research in 1996 but decided to sell off a chunk of the company's server business to Sun for just tens of millions of dollars. Sun quickly turned the old Cray server line into the core of its high-end hardware business, going on to generate billions in revenue from it every year.

As SGI struggled to deal with the changing hardware, it made another mistake by deciding to phase out its proprietary systems in favor of hardware based on Intel's new high-end Itanium processor and the Linux operating system. The Itanium chip didn't live up to its original billing and hurt SGI's efforts to revitalize its business.

By 2005 SGI was warning that it could eventually face bankruptcy in regulatory filings. In addition, it laid off large chunks of staff, leaving it with less than 2,000 workers. A falling stock price pushed SGI off the New York Stock Exchange in 2005, resulting in a position as an over-the-counter penny stock. By October 2006 the firm emerged from Chapter 11 protection with about 1,600 staff.

THE STEVENS CREEK TRAIL

WHEN THE RIGORS OF CHIP DESIGN OR PROGRAMMING prove too much, athletic members of Silicon Valley head out for a walk, jog, or bike along Stevens Creek Trail. This pathway takes you past some of the area's iconic structures, including the NASA Ames wind tunnels and Microsoft's Silicon Valley headquarters. Best of all, it removes you for a moment from urban sprawl and delivers you back to a time when wide-open expanses intermingled with

Hitchhiking Sculptures

IT SOUNDS LIKE THE WORKINGS OF Dr. Frankenstein—people working to bring some Silicon Valley legends back to life and then letting them roam around the United States.

That's exactly what happened in 2006 when Michigan artist Jim Pallas crafted five wooden sculptures of Silicon Valley icons and distinguished Sun Microsystems engineer Mario Wolczko outfitted the figures with global positioning system tracking devices. The sculptures—of Intel co-founder Bob Noyce, Stanford professor Fred Terman, semiconductor whiz William Shockley, HP founders Bill Hewlett and David Packard (in a single figure), and electronics guru Lee De Forest—were created as a project for the San Francisco–based YLEM organization, which focuses on combining art and technology. Wolczko's wife and YLEM member artist Julie Newdoll oversaw the project.

Each wooden figure was given a mission. The Terman figure, for example, was sent to MIT with a note attached to his back, saying that Terman wanted to "hitchhike" out to Stanford. Via the kindness of many strangers, Terman did in fact make it out to Stanford in just over two weeks. Observers of the project could track Terman's route thanks to the attached GPS device. Terman would peri-odically send off a signal marking his location; software written by Wolczko pumped that data onto a Web site. Those visiting the site could watch an animation reflecting Terman's journey and that of the other figures. Pallas had actually been building these types of hitchhiker figures for years but had never used GPS tracking technology before the YLEM effort.

The hitchhiker project received a mountain of press, and Newdoll kept things interesting by posting notes and pictures sent in by the people helping the figures make their way to and around Silicon Valley.

In an embarrassing moment, HP officials declined to receive the Hewlett and Packard figure when it stopped by the company's Palo Alto campus. A couple of days later, after learning of HP's decision, Sun stepped in to buy the sculpture for $6,000. Sun then posted a number of photos of the figure working its way around the company's headquarters searching for "HP's sense of humor."

There's more information on the project available at www.ylem.org/hitchhikers.

orchards instead of sweeping corporate complexes. Locals hold Stevens Creek Trail close to their hearts and count it as one of the perks behind calling Silicon Valley home.

The Stevens Creek Trail kicks off at Yuba Drive and follows Stevens Creek for 3.8 miles past the Microsoft campus, NASA's Ames Research Center, and several mobile homes. Eventually it meets up with the Bay Trail, which sits behind the Googleplex, Shoreline Amphitheatre, and old SGI headquarters and winds all the way to Palo Alto.

In fact, the Stevens Creek and Bay Trails stand as just two of the interlocking paths that run near the edge of the San Francisco Bay and tie together Silicon Valley suburbs. Over time, city planners hope to extend the stretch of trails from Palo Alto through Mountain View to areas such as Santa Clara, San Jose, and Alviso—and eventually beyond. Such a network would let a fit jogger take in numerous wildlife refuges and wetlands in one run.

Yuba Drive provides the southernmost access to the Stevens Creek Trail, but there are also entrances at West Dana Street, Creekside Park, Central Park, Evelyn Avenue/Central Expressway (easy access from the Caltrain and VTA Light Rail stations), Central Avenue, Middlefield Road, Whisman Park, Moffett Boulevard, L'Avenida, and Crittenden Lane.

You can find out more about the Stevens Creek Trail, including maps, at www.stevenscreektrail.org.

To reach Yuba Drive, take Highway 85 to El Camino Real. Travel northwest on El Camino Real. Yuba Drive will appear on the right, and you can park along the road. Only bikes and running shoes are allowed from here on out.

MILE BY MILE ALONG THE TRAIL

From the southernmost entrance at Yuba Drive, the Stevens Creek Trail runs north. While eucalyptus trees beautify the first stretch, within 0.1 mile the path rises into a massive concrete bridge straddling Highway 237. On your right, Highway 85 parallels the bridge.

The noise of the traffic drowns out all but the loudest of iPods. The first 0.3 mile of the trail, similarly, offends the eyes and nose.

Then, however, you'll cross under the Dana Street Bridge to come out on the other side, where majestic foliage hides the urban sprawl and residential areas. Stevens Creek appears at left. The trails bridges the creek for the first time just past Dana Street, then splits to circle a small grove of trees as it hugs the Highway 85 sound wall to the left. At 0.7 mile an 1,100-foot pedestrian bridge soars over Central Expressway and its CalTrain and VTA Light Rail tracks. Toward the center, the bridge bounces with the footfalls of joggers as if to motivate them to run faster to the other side.

Pines flank the stretch beyond the bridge. On the left of the trail, a makeshift dirt stunt course tempts the daredevils on bikes. At 0.9 mile the trail meanders left to again bridge the creek. At 1.0 mile a bridge splints off to cross the waterway and provide access to Creekside Park. At the corner of Easy Street and Gladys Avenue, the park provides a playground and picnic areas.

Another 0.2 mile down the trail, the path forks, with the right side sloping up to the Middlefield Road Trail entrance and the left tunneling under the Middlefield Road ramp. A chain-link fence separates the trail from Highway 85 but does nothing to block out the roar of traffic. It is again appropriate to pump up the iPod, though only briefly. Another sound wall starts just after the tunnel, muffling the disturbing noise of the highway, while pines hide the urban sights.

The trail continues past Whisman Park and School. A bridge crosses the creek to the park, which has its main entrance located on Easy Street south of Walker Drive. At 1.6 miles along the trail, you'll find the only street to intersect the trail. A stoplight with a pedestrian cross signal directs traffic along Moffett Boulevard. On the other side of the street, a grove of redwood trees welcomes back the joggers.

The creek slides back into view. Here the trees stand farther from the path, allowing more sun access. The small dam to the right contains a fish ladder to help the suckers swim upstream.

The trail sneaks under the bustling US 101 freeway. (High water levels sometimes cause this underpass to close, especially during the rainy season.) At 2.2 miles from the Yuba Drive entrance, you'll spot NASA's giant wind tunnel behind apartment buildings owned by the NASA Ames Research Center. The L'Avenida Trail merges with the Stevens Creek Trail here. Rows of benches arched like an amphitheater decorate the right side of the path. A bit farther down, a mobile home

park on your left takes the nature out of the Stevens Creek Nature Trail. A detour along L'Avenida to the right brings you alongside the Microsoft campus.

Continuing, NASA's outdoor engine test stand appears, looking very much like a large hangman's scaffold. It's hard to miss the gargantuan twenty-one-story NASA Ames steel hanger, which housed the USS *Macon* before the dirigible was lost at sea in 1935.

Several trails collide 3.1 miles from the Yuba Drive entrance, including the Crittenden Lane trailhead. Crittenden Lane marks the way toward the Shoreline Amphitheatre. The shallow pond on your right, 3.6 miles along the path, bears the title Crittenden Marsh. It covers the majority of Midpeninsula Regional Open Space District's fifty-five-acre Stevens Creek Nature Study Area. Moffett Field's fresh water runs off into the marsh, allowing a mix of fresh- and saltwater wildlife to inhabit the area.

The public trail ends 3.8 miles from its start. A tiny stop sign warns that venturing onward is both dangerous and a trespass onto Cargill Salt Company land.

ANYONE PASSING BY MOUNTAIN VIEW ON THE US 101
freeway will look out their car window and wonder what the heck
goes on inside all the weird buildings near the Moffett Field exit.
The NASA Ames complex features massive hangars, wind tunnels,
spheres, and giant concrete office buildings. You won't find a stranger
collection of structures anywhere, and the research going on at the
center matches the diversity and oddity of the surroundings.

NASA Ames projects cover a lot of scientific ground. Groups
work on robotics, flight simulation, supercomputing, space shuttle
designs, and air traffic control operations—among many other
things.

In the good old days, NASA Ames welcomed visitors with open
arms. The public could pick from a number of different tours and had
plenty of access to the various facilities. Alas, budget cuts and security concerns have now eliminated this open tour program. Today
you need to secure special access to the center, meaning that only
dignitaries and researchers can take in all Ames has to offer. Some
of the more prominent Ames visitors include the US president and
the governor of California, who land at Moffett Field when visiting
Northern California.

Average Joes, however, can get an almost up-close-and-personal
NASA Ames experience by visiting the Exploration Center museum
just outside the main gates. Don't confuse yourself by looking for
something that actually resembles a museum. Instead, look for
the ultra-plain, tent-like structure. It's a celebration of space done
in budget-cut mode. Even so, the center has all the goodies you
might expect—models of space rovers, space suits, shuttle exhibits . . . Some of the more impressive displays show off glorious photos taken from space.

The museum is located just outside the Moffett Field main gate, accessible from the 101 freeway. For more information about the Exploration Center, see www.nasa.gov/centers/ames/about/aboutames-visiting.html. The visitor center phone number is (650) 604-6274. The NASA Ames Web site is www.nasa.gov/centers/ames.

Schools often visit the Exploration Center. The kids make their way around the exhibits, ending up at a large makeshift theater that plays various educational programs about space.

The Exploration Center is open Tuesday through Friday 10 a.m. to 4 p.m., and on weekends noon to 4 p.m. Parking and admission are free. You can secure some space ice cream and other NASA gear at the nearby gift shop. NASA also holds periodic lectures at the facility. True astronomy fans might spend up to an hour here.

THE AMES AERONAUTICAL LABORATORY

NASA Ames opened in 1939 with a singular focus to pursue aeronautical research. Charles Lindbergh had been commissioned by the government to assess the flight capabilities of the United States and other countries in the early 1930s. He came across a large German air force and decided the US had to do something to keep pace. Lindbergh recommended the construction of additional centers to complement the Langley Memorial Aeronautics Laboratory that housed wind tunnels at Langley Field, Virginia. After surveying more than fifty sites, a committee headed by Lindbergh settled on Moffett Field as the best location for a second site and began work on the Ames Aeronautical Laboratory, named for aeronautical science pioneer Joseph Sweetman Ames.

NACA—the precursor to NASA—liked Moffett Field for a few reasons. Placing a second research center far from Langley would provide some protection from an enemy attack. In addition, the US military already owned the land and had built the massive Hangar One—still a major Silicon Valley landmark—on the site in 1933. And it certainly didn't hurt that Moffett Field offered up great flying weather, proximity to top-notch universities, and access to relatively cheap power supplies.

The cheap power, in fact, was essential to NACA's goal of creating a high-speed flight research center. It needed to fuel what would become the most impressive collection of wind tunnels on the planet.

Backed with close to $15 million in federal funds, a group of young engineers began their aeronautical experiments. Aided by the impressive wind tunnels, the engineers delivered a number of breakthroughs in flight research.

THE FINAL FRONTIER—AND BEYOND

In 1958 the Ames Aeronautical Laboratory took on a new name—NASA Ames Research Center—and a fresh set of goals. The US government pushed the center to use its aeronautical expertise for the creation of vehicles that could travel in space. Specific innovations pioneered at NASA Ames include the "blunt body" concept used by spacecraft to prevent burning when reentering planetary atmospheres, the Pioneer craft that were the first to leave the solar system, and the Viking craft that landed on Mars. The researchers' study of airflow and reentry systems then pushed the center toward grappling with improved materials for spacecraft, which led to a budding nanotechnology group.

The NASA Ames crew has also been pushed in a variety of other directions as an indirect result of flight study. According to facility historian John Boyd, "Starting with tunnel data to study handling characteristics, Ames people modified flight test aircraft, and then built simulators. Simulators led Ames into the human factors, including fatigue measures and data display, and into basic research on adaptability to microgravity, which paves a path into exobiology and ultimately the exploration for life on Mars."

In keeping with its roots at the heart of Silicon Valley, NASA Ames has also played host to solid computer technology research. "To better mine the data from [the] wind tunnels, Ames moved boldly into digital data computing, which led into supercomputing, then computational fluid dynamics, then into internetworking, then air traffic safety, and artificial intelligence and robotics," Boyd wrote. "At the birth of the commercial internet in the early 1990s, one-quarter of all the world's internet traffic moved through Ames servers. Meanwhile, using its expertise in handling massive amounts of data, Ames did fundamental work in infrared astronomy, earth sensing, robotics, remote visualization and now nanotechnology." NASA Ames also plays host to one of the world's largest supercomputers—the 10,000-plus-processor Columbia system, built in 2004 with the help of Intel and SGI.

"We have evolved or transformed two or three different times," Boyd said in an interview. "But the basic work we started in the '40s and '50s is behind almost everything we still do."

NASA AMES TODAY

In recent years Ames has faced the same budget constraints as other NASA centers. To help offset the financial constraints and make use of a large amount of prime real estate, NASA Ames has forged ties with the private sector in Silicon Valley, creating a type of research park where start-ups and nonprofits can set up operations and work in tandem with the NASA staff. Current projects pursued through the research park include fuel cell and nanotechnology ventures.

In addition, NASA Ames works closely with the University of California–Santa Cruz, Carnegie Mellon University, Stanford, and (to some degree) Berkeley. More recently it announced a broad partnership with Google. NASA intends to increase its cooperation with the public sector in the coming years and sees areas such as life sciences, robotics, and nanotechnology as key to the next phase of Ames.

Many of NASA Ames's most impressive structures lie dormant today, while groundbreaking research occurs in the more bland facilities. The massive 1933 hangar, for example, was shuttered in 2002—when toxic chemicals were discovered in the building's material. NASA has struggled since to discover a means of removing the chemicals while still preserving the iconic structure. (As of this writing, the future of Hangar One hangs in the balance, with the Navy examining proposals to destroy the structure while some locals fight to keep it.) Most of the giant wind tunnels scattered across the Ames campus have been mothballed as well. Like the hangar, the wind tunnels stand as impressive architectural oddities.

The bland concrete office buildings that dominate the campus prove less impressive to the eye but play host to Ames's most revolutionary research. One such building houses an air traffic control research center. In tandem with SGI, NASA outfitted a room with a 360-degree display. Groups from major airports including San Francisco and Chicago's O'Hare visit this center to train air traffic controllers and to model hypothetical problems. Researchers also use the display to explore images sent by the Mars rovers. Standing in the room you are surrounded by the Mars landscape, giving you a life-like feel for the planet's terrain.

One of Ames's best-known research buildings holds the giant Columbia supercomputer. Hundreds of researchers submit work to the massive system, which crunches away at their data. The system powers much of the research done in a broad variety of disciplines at Ames.

(((•))) THE SETI INSTITUTE

MOUNTAIN VIEW HAS THE SEARCH INDUSTRY COVERED.
Just a few miles from Google's earthbound search engine headquarters is the SETI Institute—the main hub for hunting down extraterrestrial life.

While the possibility of alien life has been debated perhaps for millennia, the official Search for Extra-Terrestrial Intelligence was first discussed in 1971, when Hewlett-Packard's chief engineer Bernard Oliver led a team of Stanford University and NASA Ames Research Center scientists in a debate about the possible discovery of extraterrestrial life. The group produced the "Project Cyclops" report, which became the SETI bible and pushed the idea of creating an array of telescopes to detect radio signals in space.

The project gained more formal trappings in 1984 with the creation of the SETI Institute. Originally funded by NASA, the project now relies solely on private donations—most notably those from Silicon Valley entrepreneurs. Prominent backers have included Hewlett-Packard, Sun Microsystems, former HP CEO Lewis Platt, Microsoft co-founder Paul Allen, William and Rosemary Hewlett, Gordon and Betty Moore, and the David and Lucile Packard Foundation. HP's Oliver left close to $20 million to SETI when he passed away. Without question, the Silicon Valley elite have kept the search for extraterrestrial life alive.

You'll find the SETI Institute near NASA Ames at 515 North Whisman Road; or on the Web at www.seti.org. The organization can also be reached at (650) 961-6633.

Today SETI employs more than a hundred people and conducts a number of research projects at any given time, including its well-known scanning of space for radio signals.

Sadly, the SETI Institute building doesn't present anything terribly out of this world to the casual observer. An elegant, curved silver entrance outfitted with a healthy amount of glass anchors an otherwise average office building. Nokia works out of an exact replica of the facility across the courtyard.

The SETI Institute, by the way, is not to be confused with the SETI@home project run out of UC Berkeley. SETI@home allows computer users around the globe to download special software that processes information from telescopes during otherwise idle periods. This model of computing—known as grid computing—has been emulated by other organization to make the most of free processor cycles.

So, er, have we heard from any aliens just yet? According to SETI:

NO SETI SEARCH HAS YET RECEIVED A CONFIRMED, EXTRATERRES-TRIAL SIGNAL. IF WE HAD, YOU WOULD KNOW ABOUT IT.

IN THE PAST, THERE WERE SEVERAL UNEXPLAINED AND INTRIGU-ING SIGNALS DETECTED IN SETI EXPERIMENTS. PERHAPS THE MOST FAMOUS OF THESE WAS THE "WOW" SIGNAL PICKED UP AT THE OHIO STATE RADIO OBSERVATORY IN 1977. HOWEVER, NONE OF THESE SIGNALS WAS EVER DETECTED AGAIN, AND FOR SCIENTISTS THAT'S NOT GOOD ENOUGH TO CLAIM SUCCESS AND BOOGIE OFF TO STOCKHOLM TO COLLECT A NOBEL PRIZE.

WHEN WILL SUCCESS OCCUR? NO ONE KNOWS. IT COULD HAPPEN TOMORROW, OR IT COULD TAKE MANY YEARS. MAYBE IT WILL NEVER OCCUR. BUT THE ONLY WAY TO FIND OUT IS TO DO THE EXPERI-MENT.

NETSCAPE

NETSCAPE'S ASTONISHING 1995 IPO SET THE TONE FOR SIX years of overzealous investing and unrealistic expectations around Internet-anything companies. (No public tours available.) By the end of trading on August 9, Netscape shares—which started the day at $28—had soared past $70. The biggest initial public offering in history, it single-handedly ignited the dot-com boom.

In true Silicon Valley style, by 2003 only the carcass remained.

A short hop down Ellis Road to 466 Ellis reveals a pair of large, college-campus-style buildings that also housed Netscape staff. Other companies have since seized this property as well.

An AOL site is nearby farther down Ellis Street. In this area, you will also find the former Veritas headquarters—now branded

Symantec following the companies' merger. All of these structures were once part of an enormous Fairchild Semiconductor site that had been shut down due to ground pollution concerns. A large cleanup effort paved the way for new tenants.

BROWSER WARS

From a technology standpoint, Netscape hadn't done anything terribly spectacular to trigger all the initial fuss. It simply piggybacked on a University of Illinois software project that had resulted in the Mosaic Internet browser. Previously the Internet and its World Wide Web layer had largely belonged to technophiles who knew their way around command line interfaces and databases. The graphics-happy and user-friendly Mosiac broke down some of these barriers, making the Web more accessible.

To see the old Netscape complex, head to the intersection of Ellis Street and East Middlefield Road. Near its peak with more than 1,500 employees, Netscape used to occupy the building located at 487 East Middlefield—currently the head-quarters for Verisign. You can't miss this structure, since it has a bright blue tiled fountain out front. No public tours are available, however.

Marc Andreesen had done much of the early work on Mosaic and in 1994 partnered with SGI co-founder Jim Clark to create a company around a new version of the software. They set up shop in Mountain View and, after the University of Illinois wrestled away the Mosaic brand in court, formed Netscape Communications.

These were the years when many folks were still questioning whether this Internet-thing would ever take off. Most notoriously, Microsoft chairman Bill Gates published a book called *The Road Ahead* in 1995 that barely touched on the Internet. It had to be revised in later editions to make up for the, er, slight oversight.

Others, however, had started to wrap their minds around the idea of connecting millions of people via easy-to-use software. These people were waiting for a sign that the next boom had arrived. Enter Netscape, which set up its massive complex in Mountain View and actually posted decent results. As other companies such as Yahoo! and eBay appeared, the good times only continued.

However, Microsoft—and Gates—eventually caught on to this Internet doohickey and released its own browser, Internet Explorer. So began the browser wars.

While Netscape enjoyed a technology lead, Microsoft had a monopoly in the PC operating system market and gave away its browser software for free. By 1997 Netscape owned less than 5 percent of the browser market; Microsoft had almost all the rest. Netscape's struggles would become a central theme in the US government's antitrust case against Microsoft.

In 1998 American Online agreed to buy Netscape in a stock-for-stock deal valued at $4.2 billion. (Microsoft later settled with AOL over numerous issues, including Netscape, to the tune of $750 million.) Even with AOL behind it, Netscape could never recover from the market share losses to be a real force in the browser market. It went through a couple of rounds of layoffs and more or less evaporated in 2003. Most of the Netscape staff were fired, while the rest were folded into AOL.

Even the Netscape logo was yanked from its former headquarters.

GOOGLE

JUST WHEN IT SEEMED THE INTERNET HYSTERIA HAD ENDED, along came Google.

"In September 1998, Google Inc. opened its door in Menlo Park, California," the company says on its Web site. "The door came with a remote control, as it was attached to the garage of a friend who sublet space to the new corporation's staff of three."

The Segway

IT'S 2001 AND RUMORS OF "GINGER" have swirled around the Internet for months. Everyone wants to know what this "world-changing" invention from Dean Kamen really is.

In December, *Time* secures a mega scoop by getting the first look at Ginger and reveals it to the world in a puffy, hype-filled story. As it turns out, Ginger is the Segway Human Transporter—a glorified scooter.

The Segway captured the attention of some of Silicon Valley's biggest names. Apple co-founder Steve Jobs told *Time* that the scooter could be bigger than the PC. Famed venture capitalist John Doerr reckoned it might be bigger than the Internet and then went a step farther by saying the company behind the Segway would reach $1 billion in sales at a quicker clip than any other firm in history.

Hindsight can be so cruel.

As a result of an embarrassing product recall in 2006, Segway Inc. was forced to reveal that over the past four years, it had sold all of 23,500 scooters. Consumers have shied from the pricey device, which is banned from sidewalks in many metropolitan areas. Only police officers and the military have demonstrated more than a mild interest.

That said, the Segway has managed to carve out a healthy or unhealthy following, depending on your perspective, in Silicon Valley. Apple co-founder Steve Wozniak can often be heard extolling its virtues in interviews. And in fact, Wozniak has garnered attention as the most famous member of the local Segway Polo groups. Segway fans from around the Valley gather from time to time to engage in a distorted form of the sport that consists of them zooming around a field and hitting a large, plastic ball with mallets. It's awkward. It's not terribly athletic. But some people love it. If you think Segway Polo might be your thing, have a look at the Bay Area Segway Enthusiasts Group's Web site at www.bayareaseg.com.

Of course, if you have the technology know-how, there's a way to avoid the price tag ($3,000–5,000) for a Segway: Trevor Blackwell, an inventor who works in Mountain View, has constructed a homemade replica for less than half the going rate of the real deal. You can catch Blackwell riding the more modestly named "balancing scooter" around Mountain View and find more information on his device at www.tlb.org.

The next year, Google moved to an office near Stanford on University Avenue. The new digs didn't last long—the firm headed for an old SGI building later that same year.

Today Google—the fastest-growing Internet company of all time—lays claim not only to the old SGI building but also most of the buildings around it. Just about every standing structure near the Shoreline Amiptheatre has a Google stamp. Every day, hundreds of workers pour into the complex, creating gridlock on Shoreline Boulevard, which feeds the Googleplex, in Mountain View.

Right off the bat, the Googleplex comes off as an unusual headquarters. Large purple, green, and yellow towers shoot up and out of a space-age structure featuring healthy amounts of glass and slick silver sides. The complex gives off a corporate-playground feeling, with liberal splashes of color. It's as if a modern architect teamed with a kid and his box of crayons.

Google, however, can't claim points for originality with its now famous headquarters. The building—described by some as the Taj Mahal of Silicon Valley—was the brainchild of former Silicon Valley hardware powerhouse Silicon Graphics Inc. (SGI), which has been forced to part with numerous real estate assets in the area to stay afloat.

The inside of the Googleplex matches the playful outside. Dot-coms once took pride in offering workers free sodas and meals. They also flaunted the occasional massage, party, or video game lounge as a perk befitting the technology worker lifestyle. Google observed these practices and then elevated the art of spoiling employees to a whole new level.

Some of the sillier signature Googleplex items are colored plastic balls, bean bags, lava lamps, toys, and inflatable doohickeys. Most, however, straddle the line between perk and productivity enhancer. Google, for example, set up a technology support store where staff can repair computers and other devices. Employees can also save a bit of time by getting a cut-rate haircut from on-site stylists. And if you need to bring your child to work for a bit, it's no problem: Kids' areas are packed full of toys.

Google's Free Lunch (and Dinner, and Breakfast)

GOOGLE FAMOUSLY PROVIDES THREE gourmet meals a day to its workers—at no charge. A top-class chef prepares the food, which might include dishes like these:

- Santa Cruz surfer's pie. Layers of sautéed organic Swiss chard, cannellini beans, seitan, garlic, fennel, oregano, molasses, mirepoix, and thyme, baked in the oven and finished with a mashed potato crust.

- Butter lettuce and beef. Organic butter lettuce chopped with grilled sliced flank steak and dried cranberries.

- Chicken adobo a la Velasquez. Braised free-range chicken with garlic, ginger, organic tamari, lime, cider vinegar, spices, hard-boiled eggs, and chipotle dressing.

- Frikkadelle (South African meat loaf). Ground Colorado lamb, ground pork, mint, parsley, carrots, eggs, bread crumbs, garlic, cloves, coriander, and milk, all served with a mushroom miso gravy.

Not exactly slumming it, are they?

On the health and diversion front, you'll find two swim-in-place pools—lifeguards and all—for catching a few laps between projects, lounges with pool tables and snack cafes, and beach volleyball courts. Workers can also partake in Google-subsidized massages and bring their dogs to the office. (No cats allowed.)

Some wonder how long Google can maintain this fanciful setup. A number of critics contend that Google has held too tightly to its child-like dreams since becoming a public company. Many of these critics would like to see a more professional work environment and expect the firm to cave when its growth slows and investors turn feisty. Until then, however, Google plans to keep its workers happy.

When the company did go public, it turned hundreds of staff into paper millionaires. The prospect of making serious dough off Google stock has allowed the company to attract top talent in an unrivaled fashion. Unlike the boom-time dot-coms, Google doesn't have any major competition from a market perception standpoint. It's been able to poach most of the talented engineers looking for work.

A SYSTEM **DUBBED** BACKRUB

Google began as an idea in the minds of Stanford University graduate students Sergey Brin and Larry Page during the height of the dot-com boom. While pursuing their doctorates in 1996, the pair developed an Internet search system. They dubbed it BackRub for its analysis of backlinks that point to a given Web site from other sites.

Up to that point, most of the popular search engines used a simplistic method for ranking their results that relied for the most part on seeing how many times a given term appeared on a Web page. It didn't take site designers very long to discover methods of gaming this search system. They would, for example, hide black text on a black background, repeating terms over and over again.

The BackRub system worked around this problem by gauging a given Web site's relevance based on how many other sites linked to it, tacitly providing their seal of approval.

You can find the Google headquarters (650-253-0000) at 1600 Amphitheatre Parkway; no public tours are available. Google's founders also purchased the house in Menlo Park where they got their start working in the garage. The house is located at 232 Santa Margarita Avenue.

By 1998 the groundwork had been laid for the typical Stanford mega start-up story. Brin and Page paid more attention to their budding project than their schoolwork and started to set up a makeshift lab. Where Hewlett and Packard had their garage, Brin and Page had Page's doom room stacked with servers and storage. The pair consulted with fellow Stanford alum David Filo, who'd started Yahoo! years earlier with yet another Stanford student, Jerry Yang. Filo encouraged the upstarts to develop their search technology and strive to start a company.

Having maxed out their credit cards, Brin and Page tried to drum up interest for their technology by showing it to the major portal companies of the time. In 1998 the portal market was hot, and many mediocre companies had tens of millions at their disposal. The portal crowd, however, didn't grasp the merits of paying for better search technology when the existing systems worked well enough.

Andy Bechtolsheim, a Stanford alum and co-founder of Sun Microsystems, disagreed. He found search to be a "broken" part of the Internet. "We met him very early one morning on the porch of a Stanford faculty member's home in Palo Alto," Brin recalls on Google's official history Web site. "We gave him a quick demo. He had to run off somewhere, so he said, 'Instead of us discussing all the details, why don't I just write you a check?' It was made out to Google Inc. and was for $100,000." Bechtolsheim's goal was simply to find things more easily on the Internet. His move did, of course, also turn out to be a sound investment.

GOOGLE BECOMES GOOGLE

The Google founders had yet to set up a formal corporate entity, which made it hard to deposit Bechtolsheim's check. So Brin and Page worked to incorporate Google and tapped friends and family for more cash, ultimately bringing in $1 million. By September 1998 Google had set up shop at the Menlo Park garage and hired its first employee.

Even in those early days, Google garnered the attention of thousands of Internet users and the mainstream media. The company offered a search box and nothing more. Yet that search box worked better and faster than any other service.

In 1999 things really took off for Google as it started answering hundreds of thousands of requests per day and received $25 million in venture funding from two of the most prominent Sand Hill Road firms—Sequoia Capital and Kleiner Perkins Caufield & Byers. That same year Google moved to the now famous Googleplex in Mountain View. Even as the dot-com bubble began to pop, the firm became the de facto search standard and edged into the black. Still, it wasn't clear that Google would become the next billion-dollar success story in Silicon Valley. Many failed to see how Google would make serious cash off its search model.

All that changed in 2002, when Google rolled out AdSense—a system allowing people and companies to bid on certain search terms to ensure that their ad appeared near Google's official search results. Instead of bringing in a few cents from each ad as Brin and Page first expected, the company was able to secure dollars per ad for the most popular terms. The subsequent revenue stream fueled Google's rise as a public company. Indeed, Google was in many ways the ultimate Internet company for Wall Street: It was already profitable when it started trading and didn't have to share hype with other companies. All eyes focused on the darling of the moment, whose stock soared.

By 2005 Google's success triggered a second wave of dot-com hype. Venture capitalists started funding a variety of dot-coms with flimsy business models, and large companies poured hundreds of millions into immature start-ups. It remains to be seen if Google can come close to matching the growth expectations of Wall Street over the long term. Without question, however, the company has established itself alongside the likes of Yahoo! and eBay as an example of an Internet-based operation with staying power.

DON'T BE EVIL

Like any successful company, Google has endeared itself to some and become repugnant to others. As is often the case, both the pro and con camps focus on the same issues.

Much of the Google adoration stems from a combination of the company's superior search technology and its whimsical corporate spirit. Google fans celebrate its R&D-friendly environment, where workers get a set amount of time per week to explore their own projects. They also admire Google's fondness for open-source software and its image as a benevolent leader in the search market.

Critics contend that something more sinister lurks beneath Google's happy-go-lucky attitude. Any entity that keeps track of individuals' search requests, e-mails, photos, and personal files deserves

Google's Party Plane

GOOGLE'S CAREFREE ATTITUDE TOWARD business turned downright silly during an episode in 2006 involving its so-called party plane.

Corporate jets have become commonplace, although wide-bodied corporate palaces remain something of a rarity. Google acquired such a beauty in 2005 when it bought a used Boeing 767-200 from Qantas. The size of this jet—the 767 model can carry up to 180 passengers—proved amusing enough to gossip-mongers who caught wind of the beast. Little did they know that the plane's girth was only the beginning of the story.

Thanks to a lawsuit between a Google holding company and the man commissioned to customize the corporate 767, the public learned of some of the unconventional desires of the Google brass. Aviation designer Leslie Jennings charged that Google's founders Sergey Brin and Larry Page wanted such extravagances in their jet as hammocks dangling from the ceiling, dining rooms, and quasi cocktail lounges. The founders were so impassioned by their jet's features that they engaged in an argument over what types of beds should fill out their private sanctuaries, according to the designer. Google's CEO Eric Schmidt had to step in during the discussion to make sure that Page got his California King bed.

Google and Jennings settled their lawsuit shortly after the plane discussions were made public in the press. According to the Google public relations team, the company looks to use the jet less as a flying party bus and more as a unique company transport. Its size will enable the firm carry up to fifty people and make longer nonstop trips than typical corporate jets. Google can also entertain significant groups of people on the plane while parked overseas.

But no matter the practical spin Google puts on the jet, most will see it as an example of the largesse that seems to accompany every Silicon Valley darling during its moment in the spotlight.

a healthy amount of skepticism. Is this company responsible enough to protect personal information? Some also charge that Google is little more than an ad broker that got lucky by stumbling into a multibillion-dollar business, which removes a bit of its inventive luster.

One particular moment stands out in the Google debate. In the paperwork accompanying its IPO, Google revealed that a core tenet of the company was "Don't Be Evil." Google fans latched on to the slogan, impressed that a technology giant would have the guts to make such a proclamation in its corporate filings. Google backed up its philosophy, too, by vowing to set up a large fund for good works. In addition, managers warned that they would not be guided by a desire to always benefit investors in the short term. The company would pursue the advancement of its technology at all costs, even if this meant disappointing Wall Street on occasion.

One set of critics in the financial community found the "Don't Be Evil" slogan and other seemingly "unserious" aspects of Google's move toward being a public company appalling. They argued that, while the business community should have lofty social goals, it should express such ambitions in a more professional manner.

A second set of critics posited that the "Don't Be Evil" notion would come back to haunt the company. And while evil is a nebulous term, Google's corporate morals have indeed come into question on several occasions. In 2006, for example, its decision to do business in China despite the government demanding that it censor search results proved controversial. In addition, US government regulators demanded the search results of many major Internet players. This

Steve Jobs Speaks

- "It's really hard to design products by focus groups. A lot of times, people don't know what they want until you show it to them."—*Business-Week*, May 25, 1998.
- "The products suck! There's no sex in them anymore!"—Jobs' take on Apple's gear under Gil Amelio's leadership—*BusinessWeek*, July 1997.
- "The desktop computer industry is dead. Innovation has virtually ceased. Microsoft dominates with very little innovation. That's over. Apple lost. The desktop market has entered the dark ages, and it's going to be in the dark ages for the next 10 years, or certainly for the rest of this decade."—*Wired magazine*, February 1996.
- "Do you want to spend the rest of your life selling sugared water or do you want a chance to change the world?"—Jobs' famous pitch to tempt John Sculley to leave Pepsi and become Apple's CEO, *Odyssey: Pepsi to Apple*, by John Sculley and John Byrne.

led some to wonder whether Google's policy of keeping track of user data for extended periods of time was a solid idea.

Beyond these elements, Google also maintains a strict code of secrecy reminiscent of fellow Silicon Valley giant Apple. Google has blocked reporters it doesn't care for from speaking with company executives and tends to allow only select groups of journalists into company events. Some question why such a company that gives off a playful vibe would be so reticent to discuss its technology and policies with the media.

Many wonder just how far Google's tentacles can stretch. It has demonstrated intentions of getting into everything from providing Microsoft Office–like software to running its own communications networks. The company's wealth and vast talent have also given rise to the notion that it could become a sort of Microsoft for the Internet—a massive force that rivals struggle to match. The company's biggest fans seem content with this proposal, viewing Google as a kinder, gentler entity than Microsoft.

The search company, however, has yet to demonstrate that it can develop successful new businesses to complement ad sales. Google faces no shortage of challenges to this core ad business and has struggled to keep a pristine aura around the "Don't Be Evil" philosophy. The coming years will test Brin and Page's idealistic objectives in a massive way.

CA-84
CA-238
US-101
G-3
I-880
SUNNYVALE
CA-238
I-680
I-280
CA-82
FOOTHILL EXPRESSWAY
LAWRENCE EXPRESSWAY
CA-85
CA-87
CA-130
SANTA CLARA
CA-82
GUADALUPE PARKWAY
CA-35
CA-17
US-101
CA-85
CA-9
CA-9

0 | KILOMETERS 5 |
0 | MILES   5 |

SANTA CLARA *and* SUNNYVALE

SANTA CLARA AND SUNNYVALE OFTEN GET knocked for being more about business than pleasure. And indeed, these two spread-out suburbs cannot claim quaint central shopping districts or clusters of eclectic eateries. Instead they intersperse generic shopping centers with business parks and fast-food chains. There are hardly any remnants of the glorious orchards that once dominated the area.

The sprawl started as companies such as Intel took advantage of once cheap land and began building out large campuses. The strategy of moving between Stanford's home in Palo Alto and the larger San Jose was risky at the time. It has, however, worked out well for the numerous companies with headquarters in Santa Clara and Sunnyvale.

In fact, locals can be proud of a couple of the giant campuses in the area. Sun Microsystems and Advanced Micro Devices both enjoy plush digs. Myriad start-ups have since filled out the business parks as well to complement these larger firms.

Along with the businesses, you'll find a number of modest-size convention centers scattered around the two suburbs. For those who can't handle the fast-food glut, Sunnyvale offers a culinary treasure in the Lion & Compass—a true Silicon Valley institution. On the more ostentatious front, Santa Clara is the home of Paramount's Great America, the largest amusement park for miles and miles. Those searching for a new house will find much-reduced prices in these two areas, at least when compared with the likes of Palo Alto and Mountain View. Of course, no property comes cheap in Silicon Valley.

CHAPTER 3

Overall, these two suburbs combine to provide much of the workforce that makes Silicon Valley tick.

⏻ INTEL

HISTORIANS LOVE TO SINGLE OUT AN INDIVIDUAL OR A corporation as the key symbol of an era in business. Such icons provide quick and easy insight into what made a certain place, industry, and period of time tick.

Those looking to define the rise of Silicon Valley will forever point to Robert Noyce and Intel as the region's most obvious icons. Noyce—as a co-founder of both Fairchild Semiconductor and Intel—embodied the entrepreneurial spirit that many associate with the technology industry. Both scientist and businessman, he had the vision to see where semiconductor technology could end up and pushed his troops toward that goal. He served as the charismatic figure needed to kick-start the silicon gold rush.

Intel delivers something more concrete to Silicon Valley lore. It has pursued the goal of making products cheaper, smaller, and faster with unmatched vigor. Intel has managed to slot its processors into the vast majority of personal computers, giving it one of the most prized positions in the technology industry. In so doing the firm has touched both consumers and businesses en masse. The chip giant helped kick-start Silicon Valley's rise and has remained the most consistent performer for more than three decades.

Two things prove striking about Intel's main campus in Santa Clara. It's big and blue.

You won't be impressed by much else about the rather bland office building giants when barreling down Mission College Boulevard. The lackluster Intel headquarters doesn't seem to fit with other aspects of the company's culture. A high level of marketing savvy, a strong brand, and first-rate attention to detail have long been traits associated with Intel. You might expect this polish to result in an aesthetic gem of a central compound.

Instead, Intel has turned out a structure closer to its engineering roots. Large, blue boxes with miles of glass link together, covering some 3 million square feet. The blue glass mass gives off a practical air that speaks more to efficiency than artistry.

In its defense, Intel did not have much time to think out the design of these headquarters. The company started on 365 Middlefield Road in Mountain View. The smallish office worked fine for a couple of years, but then Intel started to grow. Taking a risk, management shifted to a twenty-six-acre Santa Clara pear orchard in 1971. At the time, moving away from nearby Stanford University and the Stanford Research Park didn't seem like the smartest decision. Still, in retrospect the idea of picking up a lot of land at low cost looks bright. And in any event, within a few short years Silicon Valley would stretch past Intel's headquarters to San Jose, leaving the company in the middle of the technology bustle.

Thousands of Silicon Valley's sharpest folks have devoted their working hours at this expansive campus since 1971. Intel has remained a constant force in Silicon Valley. The big blue buildings may be boring, but they reflect a consistency and a force that Intel has carried all these years.

A NOYCE **GUY** FINISHES **FIRST**

In 1956 William Shockley set out to capitalize on the transistor he had co-invented by recruiting many of the finest young minds that he could find for his new venture, Shockley Semiconductor Laboratories. For this group of scientists and engineers, life at the Mountain View start-up was filled with ups and downs. On the positive side, the researchers were able to pursue work in a groundbreaking field in the company of a remarkable group of peers. The height of working for Shockley may have come when he shared a Nobel Prize

ROBERT NOYCE
"A gentle, caring spirit"

WHILE HE'S OFTEN REFERRED TO AS "the Father of Silicon Valley," Robert Noyce would have shied away from such oversimplified praise. The son of a preacher, he grew up in Grinnell, Iowa, in humble surroundings. Excelling both academically and socially in his youth, he reached even greater academic heights at Grinnell College. In particular, he became fascinated by then brand-new transistor technology.

Noyce would continue this study at MIT and, later, while working for Philco. His reputation in the field was enough to capture the attention of one of the transistor's inventors—William Shockley, who called the younger man in January 1956 to offer him a job. "It was like picking up the phone and talking to God," Noyce would remember.

Noyce's relatively deep transistor knowledge elevated him to a position of prominence at Shockley's fledgling labs. Quickly, however, the older man's many eccentricities as a manager led to deep divisions within the laboratory staff. In 1957 Noyce and seven others left to start Fairchild Semiconductor.

Without question, the Fairchild group worked as a team, and each discovery added to its overall body of knowledge in the burgeoning field of semiconductors. Noyce, however, was the lone staffer to come up with the explicit idea of an integrated circuit—a single silicon chip containing numerous transistors. As the company's success increased, Noyce took on more

and more of the managerial duties. He combined a gentle, caring spirit with an ability to set lofty goals for employees and then nudge them toward these objectives. According to biographer Leslie Berlin, "He was everything that they wanted to be.... When they would think about who had influenced them, it was this incredibly charismatic, attractive, successful man who had taken them under his wing when they were little tykes."

In July 1968 Noyce again changed course and—with longtime collaborator Gordon Moore—turned his energies toward the founding of yet another new firm. Intel's tremendous success secured Noyce's legacy as a researcher, entrepreneur, and manager. The youngster from Grinnell who'd spent his early years borrowing money from relatives had become rich beyond his wildest dreams. Noyce's personal fortune allowed him to purse activities such as extreme skiing and flying with gusto.

While Noyce eventually turned over the CEO role to Moore, he remained active at Intel for many years as well as funding numerous start-ups, keeping track of his investments on scraps of paper stored in shoe boxes. In his later years also played a central role in the US's battle to remain a major player in the semiconductor market against increasing competition from Asian suppliers.

Robert Noyce died suddenly of a heart attack in 1990, a Silicon Valley legend in his own time.

in physics for his invention. The young scientists were in the presence of a living legend.

In many ways, however, Shockley's personal success led to failures at the lab. The great scientist was forever torn between pursuing academic endeavors and running a business. While his staff urged Shockley to focus on building simpler, more usable transistors, he wanted to focus on an experimental diode. Shockley's inability to stay centered on one project frustrated the researchers.

Seven of these staffers eventually decided to leave the company and look for work elsewhere, hopefully together. Ultimately they were joined by an eighth defector—the brilliant scientist-manager Robert Noyce. The "traitorous eight" co-founded Fairchild Semiconductor in 1957. With Noyce's subsequent invention of the integrated circuit, Fairchild's future looked bright indeed.

"NM ELECTRONICS INSIDE" DOESN'T SOUND QUITE RIGHT

Over the years, plenty of Fairchild employees followed the pattern set by their own bosses—leaving the company to found concerns of their own. By the late 1960s Silicon Valley was littered with close to fifteen semiconductor-focused ventures.

So a semiconductor start-up was hardly a new idea by the time Fairchild co-founders Robert Noyce and Gordon Moore mustered the courage to create NM Electronics. The two men had stayed on at Fairchild longer than you might expect given their entrepreneurial leanings and powerful intellects.

Before leaving Fairchild, Noyce had in fact entertained the idea of starting a new company to produce semiconductor memory, and had pitched the idea to Moore. Despite working well together for years, Moore did not bite right away. It took a firmer sales pitch from Noyce to seal the deal. The final straw came when Noyce was passed over for the CEO post at their parent company, Fairchild Camera and Instrument.

Both executives left in July 1968. The press largely ignored Moore's departure but heaped ink on Noyce's exit. Companies, investors, bankers, and former co-workers reached out to Noyce, hoping to glean some insight into what he would do next.

Behind the scenes Noyce and Moore had touched base with longtime investing partner Arthur Rock and agreed to put their own money into the new venture. It seemed clear that Noyce's managerial expertise would combine well with Moore's talents in the research lab to create an interesting company. Both men owned sparkling reputations in the semiconductor industry and could attract top talent. In addition, they both displayed fierce competitive streaks, although Noyce's drive was more obvious to outsiders than that of the reserved Moore.

The Fairchild folks who caught wind of Noyce and Moore's plans were quick to try to sign on. One of the most aggressive people to follow Moore was Andy Grove, who started as research and development director at Intel.

Shortly after incorporating, NM Electronics bought the rights to the Intel name for $15,000 from Intelco. The new firm then set up shop at 365 Middlefield Road in Mountain View, zeroing in on semiconductor memory as a promising technology. Intel's first product—the 3101 Schottky bipolar random access memory (RAM)—appeared in 1969, and so did the first order from Hamilton Electric. This product did little to boost Intel's early fortunes, however, as Texas Instruments and Fairchild had similar products on the market.

But another event occurred in 1969 that would shape the future of both Intel and the computing industry as a whole. Busicom—a Japanese calculator company—called on the young firm for help with a future line of high-performance calculators. The project would require Intel to design twelve customized chips each loaded with thousands of transistors. Intel took on the job with the help of Busicom engineers.

They found the work more difficult than expected, prompting Intel's staff to look for simpler, more cost-effective ways to design the chips. That's when Intel engineer Ted Hoff proposed the breakthrough idea of producing a single, general-purpose chip that could be programmed to handle different tasks such as display and printer control.

Busicom accepted Intel's proposal, but plenty of tough work lay ahead. As months passed, Busicom begin to query Intel about progress on the chip. This led to Stanley Mazor and Federico Faggin refining Hoff's original design and delivering a product to Busicom.

INSIDE INTEL

With plenty of financial backing and a second memory product ready, Intel moved its headquarters to Santa Clara in 1970, buying a twenty-six-acre pear orchard. By the time 1971 rolled around, the firm had dubbed the chip it designed for Busicom the 4004 and billed it as "a new era of integrated electronics—a micro-programmable computer on a chip!" Intel convinced Busicom to return the rights to the design in exchange for refunding some of the development costs and a price break on the product.

Customers in a wide range of industries began experimenting with Intel's microprocessors, tuning their software to make the chip handle specific tasks. In 1975 Intel's third-generation 8080 chip really found its home when hobby computer kits such as the Altair 8800 started including the product.

By 1979 Intel had become a huge force. It appeared on the Fortune 500 list for the first time at slot 486. That same year, Noyce pulled back on direct involvement with day-to-day operations, becoming vice chairman and turning over the CEO and chairman posts to Gordon Moore. Andy Grove rose to president and chief operating officer. Two years later IBM picked Intel's 8088 processor to power its new line of personal computers. This sealed Intel's position at the center of the computing industry.

Moore's Law

THE MOST FAMOUS SILICON VALLEY LAW isn't a law at all. It's more of an observation.

While working at Fairchild Semiconductor in 1965, Gordon Moore penned an article for *Electronics Magazine* describing some of the trends he expected to see in the semiconductor industry in coming years. In particular, he pointed out that the number of transistors on an integrated circuit would likely increase at a dramatic rate.

"The complexity for minimum component costs has increased at a rate of roughly a factor of two per year," Moore wrote. "Certainly over the short term this rate can be expected to continue, if not to increase. Over the longer term, the rate of increase is a bit more uncertain, although there is no reason to believe it will not remain nearly constant for at least 10 years."

In short, Moore expected the number of components in a semiconductor device to double every year. In 1975 he adjusted his "law" to say that the number of transistors on a chip would double every two years.

Once put down on paper, Moore's Law took on a greater significance than its author could ever have imagined. It set an innovation target for the computing industry to create faster, smaller, and cheaper products at a relentless pace. At the time the paper was published, for instance, semiconductor products boasted about sixty transistors and resistors. In 2006 that number was more than a billion.

Historians often overlook other intriguing parts of Moore's paper, most likely because they don't deal directly with the transistor observation. The first two paragraphs of the piece prove as prophetic as the rest of the document:

"The future of integrated electronics is the future of electronics itself," Moore wrote. "The advantages of integration will bring about a proliferation of electronics, pushing this science into many new areas."

"Integrated circuits will lead to such wonders as home computers—or at least terminals connected to a central computer—automatic controls for automobiles, and personal portable communications equipment. The electronic wristwatch needs only a display to be feasible today."

The notion of a personal computer was hardly commonplace at the time, making Moore's ability to predict the future even more remarkable.

John Markoff, a writer for *The New York Times* and arguably the best-known Silicon Valley journalist, has contented that Douglas Engelbart, inventor of the mouse and all-around computing pioneer, actually made a similar observation during a 1960 presentation.

"Thinking about the idea of miniaturized circuitry, Mr. Engelbart realized that it would scale down to vastly smaller sizes than the current electronic comments," Markoff wrote in an article titled "It's Moore's Law, but Another Had the Idea First," published in *The New York Times* in April 2005. "He had that insight because earlier he had worked as an electronics technician in the wind tunnel at the Ames Research Center, a NASA laboratory in Mountain View, Calif. There, aerodynamicists made models and scaled them up into complete airplanes."

"It was an easy conceptual leap to realize that integrated circuits would scale in the opposite direction. In 1959 he put his ideas into a paper, titled 'Microelectronics and the Art of Similitude.' In February 1960, he traveled to the International Circuit Conference in Philadelphia. There he explained to his audience that as chips scaled down, the new microelectronic engineers would have to worry about changing constraints, just as aerodynamicists had to worry about the macroworld."

Moore said he was familiar with Engelbart's presentation. Many historians, however, maintain that Moore should still be declared inventor of the "law" because of his calculated graph showing transistor improvements, and because of Fairchild and Intel's push to turn theory into reality. Regardless of who came up with the idea first, Moore had the benefit of having friend and fellow semiconductor guru Carver Mead coin the phrase "Moore's Law" in his honor. Or, at least, that's the common wisdom.

"Gordon thinks I came up with the phrase," Mead said in an interview. "My memory is very foggy on this.

"I do remember spending a lot of time with Larry Waller who was a very good writer for *Electronics Magazine*. I think it was during an evening with a very open, relaxed discussion where we talked about this phenomenon that was happening. I would never have premeditated something like that. It would have only been something that came out of a discussion. Then, it became sort of a fun thing. It isn't a law like a law of physics. It's more like law of human nature. It's a positive thing."

Industry observers now say the number of transistors doubles every 18 months to two years. This trend more or less translates into computing power doubling about every two years. That has proven to be an incredible driver for almost every industry in Silicon Valley, as component makers of all types try to keep up with the semiconductor firms.

The processor power advances have also proved lucrative to Silicon Valley firms. Faster chips allow software makers to create more sophisticated—or at least bulkier—applications. In turn, this means consumers are more apt to seek the latest and greatest machines every couple of years to power the demanding software.

On a somewhat philosophical level, Moore's Law has hung over the computing industry's head like a commandment to innovate.

"The human race has spent its life believing things that are negative," Mead said. "The fact that a whole generation or several generations now actually believe this law enough to put their lives and careers into it is astounding. "It turns out

SILICON VALLEY SOUNDBYTE (continued)

that if you just think there is no limit, if you're willing to find a way around the obstacles people put in your way, then amazing things can happen."

Rather amusingly, Moore's original *Electronics Magazine* article had a comic attached to it, making light of the proposed ideas that personal computers would eventually be commonplace. The comic shows a store selling "Notions," "Cosmetics" and, of course "Handy Home Computers." A salesman holds up a toaster-sized computer in front of perplexed consumers. Such a scenario isn't that far off in today's stores.

Over the years engineers have periodically feared an end to Moore's Law. Yet they always manage to come up with some design breakthrough that allows them to shrink semiconductor components further and pack more electronics on a single chip. Intel expects Moore's Law to hold through 2015, as of this writing. At that time the transistors will become so small—just a few atoms—that problems could arise in the manufacturing process. Researchers are considering other materials besides silicon and new manufacturing techniques to avoid such issues.

Along with its business success, Intel made other key strategic decisions during its early years. To avoid the talent drain they had witnessed at Fairchild, Noyce and Moore used liberal stock compensation to tempt Intel workers to stay on and share in the company's future success. Then, given heavy pricing pressure from Asian competitors, the firm decided to exit the memory business in 1985. Management described giving up on Intel's original product as a "painful decision," but it proved the right one, allowing Intel to focus on the much more lucrative PC processor market.

Through the 1980s, Intel experienced a number of highs and lows—expanding across the globe while also facing its first protracted slump. In 1987 Gordon Moore turned over the CEO post to Andy Grove and became chairman; Noyce retained the vice chairman title.

The average consumer will be most familiar with the Intel of the 1990s. It debuted the "Intel Inside" slogan in 1991, branding every

PC possible with the phrase. It rolled out new processor after new processor and became the largest semiconductor company in the world. It also managed to expand well beyond PCs into server computers, networking devices, and consumer gadgets. The company's dominance in the PC processor market—it held close to a 90 percent market share at times—did not go unnoticed by regulators or competitors. Antitrust charges have followed Intel in the United States and overseas since the late 1990s.

Along with legal troubles, Intel has faced periodic bouts of product difficulties. The company, for example, suffered an embarrassing recall of an early Pentium chip. It has also been forced to kill off or delay numerous products in recent years in hopes of keeping pace with main rival AMD.

That said, Intel has established itself as a manufacturing powerhouse and is overall considered a marvel of efficiency given the enormous volumes of complex products that it cranks out. Today it's one of the most recognizable brands and companies on the planet and continues to grow. Without question, it has been a steadying presence in Silicon Valley during the region's tremendous growth. Intel's constant drive to make processors faster and smarter has helped push the technology industry as a whole.

► THE INTEL MUSEUM, SANTA CLARA

NOT SHY ABOUT CELEBRATING ITS PROMINENT PLACE IN COMPUTING history, Intel has constructed an Intel Museum at its big, blue Santa Clara headquarters. The modest, one-room structure manages to deliver an immense amount of information about Intel's founders, the making of processors, and the role processors have played in a wide variety of industries. The learning, however, does come with a cost. This is a place for Intel, by Intel, and all about Intel—so the propaganda quotient runs high. But when you're on the home turf of one of the world's most successful and inventive companies, such hubris is forgiven.

CLICK HERE **Climbing the Valley**

ROCK CLIMBING ENTHUSIASTS CAN GET their fix at a couple of spots in the Valley suburbs.

Planet Granite has emerged as Sunnyvale's hot spot for the indoor climbing crowd. The 25,000-square-foot building offers up 119 top-rope climbs, maxing out at a height of 60 feet. Classes are held for beginners, as are sessions for corporations hoping for some shared fun. Experts, too, can pick from special programs. A day pass starts at about $17, while children and students enjoy healthy discounts. Planet Granite also sells monthly and yearly memberships that include unlimited climbing along with access to the fitness facilities. Real go-getters can even tap yoga and cycling classes.

You'll find Planet Granite at 815 Stewart Drive, Sunnyvale; (408) 991-9090; or on the Web at www.planetgranite.com.

Gymnastics house Twisters Gym in Mountain View also takes its rock climbing very seriously. The gym specializes in classes for youngsters, offering beginning courses right on up to competitive training for climbing events.

The gym is located at 2639 Terminal Boulevard, Mountain View; or you can visit www.twisterssportscenter.com.

Those who prefer to venture outside will want to hit up the famed Castle Rock State Park. Along with 32 miles of hiking and horseback riding trails, Castle Rock has numerous curious rock formations that have proved popular with climbers. At the crest of the Santa Cruz Mountains, the park is located at 15000 Skyline Boulevard in Los Gatos. More information on the park is available at www.parks.ca.gov.

You might expect a corporate museum to come off as pretty hokey and uninspiring. The Intel Museum defies such suppositions with a professional, well-designed setup. Bright blue, orange, and green displays draw you in and keep your attention with text, audio, video, and hands-on components.

After entering the museum, you'll find one of the many—this place is well staffed—Intel workers offering up a guided tour; you also have the option of an audio tour. Those who pick the latter receive an Intel-chip-powered handheld device that handles video and audio duties. You're free to pick from history-focused or technology-focused tours and can alternate between the two as you like.

Don't be dismayed by the first exhibit—the Intel time capsule. This "display" consists of a hole in the wall that looks out onto the courtyard of the Robert Noyce building, where Intel planted a time capsule in 2003. The offering will be opened up in July 2018 on Intel's fiftieth anniversary. Future Intellians will find a Pentium 4 chip, some Costa Rican newspapers, hats, bracelets, and other knickknacks.

The real education process begins at the next display, where you can hear stories of Intel's past as told by the founders and early employees. This leads right into a knockout exhibit on Fairchild and Intel co-founder Bob Noyce.

The information at the museum expands on many of the well-known stories about Noyce's role as the visionary leader of Intel, his invention of the integrated circuit, and the paradoxical nature of his humble yet adventurous spirit. Those wanting to dig deeper can flip through a virtual copy of Noyce's journal, where it's revealed that he was suspended for a semester from Grinnell College in Iowa for stealing a pig from a local farmer for a party. Noyce returned to the farm the next day, confessed, and offered to pay for the pig, but was punished anyway. In a note to the school, Noyce's father offered up some pleasantries about the suspension but added that the school seemed more focused on the well-being of pigs than of students. Exhibits do spend more time celebrating Noyce than Gordon Moore or Andy Grove—perhaps because the latter are still kicking and have an active role with the company.

Intel's Long Voyage on the Itanic

WHILE ONE OF THE MOST RESPECTED companies in the technology industry, Intel has suffered through its share of foibles, gaffes, and complete meltdowns. Such flaps have included chip recalls, extensive product delays, and the failure to create new technology ahead of rivals. In most cases, Intel has managed to correct the issues in short order and maintain its efficient, ruthlessly competitive image.

Still, the company has endured a lengthy struggle to shake the curse of one product. It's a processor so mocked, knocked, and ridiculed that Intel executives cringe when reporters bring it up as a topic. Its name is Itanium, but many people refer to it as Itanic.

Intel does not stand alone as the only Silicon Valley giant to back the Itanium chip. In 1994 it announced the product in partnership with Hewlett-Packard, which had been working on the Itanium architecture since 1988. HP felt Itanium would replace its own PA-RISC chips in the years to come, becoming the industry standard. Backers billed it as a "20 year architecture"—the chip of the future.

Many companies and pundits bought this sales pitch. Large server makers vowed to rewrite their software for Itanium's unique architecture—a monumental task. Companies such as HP, Compaq, and SGI agreed to phase out their own processor development and move toward using Itanium-only for big jobs. Some reporters got really into the hype game, saying this amazing product would make its way down from servers into PCs and even laptops.

Then the problems started. First off, the original Itanium—a chip code-named Merced—was scheduled to ship in 1999. Intel and HP then pushed this date back to mid-2000 and eventually released it in May 2001. Instead of revealing a high-performing dynamo at that time, Intel released a dud. It didn't even recommend that customers use servers based on the chip in their businesses. Instead, the Merced-based gear should be used for the software rewriting and testing work that needed to be done. Analysts knocked the product launch as unimpressive.

Intel vowed that a second version of Itanium—code-named McKinley—would prove the merits of the processor. This product—once due in 2001—came out in the middle of 2002. It was, in fact, a good product. Alas, in the meantime the dot-com boom had busted. McKinley was too little, too late. Itanium server sales figures turned into an industrywide joke. Expecting to move tens of thousands of servers, for example, IBM sold only thirty-four of them one quarter.

Intel and HP pumped billions of dollars into Itanium promotions, hoping to rejuvenate interest in the chip. They gave away products to customers, paid for the software rewriting and spent millions on advertising.

These efforts along with improvements to the processor did help matters a little. But the sales of Itanium were still far below expectations. By 2004 all of the Itanium server makers combined—folks such as IBM, Dell, HP, and SGI—sold as many Itanium servers in an entire year as Sun sold of its own systems in about six weeks.

Eventually, two of the chip's most crucial supporters—IBM and Dell—exited the Itanium "ecosystem" and pulled their servers off the shelves. HP shut down internal work on Itanium, transferring its engineering teams to Intel. Then, in 2005, Intel announced more delays for new versions of the chip and was forced to admit that a plan to reduce the price of the expensive product was struggling.

In 2004 HP pledged to put another $3 billion into developing software for Itanium and marketing the chip. In 2006 a group of companies—including HP, Intel, and SGI—agreed to shell out $10 billion over five years to promote the chip even more.

It's anyone's guess as to the grand total of cash that has been forked over to save the Itanium chip since 1994. Neither Intel or HP has ever been willing to disclose the full scale of their investments in the product.

As of this writing, their efforts continue.

Aside from the founders, you can learn a lot of about chip basics here. There are exhibits that detail how transistors work and what they look like, the different types of processors Intel has made over the years, and explanations of Moore's Law—the famous observation that transistor counts would double every eighteen to twenty-four months.

Visitors will also find displays on Intel's ultraclean, multibillion-dollar chip fabrication facilities. Brave guests can even try on a "bunny suit" worn by staffers to keep their hair, dead skin, and dust from affecting the chip-making process. The entire museum sits on a raised floor design that mimics the ventilation systems found in the chip plants or data centers. It's a nice touch.

In total, the museum provides insight into the culture of a great company and goes a long way toward explaining the basics of processor technology. Most visitors should feel a bit wiser about the silicon game after spending an hour or two here. On your way out you can pick up paraphernalia at the gift shop . . . assuming you have a special someone in need of an Intel-branded shirt, folder, or mug. The museum also offers soaps, candles, and gift cards, but they're Intel-logo free. Go figure.

The museum—open since 1992—is free, and so is parking. It's open from 9:00 a.m. to 6:00 p.m. Monday through Friday, and 10:00 a.m. to 5:00 p.m. on Saturday. On weekdays guided tours are available at 11:15 a.m., 1:15 p.m., and 3:15 p.m.; on Saturday they start at 10:30 a.m., 12:15 p.m., 1:45 p.m., and 3:30 p.m. Should you miss those times, there's a decent chance that an Intel staffer will provide a tour anyway.

Close to sixty people visit the museum on an average day. Students make up a good portion of these visitors, and Intel offers additional classes on technology to schools that book in advance. At "binary beading" sessions for second graders, for instance, the children are taught the basics of the "on" and "off" states of switches while making beaded key chains. Older students can work on mathematical reasoning puzzles and other challenges set up by Intel.

COMPANIES SUCH AS INTEL, APPLE, AND GOOGLE WILL register with the casual technology observer more readily than will Lockheed Martin. This giant military contractor, however, was actually plodding away in Silicon Valley before the other highfliers came into existence.

A MAJOR **SILICON** VALLEY **EMPLOYER**

Two Los Gatos boys—Allan and Malcolm Loughead—got an early start on their way to creating Lockheed. They were considered aviation pioneers after building and landing a hydroplane in the San Francisco Bay, along with creating other craft. Despite their Northern California roots, the brothers decided to head south to Santa Barbara to start Loughead Aircraft Manufacturing Company. They later changed the name to the easier-to-pronounce Lockheed.

The Lougheads would go on to establish their reputation as world-class plane designers and secured myriad military contracts. Amelia Earhart flew a Lockheed Vega across the Atlantic in 1932, Wiley Post made the first solo flight around the world in a Vega the next year, and the Lockheed P-38 became one of the most popular fighters during World War II.

By the 1950s Lockheed had moved into new fields such as missile development. This expansion of markets prompted the creation of the Lockheed Missiles & Space subsidiary and the creation of a large manufacturing facility in Sunnyvale. The Northern California site gave Lockheed quick access to workers at NASA Ames down the road in Mountain View. The subsidiary soon became Silicon Valley's major employer, with tens of thousands of Lockheed staff dominating the area. Locals recall that the Valley was either booming or busting back then, depending on Lockheed's success at winning government contracts in a given year.

Rooster T. Feathers Comedy Club, Sunnyvale

EVEN THE COMEDY CLUBS IN SILICON Valley have a geeky bent.

For close to three decades, Sunnyvale's Rooster T. Feathers has hosted comic pros, hopefuls, and amateurs. The likes of Jerry Seinfeld, Robin Williams, and Drew Carey have played at the cozy venue situated near a series of strip malls. Rooster's also provides a showcase for touring comics and less seasoned pros during open-mike night each Wednesday. Every so often the place really embraces its Silicon Valley roots with a "Geek Comedy Showcase." This event typically features about five comedians showing off their technology humor. At just $10 for the night, most engineers can afford the entry fee.

Rooster's ties to Silicon Valley's history run deep. The comedy club used to be a pub called Andy Capp's where Atari founder Nolan Bushnell installed one of the first Pong video game systems. Pong proved almost too popular, with the game machine shutting down when it was pumped full of quarters and nondrinking patrons waiting for the tavern to open just to get a shot at it.

You won't find any mentions of these video game roots at Rooster's today, though. The no-frills club has a small stage, a bar, a few booths, a number of tables . . . and that's it. The intimacy is appreciated, giving every patron a great view of the comics.

Rooster's is a full-service comedy club. Those just looking to catch a show are urged to make reservations for the Wednesday through Sunday performances. The shows start at 8:00 p.m.; there are also second performances on Friday and Saturday at 10:30 p.m. Tickets will run you $10–15. College students get in free on Thursday. The club also offers comedy workshops and can arrange to have comedians show up at your event.

You'll find Rooster T. Feathers at 157 West El Camino Real, Sunnyvale. Reservations can be made by dialing (408) 736-0921. More details are available at www.roostertfeathers.com.

The Lockheed and NASA partnership has produced a number of significant accomplishments. The two organizations teamed on the space shuttle design, with Lockheed's models being sent over to Ames for testing in the wind tunnels. Lockheed also produced the Hubble Space Telescope.

Lockheed combined with Martin Marietta in 1995 to form Lockheed Martin. The company owns the Space Systems Technical Operations in Sunnyvale, the Space Systems Advanced Technology Center in Palo Alto, and Integrated Systems and Solutions in San Jose. It also runs Sandia National Labs in Livermore.

(¹) SUN MICROSYSTEMS

IF YOU WERE CHALLENGED TO PICK A SINGLE COMPANY THAT exemplified the great, the decent, and the bubbliest aspects of Silicon Valley, Sun Microsystems would be a fine choice. You'd also be hard pressed to find another corporate campus that contains as much beauty and history as Sun's HQ.

There was a time when you couldn't escape Sun's offices in Silicon Valley. Large towers with the firm's trademark purple logo dotted freeways and lined backstreets. The company's workforce exploded along with sales during the boom, leaving Sun trying to gobble up as much prime real estate as possible.

Sun, however, eventually realized that the office sprawl was too expensive and inefficient, so it turned to a campus plan that would collect many workers in fewer locations. The firm's Santa Clara headquarters now stand as the idyllic centerpiece of all the campuses.

More than twenty Sun buildings here are set amid beautiful grounds. The eighty-two-acre site displays a wide variety of different trees including towering palms, elms, lindens, and evergreens that have thrived on the land for more than a hundred years. But perhaps the most striking features of the campus are four historic buildings that once belonged to the Agnews State Hospital for the Insane.

Agnews opened its doors in 1889. Dubbed "the Great Asylum for the Insane" and named for local landowner Abram Agnew, the facility served as California's third major location for treating the mentally ill. A five-story redbrick building dominated the original site. During the Great Earthquake of 1906, tragedy struck as the main building collapsed and killed 111 patients and one employee. More than 860 other patients

CLICK HERE **Halted's Hardware Heaven**

HARD-CORE TECHNOLOGY BUYERS KNOW just where to go in Silicon Valley: Halted Electronic Supply. HSC caters to a mix of hobbyists, engineers, and entrepreneurs with warehouse-style stores filled by rows and rows and rows and rows of electronics components, computers, and testing equipment. The average person would likely consider HSC's wares junk, but others consider it the stuff that dreams are made of.

HSC opened its doors in 1963, looking to serve government contractors with surplus vacuum, hydraulic, and testing products. Over the years Halted matured with Silicon Valley and expanded its hardware line to accommodate the growing computing industry.

"We have featured everything from I.C.'s to rocket motors, oscilloscopes to electron microscopes, soldering irons to industrial lasers, and just about everything else in between!" the company boasts. "We also feature an extensive selection of new products for technicians, engineers and the hobbyist who needs electronic parts, or who just loves to tinker!

"Come on by and browse, the coffee is always free!"

Halted will overwhelm people who don't know the difference between a SCSI controller and a diode. Still, even those outside the technology elite will get a kick out of browsing HSC's aisles. You won't find another place like it.

The main Silicon Valley shop is at 3500 Ryder Street, Santa Clara. You can hit up Halted on the Web at www.halted.com or on the phone at (408) 732-1573.

were forced to live in tents and temporary structures as a result of the damage.

Leonard Wileke, chief designer for California, created the original drawings for the new site and picked the California Mission style as his inspiration. Today the concrete and stucco structures boast tile roofs, wooden balconies and porches, and exposed rafters. The buildings exude an Hispanic influence.

At the center of Sun's campus is the Clock Tower building, which was constructed in 1908 and originally served as a treatment building. It dominates the campus with a large central section jutting up four stories. Sun chairman Scott McNealy once worked here, but it's now used primarily for meetings. From the top of the tower, you can look out across Silicon Valley and take in the mountains that surround Sun's campus.

To the right of the Clock Tower sits the Grand Auditorium, constructed in 1914. This two-story structure houses a decent-size theater where Sun holds analyst and press events. Walking into the building, you'll find a 40-foot vaulted ceiling complemented by double-arched windows and spectacular wooden floors. In the asylum days patients would flock to the auditorium to enjoy performances, social gatherings, and billiards. A small museum dedicated to Dr. Leonard Stocking, the main force behind Agnews, can also be found in the auditorium's entryway, although it's locked on most days.

The other two historic buildings are the Administration Building (1909) and the Director's Mansion (1915). Stocking lived in the latter until his death in 1931, hosting the California governor during his required annual visit to the facility.

In its day Agnews received accolades as the first modern mental hospital. Stocking worked to provide residents with soothing surroundings and used different facilities to treat patients with varying illnesses instead of lumping all the afflicted together in a nondescript, clinical setting.

The Networked Asylum

SUN'S SANTA CLARA CAMPUS PROVIDES a home to thousands of Sun staffers— and a whole lot more. One of the company's more ambitious perks, for instance, is its iWork program. Close to half of Sun's staff makes use of this program, which lets them work at home for much of the day and then come to the campus for meetings or when they really need an office. Sun believes that it can cut down on the total number of offices it needs via this arrangement.

Workers who use this "flex plan" can log onto a Web site and assign themselves an office at any of Sun's worldwide campuses. Much of this is possible because of Sun-made technology called the Sun Ray—a stripped-down computer terminal that has no fans, hard drives, or whirring parts. In addition, a call forwarding system will send calls to any number the worker picks, be it the line in a temporary office or a cell phone.

Thanks to Sun's flex plan, you'll often find staff at work in the historic Agnews buildings. Or in their homes, or even in Bangalore. Where you won't see them is in rush-hour traffic jams.

As you might imagine, the site's history has led to supernatural tales making their way into Sun folklore. Nighttime cleaning staff complain of hearing strange noises throughout the campus, and another popular story has a pretty woman appearing at night and walking her dog around the campus . . . forever.

Agnews once housed as many as 4,000 patients but stopped treating the mentally ill in 1972. The facility was used to treat disabled patients until 1998, when Sun acquired the property; the patients were transferred to another site in San Jose. The purchase was not without controversy: People complained that the land was intended for public use, that Sun received too sweet a deal for the site because of McNealy's political connections, and that the firm would tear down too many of the historical buildings. Sun paid tens of millions for the property and kept only four of the forty-nine buildings, replacing most of the old structures with its more modern offices. Sun did pay $10 million to restore the four main buildings and allows these to be used by the public.

The public can take advantage of a park that surrounds Sun's buildings and that includes the old Agnews structures. The park opens at 6:00 a.m. and closes half an hour after sunset. Residents of Santa Clara can also use the historic buildings for private events such as weddings or parties. Interested groups should contact the City of Santa Clara Parks and Recreation Department.

You won't see many of Sun's top executives in Santa Clara. The brass once worked at the headquarters but found they were making too many trips to the Executive Briefing Center located at the company's sprawling Menlo Park campus. Scott McNealy and CEO Jonathan Schwartz now have modest offices at the Menlo Park building, with many of their top executives working down the hall. When customers are in town, the executives toddle down to the briefing center, which is equipped with millions of dollars in equipment, conference rooms, and a dining area.

> Sun's Santa Clara campus is located at 4150 Network Circle. Plenty of people head there for a morning jog or to take the kids out for a walk, and it's well worth a visit. You can call Sun's main number (800) 786-0404 for more information.

THE WONDER OF THE WORKSTATION

Sun started in 1982 as the brainchild of three Stanford students and one Berkeley graduate—Vinod Khosla, Scott McNealy, Andy Bechtolsheim, and Bill Joy (Berkeley). Khlosa and McNealy were hunting down their MBAs and made up the business side of the venture, while Joy and Bechtolsheim stood as the technical brains of the operation.

Bechtolsheim had discovered a way to create a powerful computer known as a workstation that could be used by engineers, software developers, and scientists. The Sun workstation—basically a supercharged PC—stood out because it delivered strong performance at a relatively low cost and gave customers their own machine instead of forcing them to rent time on larger computers.

SCOTT MCNEALY
The Sun King

PERHAPS EVEN MORE THAN A CULT OF engineering, Sun is a cult of personality. The hard-charging Scott McNealy defines Sun's brash style and is responsible for much of the press heaped on the company. With friend Oracle CEO Larry Ellison by his side, McNealy has made a career out of bashing Microsoft. In fact, McNealy has made a career out of bashing just about anything that bothered him, from government regulation to privacy advocates.

McNealy is the proverbial riddle wrapped in a mystery inside an enigma. His conservative roots stretch back to Detroit, where he grew up as the son of an American Motors executive. He attended a rival private high school of Microsoft CEO Steve Ballmer. (The two were clearly destined to compete.) From Detroit, McNealy headed to Harvard for his undergraduate degree and then Stanford for an MBA. He has, however, always described himself as more of a "golf major" than a stellar student. (If so, at least he's good at golf. McNealy has been ranked as the top CEO golfer, shared some course time with Tiger Woods, and owned a house at Pebble Beach.)

In person McNealy comes off almost as a grown-up fraternity boy. He cracks jokes at every opportunity, dresses in jeans and a button-down Sun shirt, and maintains a haircut reminiscent of a new army recruit. He likes to talk about cars and hockey and often crushes tough questions with huge doses of sarcasm.

When it comes to running Sun, though, McNealy displays none of the herd mentality. When Sun's shares soared during the dot-com boom, analysts labeled him a counterpunching genius. When Sun fell behind by not having an Intel-based server line soon enough, analysts wrote the company off and said a slow-moving McNealy put Sun at risk of becoming "irrelevant."

As Sun's largest shareholder, McNealy's not likely to leave the company anytime soon, despite relinquishing the CEO title to Schwartz in 2006. Still, he and his firm have recently adopted a humbler tone. Sun settled its long-running lawsuit with Microsoft and, after pocketing a $2 billion payment, turned Microsoft from the bitterest of enemies to a partner. In addition, Sun must still ask customers to stick with it as it tries to redefine a new product road map and push fresh gear to market. That's a tough sell with IBM, HP, and Dell lurking.

Being a bit more reserved does little to dampen McNealy's generous personality. He remains as acerbic, comic, and charming in the flesh as ever. Like Microsoft's Bill Gates and Oracle's Larry Ellison, he defines the company he helped start.

Customers flocked to Sun's engineering marvel overnight.

Few companies up to that point had ever experienced such meteoric growth. Sun, which stood for "Stanford University Network," incorporated in 1982 and signed a $40 million deal the next year. It reached $1 billion in revenue by 1988 and shipped its millionth computer in 1993. Not bad.

Sun's initial success hinged on its ability to use off-the-shelf components to keep costs down, while engineering state-of-the-art technology to boost the performance of its systems. This recipe proved attractive to government customers and large businesses searching for the speediest, most stable computers. In addition, Sun benefited from the reputations of its two technical leads. Customers who heard that Unix operating system pioneer Joy had joined a company called asking to buy whatever Sun was selling no matter what it was.

Sun capitalized on a general improvement in components and did so better than any other player in the market. In many ways it ushered in a new era of business computers. Plenty of companies have tried to emulate Sun's formula since, but few have neared its revenue heights or influence on the computer industry.

SUN'S HIGHS AND LOWS

While once glorious, the Sun workstations started to show their age in the late 1990s as competing systems based on Intel's processors began to eat away at the company's business. Sun's hardware—based on its own Solaris operating system and SPARC processor—still held the overall performance lead but proved too expensive compared with the rival systems that just weren't that much slower.

In a funk, Sun decided to make a major buy and acquired a line of high-end servers from SGI. This move would prove fortuitous, as it helped Sun capitalize on the dot-com boom. And how.

In the late 1990s, few could escape Sun's ads proclaiming "We're the Dot in Dot Com." No other hardware company had seized the Internet boom with such vigor, and Sun had the profits to prove its place as a dot-com darling. The firm's line of high-end servers became the prized possessions of businesses looking to prove they were Internet savvy. Sun sold the systems to governments, financial services companies, service providers, telecommunications giants, and myriad start-ups. Sun's success outstripped larger rivals such as HP and IBM that had more resources at their disposal but lacked the cachet of the plucky Silicon Valley start-up.

Sun's revenues reached more than $18 billion in 2001, based on an incredible run that pushed it to the forefront of the Internet wave. It had the might to needle fellow hardware makers IBM, HP, and Dell, and the engineering savvy to knock Microsoft again and again. Sun became known as one of the most controversial and competitive forces in Silicon Valley—driven primarily by its brash CEO (now chairman) Scott McNealy.

GOOD THINGS COME TO AN END

Sundown arrived at Internet speed. By 2002 most of the start-ups once interested in

◀)) SILICON VALLEY SOUNDBYTE

Paramount's Great America, Santa Clara

FOR MORE THAN THREE DECADES, THE Great America amusement park has entertained Silicon Valley workers and their families.

Great America goes against the tradition of placing enormous amusement parks on the outskirts of large cities. The park sits right in the middle of Santa Clara, a stone's throw from Intel's headquarters and just a couple of miles from Sun Microsystems' home office. The park opened as Marriott's Great America in 1976 but changed hands to fall under Paramount's ownership in 1992. Today it offers a number of attractions, from heart-stopping roller coasters all the way to tamer rides for kids. Great America also has a water park to keep you cool in summer. Owners have pumped more than $250 million into building new attractions at this, Northern California's largest amusement park. Great America is open from April to October. Children's tickets run $34 each, while adult tickets will cost $50.

You can find more information at www2.paramount parks.com /greatamerica.

the firm's pricey but powerful gear had disappeared. Even worse, large customers stopped major hardware purchases or turned their back on Sun in favor of cheaper, more powerful Intel-based systems. Yes, Sun's server business now faced the same fate its workstation business had years earlier.

The company has struggled to reinvent itself, despite management often insisting that such a transformation is under way. Sun continues to make servers based on its Solaris operating system and SPARC processors. But it has finally opened up and embraced the Intel-processor-based servers sold by rivals as well. Sun also continues to try to expand its software business, attacking traditional partners such as BEA Systems and Oracle. New CEO Jonathan Schwartz has come up with unique pricing methods such as selling software on a flat-fee system based on the number of employees a customer has, as well as selling access to Sun's servers at $1 per hour for each processor used. While intriguing, these efforts have done little to correct Sun's revenue woes. Major software players remain dominant, leaving Sun with little more than scraps. Still, by the end of their fiscal year in July 2007, a more stable Sun reported a healthy $13 billion in revenue.

Nevertheless, Sun maintains a prominent place in the Silicon Valley mind-set. In fact, industry observers often remark that Sun

SILICON VALLEY SOUNDBYTE

Snoogle Factoid

ANDY BECHTOLSHEIM HAS PROVED AS savvy an investor as he is an engineer. The German-born hardware guru put the initial funds into Sun and reaped massive rewards for this investment. Close to twenty years later, he would invest in another start-up led by a couple of Stanford students.

Larry Page and Sergey Brin were discussing their search engine idea and money problems with Bechtolsheim in 1998 when the Sun co-founder dashed off a check for $100,000 to the pair, making out the payment to "Google." And so the next wave of Silicon Valley began. Bechtolsheim eventually turned his investment into a windfall of more than $1 billion.

And wouldn't you know it? Google's current CEO Eric Schmidt once worked as chief technology officer at Sun.

Vineyards in Silicon Valley

IF YOU WANT TO GO WHOLE HOG WITH your wine tasting, then a trip to Napa or Sonoma is a must. But folks in Silicon Valley can enjoy some world-class vineyards as well. The South Bay boasts more than fifty vineyards—some of which are true standouts.

Ridge Monte Bello is one of the most storied of the local vineyards, getting its start back in 1885—but it was Dave Bennion and three partners from the Stanford Research Institute who really put the vineyard on the map, capitalizing on the California wine boom of the late 1960s. Today Ridge wines are said to age very well and often command more than $100 a bottle. You can visit the scenic Ridge Monte Bello vineyard nestled in the Santa Cruz Mountains on Saturday and Sunday 11 a.m. to 4 p.m. for free tastings. The vineyard is at 17100 Monte Bello Road in Cupertino. The owners do not offer tours, but there are picnic tables available.

Another local favorite with a touch of technology heritage is Testarossa. The label first got going in 1993 in an all-too-familiar fashion: Rob and Diana Jensen—former tech workers—started their wine enterprise in a Sunnyvale garage. By 1994 the endeavor had shifted from a weekend project to a full-time passion play. Today you can sip wine in the Testarossa tasting room, housed in a nineteenth-century stone cellar in Los Gatos. If you buy a few bottles, the tasting is free; otherwise it's going to run $10 per person. The tasting room is open 11 a.m. to 5 p.m. every day except major holidays. You'll find Testarossa Vineyards at 300-A College Avenue, Los Gatos, or on the Web at www.testarossa.com.

Tiny Page Mill Winery spent twenty-eight years in the heart of Silicon Valley before moving to Livermore. The label churns out only about 3,000 cases per year, selling the vast majority to locals. You can visit Page Mill at 1960 South Livermore Avenue for tasting on Saturday and Sunday 11:00 a.m. to 4:30 p.m. The tastings are free. Or visit www.pagemillwinery.com.

J. Lohr is much more ambitious from a production point of view, cranking out some 700,000 cases a year across five labels. The vineyard was started by Jerry Lohr, formerly of NASA Ames.

You can visit the San Jose facility located at 1000 Lenzen Avenue every day—except major holidays—from 10 a.m. to 5 p.m. Most of the tasting options are free. More information is available at www.jlohr.com.

manages to capture more than its fair share of attention. Despite many calls by Wall Street analysts to cut back on research and development spending, for instance, Sun has refused to do so. This policy, while displeasing to some investors, solidified Sun's place as a haven for world-class engineers. To this day the company spends billions on R&D. Indeed, it's considered one of the last great independent research and development houses in Silicon Valley.

ADVANCED MICRO DEVICES

LIKE SO MANY SEMICONDUCTOR COMPANIES IN THE 1960s, Advanced Micro Devices arose out of discontent with Fairchild Semiconductor. And depending your perspective, it's is either the worst or best behaved of all the Fairchildren.

AMD lays claim to one of the grander Silicon Valley headquarters. Located just off the Lawrence Expressway in Sunnyvale is AMD's "White House." The building's main entrance has a certain wedding-cake quality, with a couple of circular layers stacked atop each other and AMD's logo in the middle of the facade. The all-white campus has an almost southern charm. Inside the main lobby you will, of course, find a bust of co-founder Jerry Sanders, smiling with pride.

PUSHING RIVALS TO THE EDGE

AMD's co-founder Jerry Sanders was fired from Fairchild in 1969, despite being one of the company's top salesmen. He counts that moment as his "biggest break."

With seven friends, Sanders followed the lead of numerous Fairchild engineers before them and started a new company. Robert Noyce, a Fairchild co-founder, had actually fired up Intel the

The Churchill Club

WHEN YOU'RE IN THE MOOD FOR HARD-core networking or IT celebrity spotting, head to one of the Churchill Club's dinners.

Every couple of weeks Churchill Club members gather at a Silicon Valley hotel to throw down a scrumptious meal and a few cocktails. After taking care of their stomachs and swapping business cards, the Churchill crowd watches as a local journalist interviews an IT industry bigwig. Guest speakers at these events have included Microsoft chairman Bill Gates, Oracle CEO Larry Ellison, Cisco CEO John Chambers, eBay chief Meg Whitman, and then Arkansas governor Bill Clinton.

A refreshing aspect of the Churchill format comes when members are let loose on the speakers, typically peppering them with a wide range of questions—many of which fall outside reporters' usual lines of interrogation. When the Q&A session officially ends, people in the audience will rush the stage to try to hand a famous executive their card or to pitch an idea in thirty seconds. Even after the guest speaker leaves, many of the Churchill members hang around to down another cocktail or two and continue their networking extravaganza.

The group is named for British prime minister Winston Churchill. Why? According to the organization's Web site: "The nonprofit Churchill Club has amassed more than 5,000 members since it started in 1985." A one-year individual membership costs $125, while a three-year stint runs just $315. Corporate memberships are available as well for considerably more dough. The House of Commons membership, for example, costs $1,000 and lets ten employees into the club. The top-tier Prime Minister—what else?—membership costs $10,000 and gives all staffers access to the club.

Members still have to pay a fee for some events. The price is usually around $35 per person. Nonmembers can attend some of the events for around $60. The event locations are typically in Palo Alto, Mountain View, Sunnyvale, or San Jose.

You can find the Churchill Club's home page at www.churchillclub .org; upcoming events are described at www.churchillclub.org/upcoming events.jsp.

year before and agreed to provide Sanders with advice and an investment in AMD. Such cooperation seems hard to fathom today given the bitter squabbles that have occurred between AMD and Intel. Sanders, however, counts Noyce as one of the great Silicon Valley entrepreneurs and notes that times were a bit different for the young chip firms back then. "We were all trying to make it on our own and there was competition and so forth, but it really was a fairly collegial environment," Sanders said in an interview.

Many of the semiconductor start-ups looked to gain an advantage by creating a brand-new type of product or by having a better manufacturing process than rivals. AMD used a different approach. It simply took rival designs and tried to improve them via engineering tweaks or better marketing. AMD did not even invent new product names for its devices. It would literally just put AM in front of competitors' existing names. A Fairchild product called the A740 would turn into the AM740, while a Motorola product dubbed the MC1500 would turn into the AM1500. Competitors sued over this practice—and lost. Moreover, it turned AMD into a customer favorite because it forced other semiconductor companies to make better products and lower prices.

It's well worth having a quick look at the campus, which is located at 1 AMD Place just off Duane Avenue. No headquarters tours are available, but there is more information at www.amd.com /us-en/corporate/aboutamd/.

The depth of AMD's competitive fire can be seen in its ongoing legal disputes with Intel. During the 1980s and early 1990s, the companies sparred over AMD's rights to produce clones of Intel's products, making it a type of second supplier for mainstream processors used in PCs and other systems. More recently, AMD filed an antitrust suit against Intel.

Historically, AMD has struggled to maintain the periodic market share gains it makes against Intel. The plucky company has managed to grab about 30 percent of the PC chip market at times, only to see Intel come back and take close to 90 percent of the market again.

SANDERS AND HIS STAFF

AMD's co-founder Jerry Sanders is often described as flamboyant. The brash, silver-haired executive hands out controversial opinions every chance he gets. He is without question the most vocal major Silicon Valley executive; only Sun's Scott McNealy comes near. Moreover, Sanders is not shy about his fondness for material wealth and likes to show off his success via tailored suits, personal jets, and lavish houses.

Sanders no longer handles day-to-day functions at AMD—he's now chairman emeritus—but does maintain an office in Beverly Hills. In true Sanders fashion, the office is a block off Rodeo Drive and delivers a direct view of the famous Hollywood sign from the plush main conference room.

Looking past the accoutrements, Sanders also infused AMD with some serious substance. The company was an early advocate of providing profit sharing to all employees and would periodically reward staff with giveaways. Sanders, in fact, once gave a worker a new Corvette and bestowed a house upon another employee.

"What drove me was to show that I was more than just a flashy dresser," Sanders has said. "I wanted to show people there was more there than what they saw superficially, and the only way to do that was through achievement.

"I feel that has been done."

YAHOO!

EVEN WHEN JUST MESSING AROUND, STANFORD UNIVERSITY students can end up making a multibillion-dollar business. Just ask David Filo and Jerry Yang, founders of a concern known as Yahoo!

The company, which started in a small Mountain View office, now calls Sunnyvale home. It has a beautiful, modern headquarters packed full of sleek, silver buildings. Architecturally, they are some of the more interesting structures you'll find for a Silicon Valley company, with sharp, angled extensions jutting out from the main buildings. You can't miss the site, either, with the trademark YAHOO! logo plastered across the campus—exclamation point and all.

"JERRY AND DAVID'S GUIDE TO THE WEB"

In 1994 Filo and Yang were in hot pursuit of their electrical engineering PhDs from Stanford when they began compiling a list of their favorite things on the Internet. With more and more Web pages popping up every day, the list of interesting sites grew at a quick clip. Eventually the pair had to create groups of related links, which gave a directory-like structure to their project.

Most accounts say the project was officially called "Jerry's Guide to the World Wide Web," although Yahoo!'s site recognizes both founders, describing the directory as "Jerry and David's Guide to the World Wide Web."

The link collection began to eat up more and more of the students' time and attracted the attention of more and more Stanford friends. It didn't take long before hits from outside Stanford started to reach the guide.

In these very early days, chaos ruled the Web. People enjoyed the idea of accessing a flood of information but didn't have the best tools for finding it. That made a useful directory a no-brainer.

Filo and Yang dug into a dictionary looking to improve the name of their guide and settled on Yahoo!—an acronym for "Yet Another Hierarchical Officious Oracle." According to official company lore, "Filo and Yang insist they selected the name because they liked the general definition of a yahoo: 'rude, unsophisticated, uncouth.' Yahoo! itself first resided on Yang's student workstation, 'Akebono,'

SLASHDOT AND ROB MALDA

ROB MALDA—WHO GOES BY THE NAME CmdrTaco—controls a geek army that numbers in the millions. Malda started a Web site called Slashdot while still in college. The site would go on to become one of the most visited destinations on the Internet and stand as an almost religious gathering point for "true" geeks and technology aficionados. In particular, Slashdot corrals many of the most ardent fans of the open-source Linux operating system—a rival to Microsoft's Windows.

Slashdot helped pioneer a way of delivering information that is unique to the Internet. Instead of writing their own articles, Slashdotters write blurbs describing existing articles at true news sites and then link to these original stories. Editors such as Malda pick the blurbs that appear on the site, with topics ranging from new IBM mainframes to rigging electronic voting machines and cooking eggs with microprocessors. Slashdot often pushes thousands of readers to the same location and manages to cripple these Web sites—a process now known as the Slashdot Effect.

One of Slashdot's most loved and mocked features is the comments section attached to every entry. Here Slashdotters battle to express their opinions on the issue at hand and often end up veering way off course. Slashdot commentators can increase the prominence of their remarks by earning "karma" points for being comical or especially insightful. Malda has spent years fine-tuning the comments technology, which separates Slashdot from many other sites.

In a recent interview, Malda noted: "I think that part of why Slashdot succeeded is that I was something of an outsider to the culture. I came at the technology universe not from a venture capitalist perspective. Not from a business perspective at all. I'm really simply interested in the joy of technology, the fun it can provide, and its potential to change the world."

One of Slashdot's premiere moments came in 2002 when Malda proposed to a lass named Kathleen via the site. The post went as follows:

Posted by CmdrTaco on Thursday February 14, @09:25AM from the typed-with-one-pair-of-sweating-palms dept.

Kathleen, I wanted to do this in this most potentially embarassing [sic] way possible, and I figured doing it here and now, in front of a quarter of a million strangers was as good a way as any. I love you more then I can describe within the limits of this tiny little story. We've been together for many years now, and I've known for most of that time that I wanted to spend my life with you. Enough rambling. Will you marry me?

Update 15 minutes 30 seconds later:

Subj: "Yes"

Message body: "Dork. You made me cry. :)" Hazah! I'm getting married! :)

Malda continues to impact Silicon Valley from afar, refusing to leave a comfortable home in Michigan "somewhere between Dexter and Ann Arbor." His creation that started as a hobby has thrived during all of the internet's ups and downs and stands as one of the web's major success stories.

If you want to have some fun, travel over to Slashdot and watch the Linux zealots tear each other apart over what many would consider the most trivial of things.

As tradition would have it, Malda agreed to an interview using a Q&A format familiar to Slashdot readers.

Q: For the unfamiliar, can you give the quick version of how Slashdot started?

RM: In 1997 I took my journal (what today would be called a blog) and moved it to a domain name that I registered for fun. I shared postings with a few friends. We talked about Linux, Technology, Gadgets, and The Internet. We grew at an insane rate.

Q: How long did it take to start crashing web sites with the Slashdot Effect?

RM: Just a few months. I've seen mention of it occurring within about 3 months of our launch.

Q: Can you give us a sense of how big Slashdot is these days in terms of readers or hits?

RM: There are a variety of measures, but I like to figure that there are more than a half a million daily readers, and several million hits each day.

Q: Would you or have you considered moving out to Silicon Valley?

RM: I like grass and snow and having a few acres of buffer between me and my neighbor. I don't think there's a company that could pay me enough to give that up right now.

Q: You proposed to your wife on the internet in front of hundreds of thousands of people. How is the most famous geek romance working out?

RM: It was scary as hell. I was shaking as I hit the button. So far, so good. For our anniversary, we're going to Las Vegas.

Q: Inquiring minds want to know. Did Slashdot leave you set for life?

RM: It sure didn't hurt, but I'm not retiring any time soon.

while the software was lodged on Filo's computer, 'Konishiki'—both named after legendary sumo wrestlers."

After about seven months in operation, Yahoo! secured its first million-hit day in fall 1994. The ability for users to add their own links helped make the service more attractive.

ALL THINGS TO ALL PEOPLE

Like plenty of Stanford graduates before and since, Filo and Yang saw a business opportunity and went looking for venture capital. Don Valentine's Sequoia Capital—a backer of Apple, Atari, Electronic Arts, Oracle, and Cisco—liked the idea enough to slide $2 million in front of the pair in April 1995.

Yahoo!'s popularity grew at a steady rate, with many Web users setting the site as their home page. In its early days Yahoo! provided the basics for users, offering up categories such as Arts, Computers, Education, Entertainment, News, Recreation, Sports, and Science. A click on one of these sections would reveal more detailed listings with tens or even hundreds of relevant Web sites and very brief descriptions of them.

A 1996 initial public offering helped kick the Internet boom into overdrive. The company's revenue would soar from $19 million to $1.1 billion in 2000.

Yahoo!'s basic design has changed relatively little over the years. The company, however, removed easy access to the Web Directory section—a true reflection of its roots—from its home page in 2006. Today Yahoo! presents a wide array of services by using a more contemporary but still basic design. Its goal is to be all things to all people on the Web, offering everything from e-mail and stock portfolio management to Web site design services, personals, and music downloads. In recent years it has also hired its own staff of journalists to fill out its Sports and News sections.

One of Yahoo!'s main early features was search. It would, however, be surpassed on the search front by Google—another start-up to emerge from a pair of Stanford graduate students. Rather ironically, Yahoo! gave up on its own search technology in 2000 and agreed to use Google's service as its core search tool. This catapulted the growing Google to a position of major prominence on the Web. Yahoo! officials would grow to regret this decision as Google's revenue from text ads tied to its search engine soared.

YAHOO! GROWS UP

In its early days Yahoo! had hired Motorola veteran and Stanford engineering department alumnus Tim Koogle as CEO in hopes of adding some adult supervision and mature business leadership. Koogle resigned following the dot-com crash, and revenues plummeted. The company had depended on Internet advertising and cushy deals with spending-mad dot-coms looking to boost their traffic by appearing on Yahoo! Web properties. Both sources of cash dwindled during the bust.

With Yahoo!'s stock price in the single digits—it had once been in the $500-per-share range—the company made the unorthodox move of hiring Terry Semel as its new CEO. The former Warner Bros. studio head took the post despite having zero experience in the technology field and never having run a publicly traded company.

Yahoo! is headquarted at 701 1st Avenue, Sunnyvale. No headquarters tours are available. You can also visit www.yahoo.com or give the company a ring at (408) 349-3300.

Semel's best decision occurred in 2003, when he ordered the purchase of online advertising broker Overture for $1.7 billion. That move allowed Yahoo! to run its own paid search service. Once again, company coffers swelled.

Yahoo! has exerted a great influence on the Internet age. On the downside, it encouraged an entire generation of start-ups to give their corporate officers ridiculous titles. The young companies modeled their titles on the Chief Yahoo! designations for Filo and Yang

Lion & Compass, Sunnyvale

WERE YOU TO GO SCREAMING DOWN North Fair Oaks Avenue, it would be easy to miss the little slice of heaven that is the Lion & Compass restaurant. The iconic eatery is surrounded by freeway access roads, boring office buildings, gas stations, and apartment complexes—the standard accoutrements of urban sprawl. It's not until you turn off bustling Fair Oaks Avenue and catch a glimpse of the palm-tree- and shrubbery-lined walkway to the restaurant that you realize something quite special lurks here.

Lion & Compass opened its doors in 1982 on the back of an investment from part-owner and Atari founder Nolan Bushnell. At the time, the fine-dining options in Silicon Valley were quite thin, and Lion & Compass quickly became the hot spot for video game industry executives and other power brokers. Even in these early days, technology types needed to feed their insatiable information appetite while filling their bellies. So every table at Lion & Compass had its own phone jack and an NYSE stock ticker.

Today Lion & Compass remains a type of barometer for Silicon Valley's overall health. When the tables are filled, you know that the technology business is booming and deals are being forged over lamb-filled French dip or chilled watermelon gazpacho. When the tables are empty, you can expect bad times to follow—the eatery tends to "feel the pain first and recover last," according to current owner Robert Nino.

Regardless of the business climate, you're guaranteed a scrumptious meal.

Upon entering Lion & Compass, you'll find a spacious, bright dining room dot-

Lion & Compass is located in Sunnyvale at 1023 North Fair Oaks Avenue. You can reach it by phone at (408) 745-1260 or via www.lionandcompass.com.

ted with antique lampposts. The restaurant lets in a ton of natural light through a unique sunroof and then softens the light with a canvas tent. This gives the dining room a garden-like quality. The restaurant has two more traditional eating areas— one dominated by tables, the other by long, luxurious booths. In addition, it boasts an expansive wooden bar with stained glass overhead and in the windows surrounding it. This glass and the lampposts were imported from the UK and a bar originally named, wouldn't you know it, Lion & Compass.

There are three private dining areas, the largest of which is the Library Room. Intel has held its board meetings in this room from time-to-time with executives climbing up on ladders to check the room for listening devices.

If you're into technology celebrity spotting, you may well see AMD's flamboyant founder Jerry Sanders, Intel co-founder Andy Grove or Cisco's CEO John Chambers enjoying a meal at the restaurant.

On warm days, go for the true garden feel by dining at the outside patio. The menu changes often, but past lunch items have included Ahi tuna sashimi, macadamia-crusted chicken breast salad, and Asian grilled rib-eye steak. On the dinner menu you might find a prawn mango salad or venison stir-fry in Japanese plum wine.

and other titles such as Ontological Yahoo! for the company's artificial intelligence whiz. Thankfully, the firm has toned down such monikers in recent years, and so, too, have the start-ups—at least the ones wanting to be taken seriously.

On the upside, Yahoo! proved that the Web could be functional and, quite frankly, useful. Before the company arrived there was no exceptional, mainstream directory for cataloging all the Web had to offer. People knew a great information tool had arrived, but they struggled to tame it. Yahoo!'s success ushered in the age of companies trying to make life much easier on the end users in hopes of turning the Web into something that could create business opportunities for a vast number of companies.

Unlike onetime Web darlings such as Netscape and thousands of dot-coms, Yahoo! has proved itself a true Internet survivor. It's been around since the earliest days and now continues to dream up new uses for its platform. Yahoo! hosts millions upon millions of users and ranks among the top five Internet destinations. The company remains an Internet and Silicon Valley icon that countless others have tried to emulate. And along with companies such as eBay and Google, Yahoo! has made sure that the next wave of technology innovation—following semiconductors and PCs—remains centered in this region.

Of late Yahoo! has expanded well beyond its technology roots and started to resemble a mix between an Internet services firm and a media giant. It also replaced Semel with Yang as CEO in 2007.

■ ■ ■

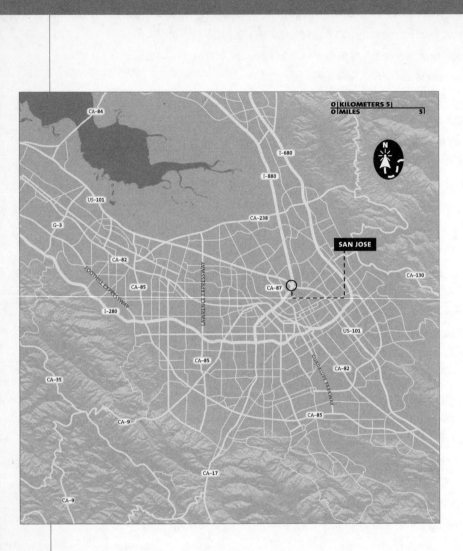

CA-84

0 | KILOMETERS 5 |
0 | MILES   5 |

N

I-680

I-880

US-101

CA-238

SAN JOSE

G-3

CA-130

CA-82

FOOTHILL EXPRESSWAY

LAWRENCE EXPRESSWAY

CA-85

CA-87

I-280

US-101

CA-85

CA-82

GUADALUPE PARKWAY

CA-35

CA-9

CA-85

CA-17

CA-9

AN JOSE HAS NO SHAME IN PROCLAIMING itself the "Capital of Silicon Valley." As the largest city by far in the Valley, San Jose has a great deal to offer on both cultural and business fronts. The city has worked hard in recent years to boost its image as a major metropolis. Locals can take in the opera, visit a variety of technology museums, stroll through a modern art museum, and see some hockey or a concert at the HP Pavilion.

While nowhere near as vibrant as San Francisco, San Jose's downtown does get its bustle on during weekends. Most of the major attractions are within walking distance, and the city puts on a number of events in its main plaza. Unlike many of the Silicon Valley suburbs, San Jose can offer up ties to its past as well. A number of older buildings reflect the Spanish roots of the area with their Mission-style designs.

The city depends a great deal on the technology economy and often plays second fiddle to San Francisco during lean times. The dot-com boom, for example, saw San Jose's convention center packed with trade shows on an almost year-round basis. Now, however, the city has to fight for these conferences, with companies often thinking visitors will prefer the more scenic San Francisco.

San Jose is the only Silicon Valley proper town that can boast near-skyscraper-class buildings in its center. It complements these giants with large corporate campuses for companies such as eBay and Cisco. In addition, it can claim a healthy nightlife thanks to the presence of San Jose State University—an urban college right in the middle of downtown. The city also hosts the ritzy Santana Row shopping and dining district.

CHAPTER 4

San Jose has done a fine job reinventing itself and seems to be better year after year. It's a convenient home base for countless workers and businesses.

THE WORLD'S FIRST BROADCAST STATION: KQW

LONG BEFORE SILICON VALLEY INVENTORS PIONEERED TV and Internet work, Charles Herrold helped kick off the radio revolution. Before his day, people used radio technology for two-way communication. Herrold, a radio enthusiast, had bigger dreams for the medium and set up the first broadcasting station in downtown San Jose.

A historic marker documenting Herrold's work can be found at 50 West San Fernando Street—the current location of the Knight-Ridder "skyscraper." (The McClatchy Company bought Knight-Ridder in 2006.)

In 1909 Herrold—a Stanford graduate—and his students at the Herrold College of Wireless and Engineering technical school created a fairly ambitious programming schedule. They would play records, host shows, and deliver news for eight hours a day, sending their radio signal 15 miles. Most of the equipment used for the show came from Herrold's own designs.

While the quality of the signal was probably pretty poor, it proved good enough to attract tourists to San Jose to listen in. Locals would also occasionally call in record suggestions, making Herrold and his student crew the first radio DJs.

Herrold had to shut down the radio station in 1917 when the United States entered World War I and the government banned nonmilitary use of radio transmitters. In 1920 he gave radio another go but couldn't make a successful business out of his station—KQW. The station changed hands a couple of times, ending up with CBS. A series of misfortunes ultimately left Herrold working as a janitor in the Oakland shipyards. He died in 1948.

DESPITE ITS NEW YORK ROOTS, IBM HAS A LONG HISTORY in the Silicon Valley area particularly with its research and development operations. In fact, IBM's Almaden Research Center, located on an idyllic San Jose hilltop, has proved one of the company's most successful research centers, developing some of the key technology used today by thousands of firms. (No public tours available, although there is a park next door to IBM's Almaden site.)

IBM takes particular pride in its research labs, which are scattered around the world in places such as Austin, Beijng, Tokyo, and Zurich. The company often receives more patents than any other in a given year. IBM has moved to place increasing emphasis on doing research that will provide some benefit to its bottom line. "In the 1950s and '60s, research labs like Xerox PARC and others did what they thought was the best thing to do regardless of whether it was the best thing for the company," said Robin Williams, associate director of the company's Almaden Research Center, in an interview. "We are very focused on doing what's right for the company." And indeed, some of IBM's most lucrative businesses—such as its DB2 database and storage operations—have come out of the research centers.

IBM has become just one of a handful of hardware makers in the United States willing to spend billions on research and development. Sun Microsystems and Hewlett-Packard are two other well-known examples.

▶ 99 NOTRE DAME AVENUE

IBM'S FIRST WEST COAST LABORATORY CROPPED UP AT 99 Notre Dame Avenue in San Jose, where Reynold Johnson had been dispatched to pursue innovative data storage methods. It took three years for IBM to reveal the RAMAC (Random Access Method of Accounting and Control)—more simply, the first device for cramming computer data onto magnetic disks. The first system to use the RAMAC technology took up about as much space as two refrigerators and held all of 5 megabytes of memory. Today, it's not uncommon to find devices about the size of an AA battery that can hold thousands of megabytes of data.

A historic marker is present at 99 Notre Dame Avenue, marking IBM's achievements. In addition, the Magnetic Disk Heritage Center has set up a display open to the public inside the building that walks visitors through some of the history of hard disks and the work done at the site.

Even more simply, this technology led to the hard drives now commonplace in business and home computers. Storage would serve as a key focus of IBM's West Coast operations for decades.

▶ BUILDING 25

IBM EXPANDED ITS SAN JOSE RESEARCH OPERATIONS WITH the creation of Building 25 in 1957. This one-story structure was somewhat of an architectural marvel at the time in that it provided pretty comfortable and scenic digs for IBM's workers. Few companies in the area placed much of a premium on their campus aesthetics, while IBM's structure gave workers a surplus of light via floor-to-ceiling windows and had design touches meant to reflect IBM's hard disk research and to make the building blend in with its surroundings.

You can find the IBM Building 25 site at 5600 Cottle Road on the northeasterly corner of the Cottle Road and Poughkeepsie Road intersection.

More recently, the building's future has come under debate with retailers looking to demolish it and create new stores and some residents fighting to preserve the site as a landmark.

▶ THE ALMADEN RESEARCH CENTER

IN THE EARLY 1980s IBM DECIDED IT NEEDED ANOTHER new San Jose research center and began construction on the current Almaden site. Workers officially moved into the elegant center in

1986, installing themselves in one of the more scenic office buildings you'll find in Silicon Valley. The research center sits atop a decent-size hill in San Jose, capping off a 700-acre spread. It's then surrounded by the 1,700-acre Santa Teresa County Park and the open lands of IBM's other nearby Santa Teresa or "Silicon Valley" Lab, which takes up close to 1,200 acres.

The Almaden building was designed with its rolling, grassy surroundings in mind. It's a low-lying structure that only comes into sight as you near the hilltop. In addition, the center's greenish hue blends into the area. Workers often head out of the office to walk around the grounds, where they can encounter wildlife such as cows, bobcats, snakes, and wild turkeys. The grounds give the IBM staff a broad view of the area, with a particularly pleasing shot of the Santa Cruz Mountains.

These plum surroundings seem to have proved inspirational to the IBM staff. The Almaden site has been one of IBM's most productive research facilities, churning out database, storage, and nanotechnology breakthroughs. The company currently has about 400 researchers working here on a wide variety of projects.

> The Almaden site is not open to the public, but you can catch a glimpse of it by heading to the Santa Teresa County Park. The two sites have land that overlaps, and it's common for joggers and hikers to climb up to the base of IBM's building. The research center is located at 650 Harry Road.

⏻ SAN JOSE CITY HALL

SAN JOSE OFFICIALS EMBRACED THE CITY'S TECHNOLOGY roots and then some with the design of their new city hall, which opened in 2005. To many, the 108-foot rotunda dominating the site looks more like an homage to a space station than a government

Microsoft: With Us or Against Us

FOR MICROSOFT, SILICON VALLEY represents a fierce battleground filled with both friends and foes.

The Washington-based software maker has spent the last couple of decades building a PC empire in tandem with local giant Intel. The two companies have suffered from the occasional squabble, but, for the most part, their shared business success has quelled much of the discord. Microsoft and Intel are in fact such tight mates that most industry watchers refer to the companies as one entity—Wintel.

Other Valley heavyweights such as Oracle and Sun Microsystems have not enjoyed a similar relationship with Microsoft. They've dedicated large chunks of their business models to eroding Microsoft's software dominance. Oracle and Sun's dislike for Microsoft reached its public peak during Microsoft's lengthy antitrust trial with the Department of Justice. Both Oracle and Sun acted as Microsoft's fiercest critics—a tactic that played into the strengths of their outspoken, charismatic CEOs Larry Ellison and Scott McNealy.

For example, Ellison hired investigators to root through the garbage of two research firms that backed Microsoft during its antitrust trial. Oracle claimed that the research organizations were misrepresenting themselves as being independent bodies, and the company sought to expose the ruse. Never shy, Ellison defended the aggressive investigatory tactics by saying, "It's absolutely true we set out to expose Microsoft's covert activities. I feel very good about what we did."

Microsoft countered in kind. "They've set new standards for hypocrisy and disingenuousness, even for Oracle," said a spokesman at the time.

Oracle and Sun also spent much of the 1990s backing technology known as a thin client, hoping the device would disrupt the Wintel PC monopoly. Thin clients are essentially smarter than average monitors that connect back to servers, which handle all of the processing and data storage usually associated with PCs. Both Oracle and Sun championed the technology, thinking it would help them sell software and servers.

Thin clients, while still available, have never inspired much customer interest. Some universities, call centers, and government bodies make use of the systems, but businesses and consumers have stuck with their PCs.

"The era of the PC is almost over, and the era of the thin client is about to begin," Ellison said in 1996.

Whoops.

office. The mesh of glass and steel gives a nod to the city's cutting-edge leanings but does not really fit in well with many of the surrounding Mission-style buildings. A more practical part of the new facility is the complementary 285-foot tower—one of the tallest structures in San Jose. This building holds the majority of the city offices.

Away from the facades, it's not all futuristic razzle-dazzle at the $382 million structure. The city hall, in fact, has a number of exhibits on San Jose's history, including photos, historical artifacts, maps, and paintings that document the city's transformation from an agricultural town to a technology powerhouse. Visitors can find everything from early Apple computers to re-creations of Doc Herrold's radio station. The exhibits, however, do change on a regular basis, making it tough to predict exactly what you'll find. You can access the displays from 8 a.m. to 5 p.m. Monday through Friday.

The city hall is located at 200 East Santa Clara Street. You can't miss it. For more information, contact (408) 535-3500 or www.sanjoseca.gov.

☕ SANTANA ROW

THANKS TO THE SILICON VALLEY BOOM, SAN JOSE HAS grown into one of the largest and wealthiest cities in the United States. Still, it lacks the cachet of nearby San Francisco and has struggled to develop the type of urban charm needed to pull in Silicon Valley types for more refined shopping, dining, and after-hours fun.

The close-to-billion-dollar Santana Row project started as a way to enliven San Jose's streets and distance the city from its strip-mall sprawl roots. The forty-two-acre center opened in 2002, combining modern apartments, high-end shops, trendy boutiques, and a bevy of restaurants.

Federal Realty Investment Trust, based in Rockville, Maryland, developed the site with the idea of adding a European flair to San Jose. And in fact, Santana Row does prove reminiscent of some high-end shopping districts in Europe. Many of the buildings display antique facades, a type of open courtyard runs the length of the street, and pedestrians outnumber cars by a large margin. Despite these European touches, Santana Row comes off less as some type of romantic district that sprang up of its own accord and more as a forced attempt at high living.

Those in search of high-end shopping won't be disappointed. St. John, Gucci, and Escada are just some of the pricey stores on site. You'll also find a number of boutiques with handmade gear that give the area a warm, local flavor.

On a Saturday night people pack these stores, along with the sushi restaurants, bistros, and Mexican cantinas. The crowd includes

CLICK HERE **Fairmont Hotel**

WHEN THE DOWNTOWN FAIRMONT Hotel opened in 1987, the city had yet to construct the HP Pavilion, the McEnery Convention Center, or even the highway off-ramps you'd think necessary to feed a luxury, suburban hotel. Still, San Francisco's Swig family embraced the risk to put up this $140 million pearl.

The hotel's fortunes have gone up and down with those of Silicon Valley. In good times the Fairmont hosts conferences, technology executives, and dignitaries. In the bad times, it has struggled to fill half its rooms at $70 a pop.

Without question, the Fairmont added a much-needed element of elegance to downtown San Jose and helped inspire others to give the city center a go. Or, as the hotel so modestly puts it, "The Fairmont San Jose opened its doors as the first luxury hotel in the Silicon Valley in October 1987 and it remains the jewel of the city's thriving downtown today." The Fairmont Tower opened in 2002, adding 264 rooms to the hotel for a grand total of 805. Today the Fairmont remains a popular destination for business travelers, with rooms hovering around the $200-per-night range.

The Fairmont calls 170 South Market Street home. Call (408) 998-1900 or visit www.fairmont.com/sanjose.

San Jose McEnery Convention Center

JUST A COUPLE OF BLOCKS FROM THE center of downtown San Jose, you'll find the McEnery Convention Center. Like its counterpart the Moscone Center in San Francisco, San Jose's major convention center caters to the local Silicon Valley powerhouses looking to put on large shows. Over the years, it has hosted some of the world's biggest software, hardware, and security events. Of course it enjoyed more action during the boom time than it does today. With fewer events to go around, the San Jose site often loses out to the more scenic Moscone.

During the largest shows, the convention center teams with the San Jose Civic Auditorium across the street to accommodate the crowds. Typically, the civic auditorium serves as the main location for the keynote speakers such as Microsoft's chairman Bill Gates or Oracle's chairman Larry Ellison, while the convention center houses the conference exhibits and lectures.

The light rail makes a stop between the two complexes. The McEnery Convention Center is the larger of the two structures—a big gray mass. A fountain out front and abstract flares to the building's facade give it a contemporary flavor. The Mission-style San Jose Civic Auditorium harks back more to the city's roots.

A number of hotels surround the two convention hot spots, including the San Jose Marriott—which is actually connected to the McEnery Convention Center. The Tech Museum of Innovation is also just a couple of blocks away.

> You'll find the McEnery Convention Center at 150 West San Carlos Street; (408) 277-5277; or on the Web at www.sjcc.com.

singles, young couples, and families. Santana Row doesn't offer the slightly seedier nightlife you'll find 4 miles away in downtown San Jose, which boasts more bars, dancing, and late-night attractions. (You'll need to be on your best behavior in both locations. San Jose's police force is notoriously strict, with officers honking and calling out at locals for minor offenses such as jaywalking. Patrol cars dominate the streets after 9 p.m.)

On top of the Santana Row retail shops are more than 500 residential units. Passersby can catch glimpses of the refined wooden fin-

HP Pavilion

LEAVE IT TO SILICON VALLEY TO NAME A hockey stadium after a computer.

Yes, the HP Pavilion is both the home of the San Jose Sharks hockey team and the brand for a broad line of HP computers. It took some effort, however, to reach what may seem like an obvious name.

In 1988 San Jose citizens once again went in search of a way to boost the economic and cultural fortunes of their fair downtown. They settled on a multipurpose sports and event facility, and the San Jose Arena opened in 1993 at a cost of $163 million. Unlike much of the plain architecture in the city, the 20,000-person stadium has a somewhat radical design. Shimmering stainless steel wraps around the building, culminating in a glass pyramid and exposed support structures. Overall, it has a modern, if boxy feel.

It didn't take long for the corporate vultures to start circling, and Compaq acquired the naming rights to the arena, turning it into the Compaq Center at San Jose (to avoid confusion with the Compaq Center in Houston). In 2002 HP completed its acquisition of Compaq, raising questions about the arena's future name. Carly Fiorina, then CEO of HP, joked during a press conference that it would become the Fi Arena before revealing that HP would take over the naming rights. The Compaq Center turned into the HP Pavilion.

The main HP Pavilion occupants are the San Jose Sharks, although the facility does play host to hundreds of events. Acts ranging from Aerosmith to the Wiggles perform at the arena, and every year a major tennis tournament—the SAP Open—takes place. As you might expect, the stadium is chock-full of advertisements from large technology companies, Hummer dealerships, and the like. Tours of the HP Pavilion are available Monday through Friday at 11 a.m. Guests visit the Penthouse Level and guest suites as well as the ice level.

The HP Pavilion is located at 525 Santa Clara Street or on the Web at www.hppsj.com. Call (408) 977-4730 to set up a tour.

ishes and modern decor that define these one- to four-bedroom units, ranging in size from 700 to 4,000 square feet. At first Federal Realty Investment Trust had a lease-only policy for the apartments, but it has since moved to sell close to half of them. At the end of 2005, prices for the units scaled from $400,000 to more than $1 million.

The very first residents of Santana Row received a huge shock when one of the most prominent neighborhood buildings caught fire

You'll find Santana Row at the southeast corner of Winchester and Stevens Creek Boulevards. You can't miss the black-and-white SANTANA ROW neon sign that stretches high into the sky. Parking is free, which is a nice plus. There's more information available at www.santanarow.com.

in the summer of 2002, just before the area officially opened. Retail outlets and potential denizens had to scale back their plans for the area when "Building 7"—with 246 apartments and 36 shops and restaurants—was destroyed.

EBAY

AS THE LEGEND GOES, PIERRE OMIDYAR STARTED WHAT WOULD become eBay in 1995 to help his girlfriend, Pam Wesley, sell Pez dispensers. Wesley had just moved from Boston to Silicon Valley and struggled to find fellow Pez collectors. In a geek's take on chivalry, Omidyar wrote some software that turned a regular Web site into an auction portal for Pez zealots, hoping this action would impress Wesley.

Countless reporters have embraced this story as they rushed to document eBay's incredible growth. And it is a helpful way to conceptualize how something so basic as a virtual auction house could transform into a multibillion-dollar business that changed countless people's lives.

Good Morning Silicon Valley

WITH COFFEE CUP IN ONE HAND AND A mouse in the other, thousands of technology workers kick their day off with a chuckle by visiting the Web site of Good Morning Silicon Valley. GMSV recaps a handful of the top technology stories with biting headlines and brief, acerbic snippets describing the goings-on in the Valley. The headlines, in particular, have established the site's reputation as a must-visit for any self-respecting technophile.

The GMSV offshoot of the *San Jose Mercury News* had much less humorous beginnings. It started in 1996 as a plain look at the main technology stories of the day. Readers could peruse a variety of headlines and digest a lot of news quickly. That staid approach died when John Paczkowski took over the site in late 1998. He went on to torment Silicon Valley companies and personalities with unmatched flair. Paczkowski left GMSV for a new project in 2007 and turned over full-time editing duties to partner John Murrell. Before departing, Paczkowski noted in an interview that GMSV enjoyed "a lot of history and a ton of readers who have been with us since 1996. When you have much history in the Valley, people begin to view you as a good source of information."

Here's a sampling of some classic GMSV headlines.

- "I'm sorry, Mr. Otellini is resting in a darkened room. May I take a message?"—to describe Intel CEO Paul Otellini's reaction to lowering the company's financial forecast

- "Capellas donates new wing to Golden Parachute Museum"—to describe former Compaq and HP executive Michael Capellas's exit package from Worldcom/MCI

- "Apple raises CEO tantrum threat level from yellow to red"—to describe ultra-secretive Apple CEO Steve Jobs's reaction to a product leak

- "Potential investors should be aware of the slight risk that management will be sent to a re-education camp"—to describe the recommended mindset of investors looking at a Chinese search rival to Google

- "Sir, could you remove the codpiece and walk through the scanner again, please?"—to describe a new airport security X-ray device that could penetrate clothing

- "New from Google Labs: Google Information Security Catastrophe"—to describe worries over Google handing users' search records to the government

You can see what the fuss is about by visiting http://blogs .siliconvalley .com/gmsv.

You'll find eBay's sprawling headquarters on Hamilton Avenue. Instead of having a campus map that points to, say, Building A or Building 31, eBay has colorful, cartoonish maps showing the way to buildings named for its various auction categories: Sports, Collectibles, Motors, Toys, and more. Other than that, however, the campus isn't much to look at. A fancier, more modern eBay complex on North 1st Street is officially the headquarters of PayPal—the online payment company acquired by eBay.

THE TRUTH OF THE TALE

The legend of eBay's founding is only half true. In fact Pierre Omidyar, a graduate of Tufts University, had been working for a couple of technology companies and daydreaming of a new way to make use of the Internet. Despite not having anything in particular to sell—or even any particular fondness for auctions—he decided that an auction site might be a practical use for the Web, allowing people to set the "real value" of an item.

He cranked out some code and set up AuctionWeb—a small section of a consulting Web site he had created called Echo Bay Technology Group. When he eventually moved to formalize his site, he found that the URL echobay.com had already been taken. So he shortened it to eBay.

Well after the site had already been established, Pam Wesley did in fact put a load of Pez dispensers onto AuctionWeb, and the candy collectibles generated a fair amount of interest. Omidyar credits the subsequent Pez fever he saw with showing him some of eBay's potential. People can be passionate about pretty basic things in the world of collectibles.

The company's first PR staffer, Mary Lou Song, grabbed hold of the Pez tale and never let go, pushing the story to reporters as the impetus behind the Web site and the company. It took a few years for the full truth to come out.

From its early days eBay traded far more than Pez dispensers. Internet users began to hear about this auction site where they could buy antiques, electronics, comics, and more. By 1996 Omidyar—hoping to morph eBay from a hobby to a business—began taking a cut of customers' completed sales. This was back in the days when just about everything on the Internet was free, and Omidyar knew the move might alienate eBay's fans. As it turned out, it didn't, and eBay grew astronomically. In short order Omidyar had taken on new hires Chris Agarpao and Jeff Skoll (a Stanford MBA—you knew the Stanford connection was coming, right?). He also had to move the business out of his San Jose living room.

OUT OF THE LIVING ROOM, INTO THE BUSINESS WORLD

Like most successful start-ups, eBay had its early struggles. Users peppered Omidyar with complaints about buyers and sellers. He encouraged them to resolve the disputes on their own but also created a type of feedback system allowing users to comment on their experiences. In addition, he set up a message board where people could offer advice about things such as the best shipping companies.

The next major milestones for eBay arrived in 1998 when the company went public and hired Hasbro executive Meg Whitman as its CEO. Alas, the company couldn't grow up fast enough.

> Look for eBay headquarters at 2145 Hamilton Avenue. No public tours are available. PayPal's complex is found at 2211 North 1st Street.

In 1999 it suffered an embarrassing twenty-two-hour outage that outraged customers and highlighted weaknesses in its technology infrastructure. Whitman has characterized June 10, 1999, as one of the best and worst days in the company's history. Without question, the incident tarnished eBay's reputation in the short term. But it also inspired Whitman to strengthen eBay's technology and helped executives come to terms with the idea that eBay would expand at an astonishing rate for years to come. They'd better start coming up with ways to solve problems no other businesses had ever encountered.

Despite ups and downs, eBay has made Omidyar and a number of early executives wealthy beyond their wildest dreams. More importantly in a broader context, it has created a new business opportunity for thousands of people. Using eBay as a type of auction platform, innovative, passionate types have developed booming businesses auctioning collectibles—or just about anything else you can imagine. Few other Internet companies have had this type of impact.

Like Yahoo!, eBay served as a stabilizing force for the Internet and Silicon Valley during the boom, bust, and recovery years, proving that Web-based ventures can turn into successful entities with the right foundations.

WINCHESTER MYSTERY HOUSE

THE WINCHESTER MYSTERY HOUSE LACKS THE TYPICAL Silicon Valley flair. You won't find any chips, software, or interactive displays at this technological oddity. Instead, you'll discover a nineteenth-century marvel that proved bigger, more advanced, and weirder than any other house of the time.

There's as much mystery surrounding the construction of this Victorian mansion as there is inside the actual building. Here's the story: Already depressed by the loss of her young daughter, Sarah Winchester snapped when her husband, William Winchester—the second president of Winchester Repeating Arms Company—died in 1881 of tuberculosis. Sarah inherited about $20 million and a large stake in the gun company, but this did little to calm her nerves.

Not sure what to do, Sarah visited a Boston psychic. The medium told Sarah to sell her New Haven, Connecticut, home and head west in a quest to end a curse tied to the Winchester gun company. Sarah needed to avenge the deaths of all the Indians killed by Winchester rifles, and the only way to do this—so the legend goes—was to build a house out west and never stop building it.

Sarah embraced this advice with gusto and made her way to California. In 1884 she acquired a six-room farmhouse that anchored a 162-arce orchard. For the next thirty-eight years, construction took place at the house twenty-four hours a day and 365 days a year. By the time of her death in 1922, Sarah had spent close to $6 million building a 160-room giant with 467 doorways, forty-seven fireplaces, nineteen chimneys, forty bedrooms, forty staircases, two ballrooms, and one shower.

Of course the strangest parts of the mansion aren't so much what Sarah built as what she didn't build. One staircase, for example, rises right into a ceiling. A number of doors open only to reveal walls. Stained-glass windows designed by Tiffany sit in the middle of hallways that receive no sunlight. And one room has a window built into the floor.

One explanation for all this, according to experts, is Sarah's lack of architectural training. They speculate that the doors were meant to open onto to new rooms, but that Sarah never got around to completing the plans or changed her mind midstream.

The other major theory posits that the owner was weird.

Without question, Sarah exhibited a penchant for the occult. The number 13 stands as a central theme at the house: There are thirteen windows in some rooms, thirteen drainage holes in sinks, and one chandelier with a crooked thirteenth candleholder awkwardly affixed. Sarah also built a séance room with three exits and one entrance to commune with the spirits.

Visitors can't help but get lost inside the mansion. The hallways connect into staircases at odd spots, and the rooms don't interlink in a conventional manner. One staircase in particular weaves back and forth like an amusement park line, taking 100 feet to rise a single story via forty-two 2-inch steps.

On the technology front, the Winchester Mystery House was ahead of its time with modern heating and plumbing systems, along with three elevators. Sarah could turn on gaslights with the press of a button; a similar push-button system allowed her to signal her whereabouts to servants. Many of the mansion's features were also designed to conserve water, including inclined countertops and an indoor plant watering area that fed runoff back to the main garden.

You'll find the Winchester Mystery House at 525 South Winchester Boulevard. For more information, contact (408) 247-2101 or www.winchestermysteryhouse.com.

Like many of the region's older structures, the mansion took a beating during the 1906 San Francisco Earthquake. The top three floors collapsed, leaving the house four stories high. Today, however, the mansion is considered one of the safest places to be during a quake. Each section has its own floating foundation, allowing separate areas to shift independently.

Few people in the area ever had a chance to take in all the mansion had to offer. Sarah was a recluse. When she died, the house and its contents went to a niece.

Disappointingly, most of Sarah's furnishings were sold off long ago. The house operators have filled a few rooms with antiques, but visitors spend a lot of time walking through empty spaces.

Still, the Winchester Mystery House provides a nice morning or afternoon outing. Just taking in the Victorian building and its gardens is a treat. You'll enjoy the strangeness of the place, its views, and its ambience. The mansion sits across the street from Santana Row, too, so make a day of it and cap off a weird morning with some lunch and shopping.

The Pulgas Water Temple

TUCKED WITHIN THE LUSH PENINSULA watershed is an unusual temple that celebrates humanity's dominance over nature and love of water.

Following the 1906 earthquake, San Francisco officials pushed the US government to grant the city water rights over the nearby Hetch Hetchy Valley. The city hoped to build a dam, turning the Yosemite National Park valley into a massive reservoir. Famed environmentalist John Muir and the Sierra Club fought for seven years to block the project. The valley "is one of God's best gifts and ought to be faithfully guarded," Muir wrote in 1908. The greenies lost their battle, though, and on October 24, 1934, Hetch Hetchy water flowed into the Pulgas Water Temple for the first time.

Today the project supplies water to residents of San Francisco as well as San Mateo, Santa Clara, and Alameda Counties. It's said to be some of the purest drinking water in the country. Yet Hetch Hetchy remains a touchy subject in the Bay Area, with various groups calling for the valley to be returned to its natural state. Even the most vocal and optimistic restoration advocates admit it would cost up to $1 billion to complete such a project, making Hetch Hetchy the kind of a hot-button issue politicians work to avoid.

To take in some of this history in person, you can travel to the temple, which boasts a Beaux Arts–style structure outfitted with fluted columns, a tree-lined pool, and some small gardens. It's all part of the 23,000-acre peninsula watershed—an area rich in coniferous forests, coastal scrub, and grasslands. The watershed—a fish and game refuge—boasts of being home to the "highest concentration of rare and endangered species in the Bay Area."

The Pulgas Water Temple is open to the public Monday through Friday 9 a.m. to 4 p.m. It's closed on weekends except for special events such as weddings. Car traffic is not permitted on Cañada Road 9 a.m. to 3 p.m. on Sunday between November and March, and 9 a.m. to 4 p.m. between April and October.

You can also hike to the temple—2.2 miles round trip—by parking where Cañada Road and Edgewood Road meet. Another route is available from the intersection of CA 92 and Cañada Road. Just hike south along the Crystal Springs Trail. For more information, check out the great Bay Area hiking site www .bahiker.com.

To reach the temple, take exit 29 (Edgewood Road) off the 280 freeway. Head west to the Cañada Road junction and make a right. After close to 1.5 miles, you'll find a parking lot on the left. There's more information at http://sfwater.org.

THOUSANDS OF TOURISTS GO TO SEE THE WINCHESTER FREAK show every year.

The Mansion Tour ($22 for adults, as of this writing) covers all the basics and runs just over an hour. You can take as many pictures as you like.

A second offering, the Behind-the-Scenes tour ($19), provides a look at the inner workings of the mansion. This tour lasts about forty-five minutes and takes in the mansion's on-site fruit-processing plant, gas production facility, garden, and basement. You get a sense of all the work that went into powering the goliath.

You can also opt for the Grand Estate Tour ($27), which combines the two. Children under five can take any of the tours for free—but note that those under nine cannot go on the Behind-the-Scenes tour for safety reasons. Tours begin at 9 a.m. but don't really run on a set schedule; guides simply set out as people show up. During the busiest times, tours begin about every fifteen minutes. The schedule changes during different times of the year; call or visit the mansion's Web site to confirm details. The Web site also provides information on special Friday the 13th and Halloween flashlight tours, which sell out well ahead of time.

SAN JOSE STATE UNIVERSITY

SAN JOSE UNIVERSITY CAN'T BOAST ABOUT PRODUCING A stream of technology millionaires like Stanford or even UC Berkeley. It can, however, celebrate educating thousands of engineers who help start-ups and technology giants thrive. Indeed, the latest figures have San Jose State churning out more engineers than its two local counterparts combined. Overall the school claims to have trained more Silicon Valley employees than any other.

Counterintuitively, San Jose State has not always called San Jose home. The university originated as the Minns' Evening Normal School in San Francisco back in 1857. Five years later the California legislature transformed this into a state school, naming it the California Normal School—the oldest West Coast public institution of higher education. By 1870 a number of cities in the Bay Area were trying to woo the school from San Francisco, and San Jose won out. A new building went up at Washington Square, with students and faculty arriving in 1871. San Jose State has since grown

You can find the university at 1 Washington Square; or on the Web at www.sjsu.edu. Campus tours are available at 11:00 a.m. and 1:30 p.m. on weekdays for prospective students. Group tours are held at 10:00 a.m. and 2:00 p.m. Call (408) 924-2786 for more information.

into a major urban university spread out over 154 downtown acres. Within walking distance of the university lie the San Jose Convention Center, the Fairmont Hotel, and the Tech Museum of Innovation. Many of the buildings at its core circle the impressive Tower Hall— one of the four oldest structures on campus. A second 62-acre South Campus sits 1.5 miles south of the main grounds and plays host to the Spartan Stadium. Close to 30,000 students enroll at San Jose State per year, 75 percent of them undergraduates.

LICK OBSERVATORY

SILICON VALLEY VERY WELL COULD HAVE MISSED OUT ON having a world-class telescope atop Mount Hamilton were it not for the convincing words of George Davidson—an astronomer and president of the California Academy of Sciences. Davidson met with eccentric millionaire James Lick during the 1870s, in part to discuss how the infirmed Lick planned to spend his fortune.

Due to some crushing snubs in his youth, Lick had developed a pressing need to prove himself both successful and larger than life. And before talking to Davidson, he had considered a couple of very grand options for honoring his own image. One had Lick paying for statues of himself and his family so large that they could be viewed from the San Francisco Bay. A second plan had Lick constructing a pyramid larger than the Great Pyramid in Egypt in the middle of downtown San Francisco.

Davidson, however, managed to fan Lick's interest in the stars and planets. Lick decided to pass on the monuments and build the world's largest telescope instead.

To get to the Lick Observatory, you have to drive more than 20 miles along a winding road. The drive can take about an hour from San Jose. At the top of Mount Hamilton, you can take in the interesting domes dotting the area and a fantastic view—on a clear day—of Silicon Valley. The observatory is open to the public every day—except Thanksgiving, Christmas Eve, and Christmas—from dawn until 5:00 p.m. You'll find exhibits in the main Observatory building, which dates back to the 1888 founding. You can also catch an informal talk about the Lick story while viewing the Great Lick Refractor held inside the 36-inch telescope dome. Tours take off from the gift shop on the half hour, starting at 1:00 p.m. on weekdays and 10:30 a.m. on weekends. The tours stop at 4:30 p.m. The talks are free and last about fifteen minutes.

The Lick staff also host a limited number of chances to look through the 36-inch refracting telescope and 40-inch reflecting telescope during the summer. These special evenings include a pair of speakers who talk about the history of the site and a topic relevant to astronomy. The talks start after sunset.

LARGER-THAN-LIFE LICK

Should you have the time or the inclination, the rest of Lick's story is worth pursuing. The East Coaster developed a talent for crafting pianos in his youth and traveled to South America, hoping to make a fortune with his craft. It took him decades, but ultimately Lick succeeded. Then he decided to pack his bags and make a go of it in San Francisco. In 1848 he carted one chest full of Peruvian gold and another full of chocolate to the Bay Area. The chocolate proved a great hit, and Lick sent a note to a Peruvian friend—confectioner Domingo Ghirardelli—suggesting that he travel to San Francisco as well. Millions of chocolate lovers remain grateful for that letter.

You can find more information on the observatory at http://mt hamilton.ucolick.org. Those interested in the summer program should visit www.ucolick .org/public/sumvispro.html or call the gift shop at (408) 274-5061.

Lick went on to become a land magnate in San Francisco and the surrounding area. Before his death he approved the choice of Mount Hamilton, nestled in the Diablo Range, as the home for his observatory. Even then hoping to attract scientific prestige to a rural environment, Santa Clara County officials agreed to shell out $73,000 to create a road up the mountain. This road made it possible to cart the men and material necessary up the 4,200-foot mountain to build the $700,000 (including the land) telescope. It took quite awhile to build the observatory—so long that Lick actually died well before its completion. One of the wealthiest Californians, Lick passed away in 1876 and was buried atop his mountain. The observatory was opened in 1888.

In its early days the Lick Observatory was heralded as one of the finest telescopes available. Thanks to constant attention and ample funding, it has remained a useful tool for astronomers.

CISCO SYSTEMS

UNLIKE TECHNOLOGY TITANS SUCH AS YAHOO!, APPLE, OR HP, Cisco Systems doesn't enjoy much face time with the average consumer. Cisco's switch and router products lurk in data centers, where they more or less serve as the glue keeping networks patched

   **The Filoli Estate**

THANKFULLY, THERE'S AT LEAST ONE mega estate out here that you're free to roam. It's the Filoli estate in Woodside, and thousands of people visit every year. The 654-acre spread is surrounded by the scenic Crystal Springs watershed—a pristine expanse largely off limits to visitors. The estate itself flaunts an early-twentieth-century mansion and sixteen acres of formal gardens.

Filoli originated as the brainchild of the Bourn family—wealthy San Franciscans enriched by a gold mine in Grass Valley. Papa Bourn's motto of choice was "Fight for a just cause; Love your fellow man; Live a good life," so he picked the first two letters from each segment of the credo to come up with the *Filoli* name.

From about 1917 to 1936, Bourn and his family pottered around the Filoli estate. Then the William P. Roth family purchased the property. In 1975 Mrs. Roth graciously donated the grounds to the National Trust for Historic Preserva-tion—thus freeing up one of the grandest estates in the area to the public.

Today Filoli thrives near the hundreds of other technology-funded personal compounds in the Woodside area. It takes fourteen full-time horticulturists and more than one hundred volunteers to maintain the gardens. Visitors can pick from guided and self-guided tours around the gardens as well as nature hikes into the vast Filoli grounds. The site is open 10:00 a.m. to 3:30 p.m. Tuesday through Saturday, and 11:00 a.m. to 3:30 p.m. on Sunday. The last admission occurs one hour before closing.

Filoli is at 86 Cañada Road in Woodside. There's more information at www.filoli.org. Contact Filoli's visitor services at (650) 364-8300, ext. 507, or tours@filoli.org for information on guided tours.

together. In this role, Cisco has become one of the most consistent Silicon Valley performers and managed to dominate its key markets. (No public tours of headquarters available.)

THE BLUE BOX

Most brief histories of Cisco state rather simply that married couple Len Bosack and Sandy Lerner started Cisco in 1984, hoping to make use of networking technology they had developed while working at

Stanford University. True enough, but such stories miss all the work that led up to Cisco's initial router.

A large amount of networking research had occurred outside Silicon Valley as engineers strove to connect both computers located near one another and those spread across the country. Staff at Xerox PARC and Stanford picked up on these efforts after seeing how much people enjoyed linking the PARC Altos—largely considered the first personal computers.

A group of Stanford researchers were able to create something called the "blue box" that let not only Altos but also computers from different manufacturers communicate. The blue box happened to have a computer board from a young Stanford student Andy Bechtolsheim—who would go on to start Sun Microsystems—and other networking components made by Stanford employees and graduate students. One of the employees was Bosack; another was William Yeager, who claims to have done most of the dirty work.

Few of the "blue boxers" were aware that Bosack and Lerner had incorporated Cisco while still working for Stanford and had been assembling routers based on the technology at their home in Atherton. They did this despite Stanford's initial refusal to let them sell the product commercially—because much of the technology development had been done at Stanford's expense.

Stanford, however, could not as a nonprofit sell the gear on its own—nor did it have a real inclination to do so. Beyond that, few of the people who knew about the blue box figured it would

Cisco's San Jose headquarters can be found at 170 West Tasman Drive. Although no public tours are available, the company's campus—made up of dozens of spacious office buildings—dwarfs any other Silicon Valley spread. It's a must-see. Just cruise up and down Tasman Drive to take it all in. You can visit www.cisco.com or call (408) 526-4000 for more information.

garner much attention given how few computers were connected at the time.

Stanford eventually realized that it could either sue its ex-employees and kill the prospect of a new business emerging from the university . . . or try to carve out some kind of arrangement. Rather grudgingly, the school agreed to license technology to Cisco in exchange for cash and products. In subsequent years, Stanford has received large donations from Cisco and its executives.

By 1989 the firm had attracted 111 employees and was pulling in revenue of $27 million. That same year the number of computers connected to the Internet cracked the 100,000 mark for the first time. Growing interest in networking computers at research labs and at businesses pushed Cisco to great heights at a quick pace. By 1994, Cisco's revenue had reached $1.3 billion. It opened up a large office complex in San Jose to house more than 2,000 staff. The firm would continue to surge at a tremendous rate, especially during the dot-com bubble. Cisco (networking), Sun (servers), Oracle (databases), and EMC (storage) were labeled the "four horsemen of the Internet."

While Cisco's profits did flatten during the bust, it never suffered from a huge collapse. By 2005 the company employed more than 38,000 people.

Despite facing plenty of competition over the years, Cisco has maintained its position as the gold standard in networking. Sticking with Cisco gear is considered the ultimate safe bet for technology buyers.

More recently, Cisco has tried to fight out of the data center shadows and touch consumers directly. Cisco bought the maker of home networking gear Linksys in 2003, and bought set-top-box maker Scientific-Atlanta in 2005. These deals were part of dozens of acquisitions led by Cisco's charismatic CEO John Chambers.

TO GET DOWN AND DIRTY WITH THE FRUITS OF SILICON
Valley, you'll want to head to The Tech and make sure your kids are in
tow. You can't miss this downtown building: It's a huge orange rectangle capped off by a giant purple dome. The gaudy structure seems
a bit out of place amid refined hotels and office facilities, but hey, it's
a gadget museum. What do you expect?

Inside you'll find hands-on exhibits, more hands-on exhibits,
and then a few more hands-on exhibits. The fun starts on the lower
level, with permanent displays on how the Internet works, space, and
the history of innovation. At one station you can arm-wrestle people
across the room or across the country using a plastic arm that con-
nects into electric sensors and then to the Internet. Screens show your
opponent grimacing or rejoicing. Another popular spot lets you play
Whack-A-Spam—an obvious knockoff of Whack-A-Mole where instead
of rodents you knock out e-mail with headlines like LOSE WEIGHT FAST! and
BUY MIRACLE PILLS. These kid-friendly items complement detailed information on the Internet's inner workings, ranging from what data packets
are and how they travel to guides for cobbling together server farms.

The space, ocean, and earth area on the lower level also holds a number of treats. You can drive a Mars rover, testing your ability to dodge obstacles from afar, or experience a fake earthquake. One of the true highlights
of this exhibit is the jet pack chair game. You lie back in a chair that has
been placed on a type of giant air hockey table and then try to align a laser
strapped to your chair with targets on the ceiling. You have sixty seconds
to hit as many targets as possible, firing your jet pack up and down and
left and right all the while. Kids will also be pleased to find museum staffers working at a science booth on this level. These folks guide museum
goers through basic experiments such as making rockets with antacid
pills or using heat to make "memory metal" return to its original shape.

On the upper level you'll find more hard science with exhibits that trace how processors are made, how genes are spliced, and how robots function. If silicon wafers and peptides aren't your thing, there's plenty of other fun to be had. You might try your hand at a design-your-own-roller-coaster station that allows you to craft a ride on a computer, then hop over to a simulator to experience your own creation—loops, corkscrews, heart-pounding drops, and all. In another area you can learn basic microprocessor logic by designing a system that alters the movements of a Mr. Potato Head based on different stimuli such as heat, sound, and light. Still another favorite exhibit lets you practice speeches on a wide range of topics in front of the US Senate. After sitting down behind a microphone-equipped desk and reading a speech from a teleprompter, you move on to another station and see your speech replayed with clapping inserted during your most eloquent moments. Of course, you'll also catch a couple of senators yawning.

Last but certainly not least for the kiddos is the Imagination Playground, where children can have their face superimposed on butterflies or play with their shadows using a colorful video display.

The museum is located at 201 South Market Street. More information is available at (408) 294-8324 or www.thetech.org.

The middle level of the museum is where you actually enter the building, and the exhibits on this floor are a bit thin. You will, however, find the entrance to The Tech's IMAX theatre. The museum shows a wide range of films from specials on the ocean or space to feature productions like *Harry Potter* or *Charlie and the Chocolate Factory*.

When entering The Tech, you'll receive an ID tag that can be worn on your wrist. At a number of displays, you slide this tag past a sensor, and it records, for example, your speech in front of Congress under your unique ID. Some of this content is stored on your own Web site provided by the museum, allowing you to replay museum moments again and again.

CLICK HERE **The California Theatre**

THE CALIFORNIA THEATRE ADDS A REAL old-school touch to downtown San Jose. Formerly the Fox California Theatre, the building languished after its closure in 1973. In fact, the theater faced possible demolition before some generous folks stepped forward to resurrect it.

Today the California Theatre plays host to the Opera San Jose, the Symphony Silicon Valley, and a variety of film events. The film agenda is particularly apt given the theater's original purpose as an elegant motion picture house. Thanks to a careful restoration, the building's facade again exudes its original 1927 charm. The structure smacks of elegance and of a time when going to see a film was a major social event.

Over the years the theater oscillated among films, vaudeville acts, and 3-D shows until its closure. A couple of attempts to revive it were made during the 1970s, but both failed. The San Jose Redevelopment Agency (SJRA) finally purchased the building in 1985, saving it from destruction. The SJRA teamed with the Packard Humanities Institute—run by David Packard, the son of the HP co-founder by the same name—to put $75 million toward restoration.

Packard insisted that the original opulence of the theatre live on, and it has. Walking through the California Theatre's front doors takes you to a different era. You'll find glorious marble columns, intricate artwork covering the ceilings, and gold-leaf cornices. In short, it's a real beauty. Seating about 1,100 people, it gives Silicon Valley residents another reason to visit downtown San Jose after hours.

The theater is found at 345 South 1st Street. You can't miss the building: Just look for the retro marquee. To learn more about upcoming shows, visit the opera's Web site at www.operasj.org or the symphony's site at www.symphonysiliconvalley.org.

The Tech is open 10 a.m. to 5 p.m. daily in summer, and Tuesday through Sunday in winter. Like any good museum, it has a store full of goodies and a restaurant. A ticket for the museum costs about $10 for adults and $7 for children—the same price as the IMAX. A combo ticket for the museum and the IMAX will cost about $16 for adults and $13 for children. Adults can make their way through in about two to three hours. With kids, you'll want to spend some more time.

IF YOUR KIDDOS STILL HAVE ENERGY LEFT AFTER GOING through the Tech Museum of Innovation, walk a couple of blocks to the Children's Discovery Museum (CDM), which picks up where some of the youngster-oriented exhibits at The Tech leave off. Children can head to Bubbalogna and create huge bubbles out of soapy water, learning a wee bit about physics as they have fun. Or they can step into yesteryear by going through an exhibit that shows what Silicon Valley used to be like when it was the lush "Valley of Heart's Delights." Then there's a pizza-making station where children can learn about recipes, measurements, and the math behind operating a cash register.

All told, the museum packs in two floors of diverse exhibits and freshens up the displays on a regular basis. Plenty of parents in Silicon Valley make a yearly pilgrimage to the CDM with their youngsters in tow.

> You'll find the CDM at 180 Woz Way. For more information, contact (408) 298-5437 or www.cdm.org.

Much of the original funding for the museum, which opened in 1990, came from Apple co-founder Steve Wozniak. The museum is now located on Woz Way. You can't miss the odd, jagged building—a purple giant that's a mix of triangles and squares and looks something like a child's funky version of a pyramid. The light rail stops nearby. CDM is open Tuesday through Saturday 10 a.m. to 5 p.m. and Sunday noon to 5 p.m. It offers specific programs for schools and for birthday parties.

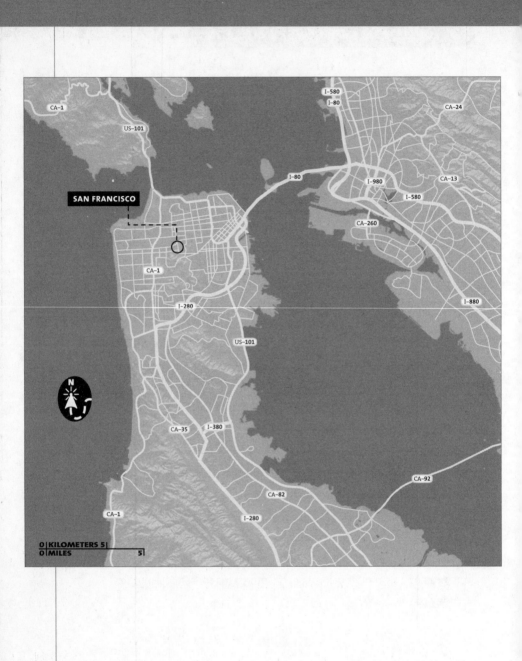

SAN FRANCISCO

SAN FRANCISCO ISN'T TECHNICALLY IN Silicon Valley, but the city has long served a major role in attracting people to the region. The proximity of such a world-class metropolis to places such as Palo Alto, Cupertino, and Mountain View can make the idea of living in the suburbs more attractive for many workers: Do your business in the 'burbs and party downtown.

San Francisco cannot claim anywhere near the number of technology corporate behemoths that Silicon Valley hosts. It has, however, always catered to the bustling dot-com scene.

During the Internet boom, San Francisco was littered with dot-coms and struggled to build enough office space to keep up with the fledgling companies. A new type of gold rush was on, and the city surged. Apartments were almost impossible to find, and the office space was some of the most expensive in the country.

That's why the Internet crash took a particularly hard toll on the city. Thousands of workers with astronomical rents were left unemployed, and huge building complexes were abandoned mid-construction by potential tenants.

San Francisco has since rebounded—in style. The dot-com mania has died down, although the city still claims a large number of the Internet survivors, including Craigslist.org. In addition, biotech firms and the likes of George Lucas seem to prefer the flashy San Francisco over Silicon Valley.

No other city in the Bay Area can match what San Francisco has to offer from a cultural point of view. It's one of the most popular

CHAPTER 5

tourist destinations in the world with an unrivaled dining scene, thriving nightlife, and elegant hotels.

During the week, San Francisco often hosts thousands of technology tourists in town for various conventions. On weekends tourists and locals can get their technology fix by visiting the long-standing Exploratorium or even the Green Street Lab where television was invented.

It's hard to imagine Silicon Valley being as successful without such a nearby treasure.

⚔ GREEN STREET LAB

A FARM-BOY-TURNED-INVENTOR WORKING OUT OF A SMALL San Francisco lab decades ago may well have outdone the likes of Intel, Apple, Sun Microsystems, and Google by creating one of the most used products on the planet.

In September 1927 Philo Taylor Farnsworth delivered up the first working television set. This feat hardly earned Farnsworth lasting fame—few people even recognize his name these days. Still, he stands as a giant among giants and a major contributor to the Bay Area's technology history.

> You'll find the building at the northwest corner of the intersection of Sansome and Green Streets.

As the legend goes, the budding technophile Farnsworth came up with a vision for the television while doing farm work on his parent's land in Utah at the tender age of fourteen. It would take Farnsworth another seven years to turn this vision into reality and make the first successful transmission of television signals.

A handful of inventors had explored the ideas that led up to the creation of TV, and Farnsworth was not the first to patent the electron scanning tube that's key to the device. The self-taught Utah inventor, however, beat out all the competition by developing a practical, functioning TV system.

During the 1930s Farnsworth battled RCA over the rights to the major TV intellectual property. One of Farnsworth's high school teachers testified that his pupil had indeed drawn out his vision for TV many years before on a chalkboard—a disclosure that helped secure a legal victory for Farnsworth.

Farnsworth's major TV work took place at the Green Street Lab, which is located just a few blocks from Wharf 15 in downtown San Francisco.

Like many Bay Area entrepreneurs, Farnsworth knew how to impress his investors. When they asked if the invention would ever generate profits, Farnsworth displayed a dollar sign on the TV screen. Ultimately, however, he grew to have concerns about his invention, saying later in life that he didn't want it to be part of his son's "intellectual diet."

While Farnsworth wasn't deeply intertwined with the other electrical pioneers in the Bay Area, his work did add to the hobbyist inclinations of people in the region. Today you'll find a historical marker noting Farnsworth's achievement outside a rather average two-story office building. Farnsworth—the "genius of Green Street"—worked in this lab with his wife and brother-in-law. He left the site in 1931 and moved his office to Philadelphia.

The marker reads as follows:

IN A SIMPLE LABORATORY ON THIS SITE, 202 GREEN STREET, PHILO TAYLOR FARNSWORTH, U.S. PIONEER IN ELECTRONICS, INVENTED AND PATENTED THE FIRST OPERATIONAL ALL-ELECTRONIC "TELEVISION SYSTEM." ON SEPTEMBER 7, 1927 THE 21-YEAR-OLD INVENTOR AND SEVERAL DEDICATED ASSISTANTS SUCCESSFULLY TRANSMITTED THE FIRST ALL-ELECTRONIC TELEVISION IMAGE, THE MAJOR BREAKTHROUGH THAT BROUGHT THE PRACTICAL FORM OF THIS INVENTION TO MANKIND. FURTHER PATENTS FORMULATED HERE COVERED THE BASIC CONCEPTS ESSENTIAL TO MODERN TELEVISION. THE GENIUS OF GREEN STREET, AS HE WAS KNOWN, DIED IN 1971.

⏻ THE EXPLORATORIUM

THE EXPLORATORIUM EXEMPLIFIES A HANDS-ON TECHNOLOGY museum. It unites science and entertainment in unmatched fashion, allowing visitors to fondle just about every exhibit within the display area. Kids will be entertained for hours while adults learn a thing or two as well.

Museum science exhibits allow you to replicate a geyser by pressing down on a large plastic platform and creating puffs of steam. You can also play gravity games by trying to launch a series of plastic balls into containers lined up below the release platform. Friends can head to the second floor and sit in opposing structures that focus sounds on the participants, making it possible to hear a softly spoken voice from 70 feet away. And of course, children can play with a huge pool of soapy water and create massive bubbles.

Those who prefer brain teasers won't be disappointed. Vain visitors can climb inside a kaleidoscope and see their images repeated ad infinitum. Another exhibit displays an always changing video of a street corner and highlights how bad people are at picking out small alterations to a scene. In a demonstration area, Exploratorium workers will show off some card tricks as well.

The Exploratorium is located at 3601 Lyon Street. You can find more information at www.exploratorium.edu or by calling (415) 561-0360.

Harder-core science exhibits delve into areas such as genetics, the effects of environmental changes on organisms, and earthquakes. The Exploratorium still covers these areas in a hands-on manner, with the addition of some laboratory setting elements. You can, for example, examine different types of flies under a microscope to see their genetic mutations, or have an up-close gander at sea urchin sperm. There's even an actual laboratory where young Exploratorium volunteers walk visitors through various experiments.

This type of interaction builds on the original dreams of Exploratorium founder Frank Oppenheimer—the brother of Manhattan Project lead Robert Oppenheimer. Frank hoped to link science and technology and make advances in these areas accessible to the public. In 1969 the spacious Palace of Fine Arts opened up in San Francisco's Marina District to house Oppenheimer's vision.

The Exploratorium proved an experiment worthy of the scenic Palace of Fine Arts. Built in 1915 for the Panama-Pacific Exposition, the building had been used for various inglorious purposes over the years—housing tennis courts, phone books, and cars. Today visitors can spend a couple of hours inside the Exploratorium and then take in the surrounding architecture and lagoon. More than half a million people visit the Exploratorium every year, making it one of the most popular museums in San Francisco. Geared toward youngsters, the 400 exhibits offer adults a good time as well.

The Exploratorium is open 10 a.m. to 5 p.m. Tuesday through Sunday. Admission is free on the first Wednesday of every month. Normally, however, adults pay $13, students $10, and kids $8. The Exploratorium is open to birthday parties and also has a Tactile Dome that can be accessed by appointment. Visitors make their way through the dome in total darkness.

THE WAVE ORGAN

TOURISTS OFTEN GET A BAD RAP IN SAN FRANCISCO. THEY clog the streets by walking slow. They hang out in cheesy spots. Worst of all, they refer to the town as "Frisco." Still, even the freshest-meat tourist can outclass a San Francisco native—at least for a moment—by visiting the low-tech, lovable Wave Organ.

San Francisco denizens have forgotten about the Wave Organ— with good reason. It's not easy to find. Unlike major tourist attractions, the Wave Organ does not claim a single sign flagging its location (unless you count the NOT A THROUGH STREET marker near its entrance).

BUT WHAT IS IT?

When San Francisco cemeteries in the city were removed and shifted to Colma in the early 20th century, piles of discarded Victorian tombstones were left behind. In 1986 the Exploratorium's artist in residence, Peter Richards, teamed with sculptor and master stonemason George Gonzales to create the Wave Organ from this rubble. The men developed a site reminiscent of a small Greek amphitheater or a humble temple to Poseidon—at least aside from the twenty-five pipes (made from a combination of concrete and PVC) snaking their way up from the water to jut out at odd angles around the shrine. These pipes suck in the sound of waves rushing into the shore and crashing against the rocks at the base of the structure, and then deliver that sound back up to observers in a distorted form. It's hard to describe the noises made by the Organ other than to note their gurgle, roar, whoosh, and burpish qualities.

To find this human-made music machine, you want to head toward the Yacht clubs located near the Presidio. In fact, you want to traverse Yacht Road (via Lyon Street) in particular and head past the Golden Gate Yacht Club. There you'll see some unusual rock formations jutting out from the end of the jetty. That's the tip of the Wave Organ.

Aficionados say the pipe system works best early in the morning—at sunrise. Even at peak performance, however, the Wave Organ does not pump the marina with a thunderous concert. Instead, you will likely need to stick your head right up against one of the many pipes to take in the unusual ocean sounds. Or you can sit in the so-called stereo booth—a roof-topped concrete bench at the heart of the Organ—and catch the subtle rushes and gurgles as you meditate on the sunrise.

The sounds are also said to vary based on how recently the pipes have been cleaned by the nearby Exploratorium.

The Wave Organ can complement a day at the Exploratorium, a walk by the Presidio and marina, or some outdoor time at Crissy Field. You can't help but be amused and impressed by the structure, and the surrounding view is fantastic. On one side of the Wave Organ, you'll catch the Golden Gate Bridge and Alcatraz; on the other lie the marina, the Palace of Fine Arts, and some of San Francisco's prettiest homes.

Best of all, you can fluster the natives when you talk about tracking down the Wave Organ and have a giggle at their curious looks. Unless, of course, you are a San Francisco resident. In which case it's time to head down to the marina and make your way to the end of Yacht Road before some silly tourist makes fun of you.

THE LETTERMAN DIGITAL ARTS CENTER

THERE IS A HEAVEN ON EARTH FOR GIFTED MOVIE BUFFS who enjoy breathtaking views and want to work in a bustling, vibrant city. The Pearly Gates to this particular paradise open at the Lombard Street entrance to the Presidio, leading to the Letterman Digital Arts Center.

Resembling a miniaturized version of a college campus, the center plays home to the special effects, video game, and corporate divisions of George Lucas's filmmaking empire. Four large, Arts and Crafts–style buildings stretch over a small portion of the twenty-three-acre site. Their efficient, nondescript architecture gives way to rolling, grassy grounds that link the structures and allow the buildings to fit in with the Presidio National Park.

Visitors can look up through the windows of one of the outer buildings and see a massive gym packed full of exercise gear. The center also holds a fancy day care center and cafeteria, not to men-

GEORGE LUCAS AND PIXAR ANIMATION STUDIOS
"These guys invented the industry out of absolute pure passion."

TO THE CASUAL OBSERVER, PIXAR ANIMATION Studios appeared out of nowhere with the groundbreaking release of *Toy Story* in 1995. No company had ever produced a feature-length computer animated film before, and few would have guessed that the movie would pull in more than $360 million, making it the top grossing picture of the year.

Far from being a sudden creative stroke of genius, *Toy Story* came to life after more than 20 years of struggling on the part of engineers, technophiles, and patrons such as George Lucas and Apple's Steve Jobs.

In the 1970s director George Lucas—and many other prominent filmmakers—had a dream of breaking from the confines of the Hollywood machine to gain more control over film production. Convinced that technology advances could play a crucial role in this quest, Lucas put large chunks of his own money into funding various technology projects in and near San Francisco, including Lucasfilm.

The engineers at Lucasfilm battled for years trying to deal with machines that—even as they cost millions of dollars—were inadequate. Graphics work by nature creates large, complex sets of data that would, in many cases, break the computers from the likes of Digital Equipment and Cray that Lucasfilm tried. Engineers stayed up for days trying to remove jagged edges from an image or to model an object better than ever before.

Through all the challenges, the engineers managed to wow their peers with custom hardware and software advances. The work never quite reached the point where Lucas could incorporate it on a large scale in his films. Nonetheless, he continued to fund the graphics efforts, believing they would eventually allow him to make better movies.

During a financial crunch, Lucas put his graphics group and the Pixar hardware they had developed up for sale. Steve Jobs, co-founder of Apple, stepped in with a $5 million bid. He then put another $5 million in funding behind the unit.

And the battles to master the machines continued. Thankfully, Sun Microsystems developed a cheaper, more powerful workstation that proved attractive to Pixar. Soon the breakthroughs began coming at a faster clip; the creation of an entire film was perhaps within reach. Jobs worked out a deal with Disney to help develop and distribute a movie called *Toy Story*. Even during that time, though, Jobs was openly wondering if he'd ever get his money back . . . at least until he watched the flick.

"I think Jobs was surprised when he finally saw *Toy Story*," said Michael Rubin, author of *DroidMaker*. "I believe it wasn't until he saw how good the movie was that he realized it wasn't just the technology that he owned but also these amazingly talented guys. . . . the graphics projects at Lucasfilm represented guys who dreamed of doing this their entire life in many cases. These guys invented the industry out of absolute pure passion."

In the end, Pixar's success with *Toy Story* and beyond vindicates both Lucas and Jobs for pursuing a very Silicon Valley model of doing business: nurturing talent for years in the belief that a payoff would come—someday.

tion state-of-the-art communications to facilitate high-speed computing and several theaters for screening completed movies or watching dailies.

Though the Letterman Digital Arts Center can hold up to 2,500 workers, you won't notice many cars surrounding the offices. That's a result of the underground parking meant to help keep the grounds around the center pristine.

Lush Presidio Park lies on one side of the campus, and a flowing walkway lies on the other. This bench-lined walkway swirls around a stream and pond and provides a chance to take in some of San Francisco's most famous sites in a relaxed atmosphere. The view from the Lucas offices spans from the Golden Gate Bridge across to the Palace of Fine Arts. Plenty of San Franciscans enjoy a weekend stroll through the seventeen public acres of the compound.

Serious *Star Wars* fans may be disappointed by the site. The only real indication of the property's owner comes from a single water fountain topped off by none other than Yoda. The already blessed workers inside have the privilege of taking in more Lucas memorabilia, with stormtroopers and starships decorating the halls.

HELPING BUSINESS, NATURE, AND ART

When it officially opened in 2005, the center went a long way toward solving two problems. First off, it helped the Presidio Trust meet its goals. This trust, created by Congress in 1996, was charged with turning the old army stomping grounds into a scenic and useful part of the Presidio. In particular, the park needs to be self-sufficient financially by 2013.

With this in mind, the trust freed up the chunk of land that used to be the Letterman Army Medical Center and invited proposals. While Lucas reportedly did not put forth the most lucrative offer, the trust decided that his reputation and intentions outweighed other bidders in the long run. Lucas currently leases the facility, helping the trust reach the self-sufficiency target. He's also put more than $300 million into the renovation project.

Second, the location allowed Lucas to meet a crucial corporate objective—improving the working environment of his Industrial Light and Magic special effects team, corporate staffers, and LucasArts games. While magnificent in its own right, the Skywalker Ranch across the Golden Gate Bridge in Marin County had proved bothersome to employees and clients. This facility, the historic home of Lucas's operations, was somewhat isolated and required a serious commute for staffers living in San Francisco and customers flying into SFO airport. The new site made life easier on Lucas's employees, and should improve their working conditions as well. Instead of having isolated teams at Skywalker Ranch, Lucas now has key groups working right next to each other and contributing simultaneously to projects.

> You can visit the Letterman Digital Arts Center anytime. It's near Chestnut and Lyon Streets and most easily accessed via the Lombard Gate of the Presidio. No public tours are available, but you can find more information on the center at www.lucasfilm.com/inside/letterman/.

MOSCONE CENTER

THE MOSCONE CENTER SITS AT THE HEART OF DOWNTOWN San Francisco and serves as the big daddy of all Silicon Valley conference centers. This giant plays host to more than 900,000 visitors per year and offers more than 2 million square feet of space for exhibits, speeches, and sessions.

The Moscone Center first started hogging space in the Yerba Buena Gardens back in 1981 when the Moscone South building was completed. Ten years later the Moscone North structure appeared, and in 2003 the smaller, more modern Moscone West building started hosting conference attendees.

Technology types can't claim a monopoly on the massive convention center. San Francisco residents often see badged tourists of all varieties funneling their way from the Moscone to nearby hotels. Organizations as diverse as 7-Eleven, the American Vacuum Society, and the American Society for Bariatric Surgery turn to at least one of the three buildings to meet their needs.

Of course, if processors appeal more than peritoneal dialysis, the Moscone Center has an event or two for you, too. Some of the technology world's largest conferences take place here, including the Intel Developer Forum, the JavaOne event, and Linux World.

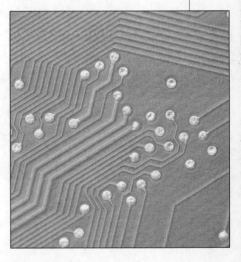

Larger conferences demand both the Moscone South and North buildings. Luckily for the attendees, the two buildings connect via a large underground pathway. This makes shuffling from session to session relatively easy. Many recent exhibitors have preferred to use the more modern and manageable Moscone West building, which sits off on its own across the street from the older structures.

It's not uncommon for organizers to tweak part of the Moscone Center to throw a bash for conference attendees during the evenings. During the dot-com boom, you'd likely find the real Neil Diamond belting ballads in the Moscone's underground chambers. In the bust world, you'd be lucky to find a second-tier Neil Diamond cover band. Should you choose to avoid the conference entertainment, there are plenty of other options near the Moscone Center, including the Metreon movie theatre and the San Francisco Museum of Modern Art.

☕ MOSCONE CENTER HOTELS

A TOP TOURIST ATTRACTION LIKE SAN FRANCISCO HAS A plethora of hotels to throw at visitors. This selection can make life interesting for business travelers trying to combine convenience with comfort. Those coming in for a conference at the Moscone Center have a number of nearby options—each with something unique to offer.

▶ THE SAN FRANCISCO MARRIOTT

THE CLOSEST HOTEL TO THE REVAMPED MOSCONE WEST IS the San Francisco Marriott. This giant has a spacious lobby and provides all the amenities you would expect of a hotel that caters to business travelers. Rooms can range from $300 on up, depending on the season and what events are in town. You're paying more for the location than luxury and will be in walking distance to all of the Moscone buildings, Union Square, Market Street, and parts of the Financial District.

> The San Francisco Marriott is located at 55 4th Street. It can be reached at (415) 896-1600 or www.sfmarriott.com.

The biggest downside to the Marriott is its sheer size. The thirty-nine-floor building has 1,500 rooms. During busy events, you can expect to wait in line for the elevator and to run into decent-size crowds in the lobby. On the plus side, entire conferences or parts of events being held at the Moscone often take place within the Marriott, which has fifty-two meeting rooms and 100,000 square feet of meeting space.

▶ THE W

THE UPSCALE W HOTEL—ON THE OTHER SIDE OF THE MOSCONE Center from the Marriott—is anything but average. On the outside you'll find a shimmering, glitter-flecked sidewalk. Inside lie a posh bar, bellhops with fancy communications sets, an elegant setting, and, of course, free apples.

As with many W Hotels, the rooms end up being smaller than those at neighboring hotels. The W tries to make up for the tight quarters by supplying the latest

You can find the hotel at 181 3rd Street. Reservations can be made by dialing (415) 777-5300 or by visiting www.star woodhotels.com/whotels.

and greatest gadgets and refined decor. Room rates start at about $340, and you'll be paying $10 or more for cocktails at the bar. The W also offers a top San Francisco restaurant—XYZ.

The W is across the street from the Moscone, next door to the San Francisco Museum of Modern Art, near Market Street, near the Financial District, and unfortunately next door to a fire station.

▶ HOTEL PALOMAR

IF THE W SCENE IS A BIT MUCH BUT YOU STILL WANT TO GO boutique, then head over to Hotel Palomar. Folks in the know treasure this gem just a few doors down from the Moscone Center West.

Boutique to its core, the Palomar has a pint-size, although elegant, lobby. Friendly staff will check you in and rush your bags up to the more spacious and even more elegant rooms in a jiffy. The Palomar decor resembles that of the swank W and provides travelers with total comfort. Rooms start at around $250 per night.

When you're ready to escape these plush confines, cruise down

You'll find the hotel at 12 4th Street and can make reservations by dialing (415) 348-1111 or visiting www .hotelpalomar.com.

to the Fifth Floor restaurant and accompanying lounge. The lounge bartenders serve some of the best drinks in town, and you can't go wrong with dishes like foie gras ravioli with caramelized napa cabbage in a duck bouillon from the restaurant.

➤ **THE WESTIN SAN FRANCISCO MARKET STREET**

THE WESTIN HOTEL COULD BE THE BEST VALUE FOR THE BUSINESS traveler looking to stay near the Moscone Center. It falls somewhere between the boutique-class hotels and the oversize Marriott. With a spacious, elegant lobby and rooms to match, the Westin really does offer more room to move than most San Francisco hotels. Secure a corner room and you'll be in heaven. Rooms hover around $250, although the hotel often offers up steep discounts during slower periods. Like the Marriott, it often plays host to conferences or helps out with Moscone overflow.

> You can find the hotel at 50 3rd Street—just off Market Street and a couple blocks from the Moscone. For reservations, contact (415) 974-6400 or www.westinsf.com.

⏻ THE METREON

TO MANY, IT SEEMED LIKE A GREAT IDEA: COMBINE SHOPS, great restaurants, and a movie theater with unique exhibits centered on quirky themes like "Where the Wild Things Are" or The "Way Things Work." Why deliver the same old shopping experience when you can guide consumers through a type of urban amusement park?

Sadly, the $85 million vision funded by Sony never really took hold. Since its opening in 1999, the Metreon—formerly the Sony Metreon—has been a movie theater first and little else second. Backers had hoped to unite a technology-rich and educational environment with shopping. Customers could stroll through the building and be entertained as they consumed. Artist types were brought in to create a new type of shopping environment that would stand as the model for more Sony creations around the globe.

For a while things looked promising. Sony, for example, managed to tempt Microsoft to open the world's only Microsoft store in the complex. It then lured some other high-end tenants and opened a couple of slick restaurants. But most of the nontraditional exhibits inside the contemporary silver complex had closed down by 2001—the same year that Microsoft bailed on the project.

On the plus side, the fifteen-screen Loews Theatres Metreon remains one the most popular movie venues in the country, pulling in both tourists and locals. In addition, visitors will find the Walk of Game—the video game industry's answer to the Walk of Fame in Hollywood.

> You can find the Metreon next to the Moscone Center at 101 4th Street; (415) 369-6000; or on the Web at www.metreon.com.

In 2006 Sony pulled away from the Metreon and sold out to mall developer the Westfield Group. Sony will, however, continue to run its Sony-themed store. These days the Metreon is pretty much a small mall in flux.

CRAIGSLIST.ORG

NO WEB SITE HAS CLOSER TIES TO THE BAY AREA—WHILE AT the same time rejecting a huge chunk of current Silicon Valley leanings—than Craigslist.org. In the age of dot-com hysteria, Craigslist and its founder, Craig Newmark, have stayed close to their humble roots. No ads. No IPO. No venture capital. No bloated salaries, sports cars, or lavish offices.

Instead, Craigslist has simply pumped out billions of pages per month to users across the United States and throughout the world. Its mix of real estate postings, personals, job offers, and everything in between has made the site one of the most visited Internet destinations. People in the Bay Area have long relied on Craigslist for everything from setting up dates to moving their old computer gear.

CLICK HERE

The Ramp

FOR THE ULTIMATE CASUAL BRUNCH experience, you'll want to head south of Market and visit the legendary Ramp restaurant. This eatery has nurtured the downtrodden spirits and bodies of weekend revelers in San Francisco for decades. It's the place you turn to when a Bloody Mary, a burger, and a breeze seem like the only things capable of making the rest of your day bearable.

Unlike the trendy hot spots that dominate San Francisco, the Ramp is a back-to-the-basics kind of place. You get plastic chairs and tables, umbrellas, easygoing staff, and a not-too-spectacular view of the bay. The food, too, is on the basic side with breakfast fare, burgers, and salads dominating the menu. But you go to the Ramp more for the relaxing ambience, people-watching, and strong cocktails than anything else. On a warm, sunny day you can expect a healthy one-hour wait. The restaurant often has live music as well.

The Ramp is located at 855 China Basin Street and can be reached at (415) 621-2378.

The site has expanded to make a few bucks from job postings in San Francisco and apartment listings in New York.

TEMPTATIONS AND DISTRACTIONS

Microsoft was the first company to approach the humble community message board commercially, asking to slap an ad on the Craigslist home page. Newmark rejected this offer and has declined similar proposals ever since. The closest any company has come to gaining a piece of Craigslist occurred in 2004 when eBay took a 25 percent stake in the company, and that was the result of an oversight. A former partner of Newmark's—Phillip Knowlton—had left Craigslist and sold his shares for millions without alerting Newmark to his plans. "I figured [handing out shares] didn't matter, since everyone agreed that the equity had only symbolic value, not dollar value," Newmark writes on his Web site. "Well, the guy later left the company, and decided to sell his equity, which I learned he had every legal right to do."

Aside from the eBay episode, Newmark has turned down huge offers to buy the Web site, insisting all along that he simply wants to make life easier on people. "We are doing well," he said in an interview. "Personally, I have

> You can find the Craigslist offices at 1381 9th Avenue. In addition, Newmark often hangs out at the Reverie Coffee Café on 848 Cole Street.

stepped away from at least tens of millions. I am not interested in running ads or doing an IPO."

While helping people out seems like a noble goal, many paint it more as naiveté. Detractors charge Craigslist with triggering huge declines in newspaper revenues, as publishers struggle to match the site's classified clout. They also claim Craigslist allows corrupt people to game the apartment rental postings and to harass individuals in the personal sections. The Web site has even been accused of increasing the number of violent dog mauling incidents in the Bay Area as a result of its popular "pets" section where folks trade pit bulls and the like.

Critics have called on Newmark to turn Craigslist into a more professional business in the hopes that a capital infusion would help the company deal with these issues. The founder, however, insists that Craigslist is doing just fine and says the site remains in keeping with his goals.

A positive spirit has endeared Newmark and his Web site to many in the Bay Area. They're proud to note that the influential site and concept originated here. Craigslist is the ultimate helping hand, showing you the best place to grab a sofa or to find a lesbian seeking love on Tuesdays.

After a few years as a Bay Area–only thing, Craigslist has pushed its peace and love vibe into US cities and large metropolitan areas around the world. Other companies have taken notice

VALLEY ROMANCE ON THE HIGH SEAS
Big Boats and Romance Novelists

OVER THE YEARS, AN UNOFFICIAL contest has cropped up between Oracle founder Larry Ellison and famed venture capitalist Tom Perkins. The wealthy entrepreneurs have pushed to build the grandest boats known to humans and to bedazzle their personal lives by marrying sultry romance novelists.

Ellison's love of sailing is no secret. The Oracle chief almost lost his life in the Sydney-to-Hobart race off the coast of Australia in 1998. He's also known for his ongoing attempts to win the America's Cup. When not racing, Ellison lives it up on the 452-foot mega yacht *Rising Sun*—said to have cost close to $200 million.

He made even more headlines in 2003 when he wed romance novelist Melanie Craft. A quarter century younger than her husband, Craft is Ellison's fourth wife.

"Melanie has been a sales clerk, a bartender, a safari driver, a pastry chef, a cocktail waitress, a housecleaner and a technical writer," Craft says on her Web site. These days, however, she writes full time from her luxurious spread in Woodside. Coincidentally, her novel *Man Trouble* is about a self-centered billionaire playboy named Jake Berenger whose business has hit the skids. It takes the pulsating love of author Molly Shaw to set Berenger straight and revive his spirits. Craft maintains that the characters are not based on her and Ellison. So there you have it.

If anyone could best Ellison at his own game, it's Tom Perkins—the one-time Hewlett-Packard executive and co-founder of Silicon Valley's preeminent venture capital firm, Kleiner Perkins. On the boating front, Perkins has no equal after constructing the *Maltese Falcon*—a 289-foot super yacht modeled on a clipper ship. The $100 million yacht is hailed as the largest and fastest personal sailboat on the planet. It took 300 workers a little more than five years to craft the beast, which boasts a push-button mechanism for raising its sails. He can also lay claim to having married a bigger name in the romance field than Ellison did: Perkins enjoyed a brief marriage to best-seller Danielle Steel. The pair spent all of seventeen months together as husband and wife before calling off their romance in August 1999. Nevertheless, they remain good friends. Steel even encouraged and helped out with Perkins's 2006 novel *Sex and the Single Zillionaire*.

Perkins admits that the idea for his novel was based on a 2003 invitation to appear in a TV reality show. The producers wanted a group of twenty-something beauties to compete for the wealthy elder statesman's hand in marriage. Perkins pitched the idea of turning the show into a novel to Steel, and she then dared him to write up the story on his own.

of this expansion and the site's success. Microsoft, Google, and Yahoo! are just some of the rivals hoping to take over part of Craigslist's territory.

Newmark downplays such competition with his typical nonchalance. "I don't care," he said. "The more options that serve the community—the better. If somebody does a better job than us, if we fall behind, then that's our fault."

 ## SILICON JUSTICE: SAN FRANCISCO'S COURTHOUSES

GIVEN THE RIGHT CASE, A PAIR OF SAN FRANCISCO courthouses will spring into action and hash out the merits of an often technology-related dispute. Complaints get their start at the Phillip Burton Federal Building at the corner of Golden Gate Avenue and Larkin Street. Lacking the architectural grandeur of the main Civic Center structures, it's a massive rectangle made of out steel and glass. The bland beast houses government organizations ranging from the General Services Administration to the Federal Bureau of Investigation.

On the sixteenth floor you'll also find the clerk's office for US Courthouse for the Northern District of California. This court handles all manner of civil and criminal proceedings. One of the best-known recent disputes to take place at the court was the war between the original Napster peer-to-peer file-sharing service and the recording industry and music publishers. The two opposing sides fought for months at the courthouse over the future of P2P technology and whether or not a company such as Napster could be held liable if users traded copyrighted songs and other material. The case garnered global attention, as evidenced by the long lines to catch oral arguments and the satellite news trucks lining Larkin Street. On several occasions the CEO of Napster, Hank Barry, or Recording Industry Association of America chief Hilary Rosen could be found holding press conferences outside the Federal Building. This same structure also hosted the likes of Barry Bonds and Jason Giambi during the investigation into BALCO Laboratories.

You'll find the Ninth Circuit at 95 7th Street (the cross street is Mission). The Federal Building is at 450 Golden Gate Avenue.

A number of decisions handed down by the District Court in the Napster matter were debated some more by the US Court of Appeals for the Ninth Circuit, which is located in the more ornate and attractive James R. Browning Courthouse less than a mile away. It is the largest and perhaps the most uppity appeals court in the nation, handling cases for California, Alaska, Arizona, Guam, Hawaii, Idaho, Nevada, Oregon, Washington, Montana, and the Northern Mariana Islands. Left-leaning types tend to celebrate the Ninth Circuit for its decisions. In addition, it has a reputation for running under its own rules and having many decisions overturned by the Supreme Court.

Advocates for Napster and the music labels went back and forth between the Ninth Circuit and the District Court for months, as did reporters and news crews covering the case.

On another technology-related note, one of the well-known Ninth Circuit judges is Joseph Tyree Sneed III—a Nixon appointee and father of Carly Fiorina, the former CEO of HP.

If pressed to pick just one of the courthouses to visit, most people would want to head to the Ninth Circuit, which is easier on the eyes.

⚜ ELECTRONIC FRONTIER FOUNDATION

IF YOU IMPLANTED A PROCESSOR IN THE BRAIN OF EVERY ACLU (American Civil Liberties Union) member, you might end up with the Electronic Frontier Foundation (EFF).

Few technology organizations elicit as much praise—or criticism—as the Electronic Frontier Foundation (EFF). One set of people see the EFF as a fighter for free speech, more privacy, and an open Internet. Others deride the nonprofit group as an ineffectual, left-leaning body that tries to block businesses from protecting their intellectual property.

The EFF was started in 1990 by software pioneer Mitch Kapor, Grateful Dead lyricist John Perry Barlow, and early Sun Microsystems employee John Gilmore. While it began on the East Coast, the EFF now keeps its headquarters in the eclectic Mission District of San Francisco. It works out of a classic San Francisco redbrick office that is one of the nicer buildings in the area.

CLICK HERE — Drink Up San Francisco's Zeitgeist

PLUNK A GRITTY BEER GARDEN DOWN in the middle of San Francisco and you end up with an instant classic. Zeitgeist is *the* place to be on a warm day or evening when you're out with a few friends and need a venue for passing around pitchers of beer. Think gravel, lots of wooden tables and benches, and some healthy-size trees providing shade. That's more than enough to separate Zeitgeist from San Francisco's often crowded indoor joints.

At the edge of the beer garden, cooks will crank out burgers, grilled cheese sandwiches, and barbecued chicken. The indoor bar is relatively small and chock-full of biker-themed paraphernalia. Most days it's also chock-full of bikers and leather fans.

Still, anyone with a fondness for beer and a good time is welcome. And should you put down one too many or find a special someone in the beer garden, Zeitgeist offers rooms in its, um, quaint upstairs guest house for $30—a deal that can't be beat in San Francisco.

With property values so high in the city, it's hard to find a spot with as much outdoor room to move. Zeitgeist is certainly a San Francisco standout.

You'll find Zeitgeist at 199 Valencia Street.

PROTECTING CYBERSPACE

Since 1990 the EFF has looked to afford technophiles certain protections. In particular the organization has tried to make it tough for government officials to obtain private electronic communications. It has also battled to keep regulators and companies from locking down computing systems, preventing research.

You'll find the EFF headquarters—wrapped in ivy—at 454 Shotwell Street. Read more about the organization at www.eff.org.

EFF members have appeared in court or in the press to champion causes such as the original Napster peer-to-peer technology. The group did not support the violation of artists' copyrights but did look to prevent the music industry and government from clamping down on peer-to-peer communications—a then promising new computing advance. Similar wars have been fought to control the spread of digital rights management technology, which governs when and on what device a person can play purchased digital music.

The EFF has enjoyed some successes. Still, many would argue that media companies and government regulators have secured more than their fair share of victories over the libertarian technology crowd.

MICROSOFT RESEARCH CENTER

MICROSOFT'S VAST CASH STOCKPILES ALLOW IT TO DO JUST about whatever it wants when it comes to hiring technology gurus. One of the best examples of this fact is the company's small San Francisco research and development hub dubbed the Bay Area Research Center—BARC for short.

At last check, the lab had just six people scurrying about offices that look out on downtown San Francisco. The main entrance to the lab leads to a meeting space of sorts, along with a couple of couches and a large white board always full of scribbling. The eight or so offices shoot off from this meeting space.

GRAY'S BARC AND BELL'S BITS

This site probably would not exist were in not for Microsoft's desire to keep database guru Jim Gray from working at any another company. Gray, a UC Berkeley graduate, built an incredible track record over the years working on database projects and transaction processing systems for the likes of IBM, Tandem, and Digital Equipment Corporation (DEC). In particular, he made large contributions to some of the most powerful and stable databases ever created.

During the 1990s Microsoft went hunting for all the computing pioneers it could find—in part because it could, and in part to help the company's image. Microsoft had been battling the US government over antitrust charges for years and found that recruiting luminaries gave it a more academic feel, adding some oomph to the idea that the company worked on groundbreaking stuff rather than just bullying and copying competitors.

The BARC headquarters is located at 455 Market Street. To find out more about BARC, you can visit http://research.microsoft.com/aboutmsr/labs/sanfrancisco. There's more on Jim Gray at http://research.microsoft.com/~Gray/ and more on Gordon Bell's My Life Bits project at http://research.microsoft.com/barc/media presence/mylifebits.aspx.

Microsoft approached Gray, who had just left DEC for a post at Berkeley, with the proposal that he lead a research effort of his choosing. Gray agreed to the idea with the stipulation that Microsoft set up a San Francisco office, as he had no intention of venturing to Redmond, Washington.

So BARC appeared in 1995 in a pretty standard office smack dab in the middle of downtown San Francisco. Over the years it has kept staffing levels to a minimum—peaking at about eight. Microsoft runs a larger research center in Mountain View.

Gray eventually snagged another big name for Microsoft when computing pioneer Gordon Bell agreed to join BARC. Bell is a renowned engineer who did much of the key work on DEC's most successful systems and taught at Carnegie Mellon. In addition, Bell started the Computer History Museum project.

Tragically, Gray went missing in early 2007 after setting out on a sailing excursion. More than 6,000 volunteers helped search for the famed researcher, but his whereabouts remain unknown as of this writing.

CLICK HERE   **Mandarin Oriental**

THOSE TRAVELING TO SAN FRANCISCO on business who come armed with a decent-size expense account may wish to consider the Mandarin Oriental hotel as their residence of choice. This hotel in the heart of the Financial District offers some of the most spectacular views you'll find at any San Francisco hotel. The Mandarin Oriental doesn't bother with putting visitors on lower-level floors. Instead you enter at street level and then travel up a few stories to reach the rooms. Almost all feature a breathtaking view of either the city proper or the San Francisco Bay. Unique to the hotel, however, are the open corridors on each floor. Expansive windows sit on either side of these walkways, providing simultaneous views of the city and the water.

The per-night charges aren't for the faint of heart, ranging from $400 right past $600 and higher depending on how much of a view you desire.

Most people won't want to stay at the Mandarin Oriental for weekend visits. The Financial District goes dead after 6 p.m. on Friday, making San Francisco basics such as walking to a nice restaurant or hailing a cab difficult. That said, the hotel isn't more than a fifteen- or twenty-minute walk from major tourist attractions such as Union Square and popular shops. The views can make up for the sleepy downtown conditions come Friday and Saturday night, especially if you brought some walking shoes.

You'll find the Mandarin Oriental at 222 Sansome Street; (415) 276-9888; or on the Web at www.mandarinoriental.com.

BARC's research currently divides into database and server work and a project known as My Life Bits headed by Bell. Gray had made it a goal to bulk up Microsoft's database and server operating system technology so that it can function under heavy loads and on large systems. Microsoft has traditionally struggled keep up with rivals on high-end types of systems. My Life Bits, on the other hand, is far more experimental. Basically, Bell and his team have tried to devise technology to let people record their entire lives in digital format, store the information on a computer, and then search that information. Such work entails keeping track of videos, e-mails, pictures, music, and documents produced by an individual.

GENENTECH

IN 1976 TWO MEN TRANSFORMED BIOTECHNOLOGY FROM a field of research into an industry.

As a venture capitalist at Kleiner Perkins Caufield & Byers, Robert Swanson had developed a deep interest in the budding area of biotechnology research. Recent advances with DNA—such as gene splicing techniques pioneered at Stanford—convinced him that a new type of business could be formed, and he pitched this idea to the venture capital firm. The Kleiner Perkins brass thought Swanson presented a solid case and told him to pursue the idea of creating a biotechnology venture.

So the twenty-nine-year-old Swanson set up a meeting to pitch his idea to Dr. Herbert Boyer, a University of California–San Francisco biochemist and DNA expert. At first Boyer agreed only to a ten-minute meeting, but "Swanson's enthusiasm for the technology and his faith in its commercial viability was contagious, and the meeting extended from 10 minutes to three hours," according to Genentech company lore.

IBM's Dirty Street Penguins

SAN FRANCISCO IS ALL ABOUT PEACE AND love—just not peace, love, and penguins.

In April 2001 IBM bombarded San Francisco with an unorthodox advertising campaign: It spray-painted hundreds of images on the city's streets, depicting the peace sign, a heart, and a chubby penguin. The images proved confusing to those outside the technology realm. What could a penguin have to do with the peace and love vibe?

True techies, however, were quick to recognize the penguin as the symbol of the Linux operating system—a rival to Microsoft's Windows. Linux is the most famous example of the open-source model, in which anyone can see and use the underlying code behind a software package. Open-source software often gets pitched as a kinder, gentler development model than proprietary software, where a single company keeps the underlying code behind a package secret.

At the time, IBM had just launched a massive campaign around Linux and thought covering San Francisco in graffiti would demonstrate just how serious it was about the open-source operating system. The stodgy technology giant hoped to endear itself to playful Linux advocates by playing off the peace and love ideals.

San Francisco city officials were less than thrilled with IBM's guerrilla marketing. They were quick to cite IBM as being in violation of a public works code and charged the company $100,000 plus cleanup costs for the stunt.

IBM blamed the peace, love, and Linux campaign on its overaggressive ad firm Oglivy & Mather. Public relations representatives insisted that the graphics were produced with a biodegradable chalk that would wash away after a hard rain. In fact the spray-painted symbols were visible for weeks, despite ongoing city cleanup efforts and plenty of rain. It took a few months for all of the logos to disappear. Ultimately, IBM received a huge helping of press for the exploit and then promised never to do such a thing again.

IBM has gone on to become one of Linux's strongest corporate backers. With big names like IBM, Oracle, and Hewlett-Packard behind it, Linux turned into the most serious threat to Microsoft's lucrative operating system franchise. For better or worse, though, the big-business push behind Linux has removed much of its counterculture feel.

Swanson and Boyer created Genentech and opened their office at a 3,000-square-foot spot in South San Francisco. Plenty of skepticism swirled around the firm during its early days, as experts wondered how the company planned to use recombinant DNA technology to fuel a profitable concern. But the founders soon shocked the naysayers with a series of successes. First off, Genentech enjoyed one of the most successful initial public offerings in history when its shares jumped from $35 to $88 in less than an hour on the market in 1980. The company backed up this investor confidence by cranking out the first human proteins via biotechnology methods. Such advances included the creation of a human insulin drug in 1982, which became the first biotech drug approved by the FDA. Genentech followed this with the 1985 release of a growth hormone for children.

> You'll find Genentech's expansive headquarters at 1 DNA Way in South San Francisco. The company can be reached at (650) 225-1000 or on the Web at www.gene .com.

After more than twenty years of success, Genentech was rewarded by the city of San Francisco for helping establish the city as a biotechnology hub. The 400 block of Point San Bruno Boulevard was renamed DNA Way, which placed Genentech's headquarters at 1 DNA Way. As of this writing, the pioneering biotechnology firm boasts a market capitalization of more than an $80 billion and close to 10,000 employees. It trades on the New York Stock Exchange under the ticker symbol DNA.

TECHNOLOGY PUBLISHERS ROW

SAN FRANCISCO OFFERS TECHNOLOGY COMPANIES A convenient place to hit up a number of technology publishers in one go. In fact, companies don't have to stretch much beyond 2nd Street to reach most of the major trade magazines.

iPodding at the 21st Amendment

TECHNOLOGY-INCLINED MUSIC FANS can head over to the 21st Amendment bar and restaurant every Wednesday to show off their iPod collections. The pub holds a Cask and iPod night in its cozy Brewer's Loft. Customers can plug their iPods into the pub's music system while downing imperial pints of cask-conditioned ale.

The iPod night fad arose almost simultaneously with the first sale of Apple's music-playing device. Two DJs who perform under the name *DJ Andrew Andrew* claim to have held the first iPod night at a West Village club in New York called APT. A number of bars throughout the United States, particularly in New York and Chicago, quickly embraced the idea of letting customers express themselves via the iPod. The trend started to gain mainstream attention in 2004 and 2005 when *Wired* and *The New York Times* spotlighted iPod nights.

Typically, customers sign up on a list and wait their turn to hook up their iPod and wow the other patrons. The time limit for playing your collection varies widely from bar to bar.

The 21st Amendment serves far-above-average pub food and supplies a proper dining room for those more focused on filling their bellies than downing beers. It's a popular SoMa hangout and just a few blocks from AT&T Park.

You'll find the 21st Amendment at 563 2nd Street; (415) 369-0900; or on the Web at www.21st-amendment.com.

Publishing giant IDG, for starters, has a large office at the corner of 2nd and Bryant. The building hosts such publications as *PC World* and *InfoWorld* and serves as IDG's West Coast hub. (IDG founder and billionaire Pat McGovern centered the rest of his publishing empire on the East Coast near Boston. The first big IDG hit was *Computerworld,* which arrived in 1972.)

Heading up 2nd Street toward Market Street, you'll run into the flashy offices of Cnet Networks. Cnet has established itself as the major online destination for technophiles hunting down news, product reviews, and software downloads. Well funded, Cnet turned its back on the idea of creating sister print publications and embraced the online world its reporters so often described. The News.com Web site, along with sites such as Slashdot.org. and TheRegister.co.uk, have become musts for geeks wanting to know the latest moves of the major technology players. Without question, most technology companies consider Cnet the gold standard of the online technology news scene and rank coverage on the site on par with many business journals.

> Publishers Row stretches along 2nd Street from Market to Bryant Streets in the SoMa (South of Market) District.

Other publishers on or near Publishers Row include *Wired Magazine*, Ziff Davis Internet, CMP Media, and the *San Francisco Chronicle*. Before their product launches, companies often make their way among these news hubs hoping to curry favor with the reporters and hawk their latest gear. Reporters will note the familiar sight of black Town Cars with tinted windows going from one spot to another over the course of a day.

THE INDUSTRY STANDARD

Archaeologists will one day uncover huge stockpiles of a bloated magazine called *The Industry Standard*. They will marvel at its girth, the quantity of its advertisements, and its incredible gloss. No technology trade magazine—in fact, no trade magazine, period—has ever approached the heights reached by *The Industry Standard* during the technology boom that closed out the last century. The magazine that started out with a smattering of items documenting the Internet economy would swell to hundreds and hundreds of pages. It charted every start-up, every share surge, and every dot-com hero. Companies clamored to make their way into its pages, doing just about anything for a spill of ink.

Back then *The Industry Standard* pretty much *was* the technology publishing industry. It operated from seven offices scattered throughout San Francisco. During those glory days, a giant billboard stretched across SoMA displaying all *The Industry Standard*'s latest

Barry BALCO

WHILE PROUD OF MOST OF ITS biotechnology firms, Silicon Valley would probably prefer to have done without the Bay Area Laboratory Co-operative (BALCO).

In September of 2003, representatives from the US Food and Drug Administration, the Internal Revenue Service, the US Anti Doping Agency, and the San Mateo Narcotics Task Force went busting through BALCO's doors. The investigators had learned that BALCO developed a number of illegal performance enhancing substances and supplied these often undetectable substances to some of the world's premier athletes. The raid and subsequent investigations kicked off a drug scandal that had profound effects on US sports. In particular, it rocked professional baseball by bringing out into the open many peoples' worst fears about steroid-fueled stars.

Victor Conte had started BALCO in order to offer athletes drug testing services and to give them supplements to aid performance. As more sports stars turned to BALCO, the company's product line expanded, culminating with the now infamous Cream and Clear substances that were undetectable to drug tests.

In 2005 Conte pleaded guilty to money laundering and steroid distribution and was sentenced to four months in prison.

BALCO operated out of a non-descript, cement-block shop set up in a strip mall close to the San Francisco International Airport in Burlingame. You can visit the old lab headquarters at 1520 Gilbreth Road.

headlines in lights. The magazine, majority-owned by IDG, also used to throw elaborate parties on the rooftop of one of its offices; there reporters, public relations types, and executives would flock to put down free grub and booze.

Ultimately *The Industry Standard* met the same fate as many of the companies it covered, filing for bankruptcy in 2001. The publication, which started in 1997, will be remembered as the fastest-growing magazine in US history, reaching 350 pages—many of them ads—at its peak and pulling in well over $100 million per year. Near the end, the magazine shriveled to around eighty pages, and the hundreds of staff hired at remarkable salaries were forced to beg for work in a depressed technology publishing market.

Since that low, the publishing game has recovered quite a bit. It's unlikely that we'll ever see a phenomenon like *The Industry Standard* again, but you can witness the more stable and functional technology publishing crew on 2nd Street.

AT&T PARK

IT SEEMS ONLY RIGHT THAT A STADIUM LOCATED WITHIN Silicon Valley would turn into a slave of the telecommunications and Internet service industries. Such is the fate of AT&T Park—the beautiful home of the San Francisco Giants baseball team. Since it opened on April 11, 2000, the park has already gone through three name changes. It was Pacific Bell (more commonly Pac Bell) Park until 2004, when it turned into SBC Park. The Texas-based telecommunications company acquired the rights to the stadium's name after buying Pac-Bell. In 2006 the name changed again after SBC bought AT&T and changed its own name to the more familiar AT&T.

The constant name swapping should settle down now that the telecommunications mergers and acquisitions have slowed. That's a blessing for locals and even more so for tourists, who struggled to keep track of the field's fortunes.

The park is located at 24 Willie Mays Plaza. As mentioned, you can get to it via CalTrain or by bus, ferry, or BART. In most cases you'll only have to walk a couple of blocks to reach the stadium. There's also room for a few thousand cars in lots near the stadium. You can find more information at http://sanfrancisco.giants.mlb.com.

No matter the name on the outside, the stadium remains a true delight for fans. Located south of Market Street near the China Basin Landing, AT&T Park opens up onto the water and offers fans glorious

CLICK HERE **Edinburgh Castle**

THE BEST-KNOWN ELEMENT OF SAN Francisco's literary tradition centers on the Beat writers who once made the North Beach District their home. These days a smaller-scale arts scene has emerged in one of San Francisco's seedier neighborhoods—The Tenderloin.

Where the Beats had City Lights Bookstore, today's authors have the Edinburgh Castle. Irvine Welsh—the author of *Trainspotting*—put "The Castle" on the literary map with a 1995 reading of his work. Since then the Geary Street pub has managed to attract numerous authors, journalists, artists, pundits, and poets to its events. Larger than most San Francisco bars, The Castle can pack in two floors' worth of drinkers. The pub's bottom layer has a number of wooden booths for your seating pleasure; naturally a remarkable scotch collection runs the length of a spacious bar. Most of the events—be they musical or literary—take place in a more secluded upstairs section that resembles a small theater. The Castle also puts on a popular Pub Quiz every Tuesday that has people coating every inch of the establishment.

The Castle has set up its own publishing arm called the Public House Press, which issued a solid anthology in 2004 containing the works of Irvine Welsh, Po Bronson, and Alan Black, among many others. If you've been put off by a recent technology news story, then be sure to skulk around this joint. A few of San Francisco's well-known technology journalists call the establishment home, while many others pay regular visits.

Also worth noting is the O'Farrell Street Bar (OSB) just a brief walk away, which features one of the warmest staffs on the planet.

Both The Castle and OSB are found in the Tenderloin—largely considered San Francisco's least desirable area. And it does have its fair share of homeless folks, drug-addled types, and strip clubs, but it's also a rich cultural scene full of great pubs and restaurants. San Francisco's undesirables tend to be pretty harmless, so just be a tad careful and everything will be fine.

The Castle calls 950 Geary Street home; (415) 885-4074; www .castlenews.com. The OSB is found about a block away, at 800 Larkin Street; (415) 567-9326.

views of the San Francisco Bay. Holding just under 41,000 spectators, it's considered an intimate stadium, with almost every seat allowing you to take in the action on the field and the surrounding area.

Perhaps its most unusual feature, though, is the way the architects kept the left-field bleachers and right-field standing area low while creating towering rows of seats behind home plate and along the first- and third-base lines. This lets the vast majority of the fans look across the field and to the bay. In addition, passersby can take in the action for free by looking through a ground-level outfield fence.

San Franciscans have perhaps been more forgiving of the name changes because they did not have to shell out any money for the new stadium. Touted as the first privately funded field since Dodgers Stadium in 1962, AT&T Park was built on the back of early season ticket sales, naming rights, and other sources. The incredible number of season tickets sold—close to 30,000—showed that fans were anxious for a real home for the Giants after sharing the frigid Candlestick Park with the 49ers football team.

The Giants like to promote a quotation from sports columnist Peter Gammons to describe the ultimate success of the private funding effort:

IT'S HARD TO SAY WHAT'S BEST ABOUT [AT&T] PARK, EXCEPT THAT IT IS SAN FRANCISCO. THE VIEW FROM THE WORST SEATS IN THE HOUSE STILL GIVES YOU A VIEW OF THE BAY BRIDGE AND THE MARINA. AS GREAT AS CAMDEN YARDS, TURNER FIELD, THE JAKE AND COORS FIELD ARE, THIS IS THE BEST FAN'S BALLPARK BECAUSE IT WAS CONCEIVED, BUILT AND PAID FOR BY GIANTS OWNER PETER MAGOWAN, A LEGITIMATE BASEBALL FAN.

AT&T Park opened in 2000 at a cost of $319 million. The stadium has helped breath new life into the South of Market district popular with dot-coms and other technology start-ups. Up until the late 1990s, the area had some businesses and a lot of run-down areas. Few locals wanted to call SoMa home.

Recently, however, a healthy amount of renovation has resulted in stylish office buildings, new bars, and luxurious restaurants. In addition, a number of apartment complexes have popped up. These apartments give Silicon Valley commuters a close link to the CalTrain Station on 4th and Townsend Street. CalTrain feeds the heart of Silicon Valley, and the station is just a few blocks from AT&T Park.

The stadium also hosts a number of other events, including large concerts, trade shows, and even weddings. Like any decent Silicon Valley venue, it provides wireless Internet access to fans and is plastered with billboards from local technology companies.

MONSTER/CANDLESTICK PARK

LIKE ITS COUSIN AT&T PARK, THE WINDSWEPT MONSTER Park has gone through its share of name changes over the years. The stadium opened in 1960 as the home of the San Francisco Giants baseball team and was named Candlestick Park for its location on a small peninsula—Candlestick Point—at the edge of the San Francisco Bay.

Pack a jacket and head out to a 49ers game by traveling to Monster Park at Jamestown and Harney Way. You can find more information about the stadium at www.monster parksf.com.

From day one, the gusts of wind screaming across the field proved troubling to the players and frigid to fans. The Beatles would endure the inclement conditions to play their last commercial concert at Candlestick Park in 1966. It was bulked up in 1971 to play host to the San Francisco 49ers football squad.

In 1995 networking company 3Com—started by Robert Metcalfe, who invented Ethernet at Xerox PARC—acquired the naming rights to the stadium. The company dubbed it *3Com Park at Candlestick Point* as a type of concession to fans who longed for the classic name. Eventually, though, the conditions proved too much for the Giants and their fans. The baseball team moved into San Francisco proper at the new Pac Bell Park—now known as AT&T Park.

Declining fortunes for 3Com led to another renaming exercise in 2002. In the midst of an economic downturn, stadium owners struggled to find a company willing to shell out enough bucks to put its brand on the structure, leaving fans with San Francisco Stadium at Candlestick Point. Then in 2004 Monster Cable—a maker of high-performance stereo cables—stepped in with some cash and earned the rights to Monster Park.

In some ways Monster Park has touching ties to Silicon Valley entrepreneurship. Company founder Noel Lee quit his job as an engineer at Lawrence Livermore National Laboratories in the 1970s and went to working creating improved cabling for music systems. His San Francisco start-up was registered as Monster Cable in 1978.

The story, however, turns less touching for a couple reasons. First off, plenty of people believe that jobs Web site Monster.com is responsible for the stadium name and have no idea that Monster Cable even exists. Too, San Franciscans have such disdain for corporations slapping their names on Candlestick that they passed a measure in 2004 banning a renewal of the naming rights deal. Monster will have to give up its rights to the stadium in 2008 when its contract expires, and Candlestick Park will come to life once again.

■ ■ ■

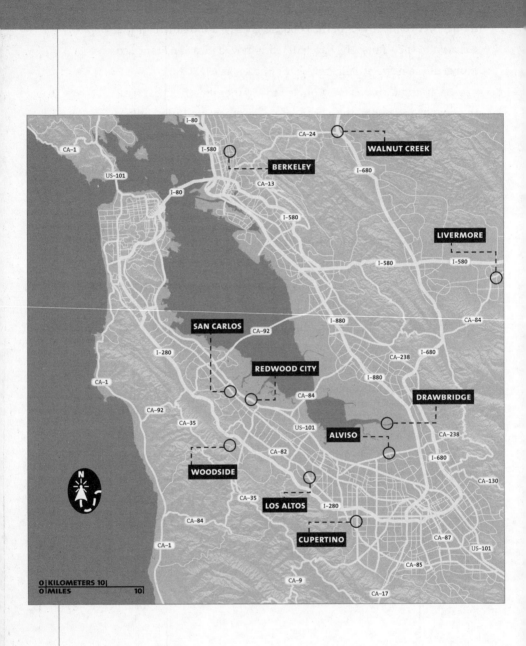

CA-1

I-80

CA-24

WALNUT CREEK

I-580

BERKELEY

I-680

US-101

CA-13

I-80

I-580

I-580

LIVERMORE

I-580

I-580

CA-84

I-880

SAN CARLOS

CA-92

I-280

CA-238

I-680

REDWOOD CITY

I-880

DRAWBRIDGE

CA-1

CA-84

CA-92

CA-238

CA-35

US-101

ALVISO

I-680

WOODSIDE

CA-82

CA-130

N

CA-35

LOS ALTOS

I-280

CA-84

CUPERTINO

CA-87

US-101

CA-1

CA-85

0 | KILOMETERS 10 |
0 | MILES   10 |

CA-9

CA-17

OUT *and* ABOUT *in* SILICON VALLEY:
THE SURROUNDING SCENE

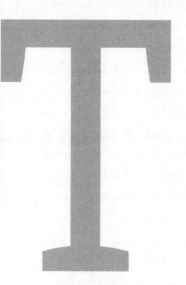HIS BOOK HAS FOCUSED ON THE main forces behind Silicon Valley. A number of other areas, however, contribute to the economy and culture of the region.

Cupertino, for example, has long been the home of Apple Computer. It thrives on this relationship, with Apple paying more taxes than any other company and providing Cupertino with a true Silicon Valley icon. Similarly, Redwood City plays host to Oracle and its grand headquarters. You can't miss the Oracle compound when driving down US 101. Well outside of Silicon Valley's official boundaries, places such as Walnut Creek and Livermore have a lot of interaction with local technology companies and research institutions as well.

Beyond the businesses, Silicon Valley offers an array of breathtaking neighborhoods and exquisite trails. Such scenery helps locals come to terms with the unreal housing costs. All the varied elements combine to provide the total Silicon Valley package. It's doubtful that the region could keep attracting so much talent year after year without such a rich support structure.

This chapter will walk you through some of the best of Silicon Valley's environs.

CHAPTER 6

UNIVERSITY OF CALIFORNIA–BERKELEY

NOT TECHNICALLY PART OF SILICON VALLEY, THE UNIVERSITY of California–Berkeley has still had a major impact on the region from cultural and technological points of view. The Berkeley links to the Valley don't, of course, come across with the same clarity as the strong ties demonstrated by Stanford University over the years. You won't find a long list of billionaire Berkeley-educated CEOs running hardware giants, software start-ups, or dot-coms. By nature, Berkeley's computer science and engineering grads don't seem to have the same entrepreneurial motivations as the Stanford student body. Nor do they have as direct access to the entire investment and development infrastructure.

Berkeley, however, has long proven itself a true science and overall academic powerhouse. It typically ranks as one of the very top state schools in the country and has filled Silicon Valley with a bevy of bright people.

Those interested in Berkeley overall can check out the university's home page at www.berkeley.edu. The school offers free campus tours seven days a week as well, and you can find more information on those at www.berkeley.edu/visitors/free_tours.html. The Visitor Services office is located at 2200 University Avenue and can be reached at (510) 642-5215.

Every aspect of the Berkeley campus proves impressive, from its numerous architectural gems to the rolling wooded surroundings. Like any good college town, Berkeley proper also delivers a colorful mix of nearby shops, restaurants, and bars for students and locals.

Those hoping to visit Berkeley to get a sense of the university's diverse research have a number of options. You can, for example, set up a tour to visit the Lawrence Berkeley National Laboratory. The tour covers some of the lab's history and travels to various sites at the 183-acre compound, which sits on a hillside near the main Berkeley campus. You can expect to see the Advanced Light Source, which studies some of the "world's brightest sources of ultraviolet and soft x-ray beams," along with other similar technology. The lab also has a Center for Beam Physics, Cancer Research Laboratories, Genomic Science Laboratories, and an Energy Sciences Network facility. It employs close to 4,300 people, mixing researchers with graduate and undergraduate students and support personnel.

You can set up a tour by visiting www.lbl.gov/community/tours .html or calling the Community Relations Office at (510) 486-7292.

Visitors may also want to check out the Lawrence Hall of Science (LHS), which is billed as both a public science center and a resource for schoolchildren. LHS has been around since 1968 and has exhibits on things such as earthquakes, dinosaurs, and insects. The museum caters to youngsters with a number of hands-on displays. In addition, visitors of all ages can check out the William Knox Holt Planetarium, which is open on weekends and holidays. The main exhibits can be seen daily 10 a.m. to 5 p.m., while specialized areas such as the planetarium, biology lab, and computer lab are open on weekends.

More information on LHS, which is just east of the Berkeley campus, can be found at www.lawrencehallofscience.org.

The Space Sciences Laboratory (SSL) and Mathematical Sciences Research Institute (MSRI) are less accessible to the public but may be worth checking out if you're interested in either field. More information on SSL is available at www.ssl.berkeley.edu, and more information on MSRI can be found at www.msri.org.

BERKELEY'S BEST **AND** BRIGHTEST

The oldest school in the UC system, Berkeley dates back to the mid-1800s. A few forward-looking thinkers were able to see past the immediate riches of the gold rush to think about setting up an institution that could one day rival East Coast universities. It took a couple of decades for Berkeley to find stable funding and set up a well-organized growth plan. Once it got going, though, it did so in style.

Through the years the Berkeley setting has proved attractive to cloistered researchers and gadabout social misfits alike. One of the first Berkeley researchers to strike with a major breakthrough was physics professor Ernest O. Lawrence. In 1930 Lawrence created what was basically the foundation for the first atom smasher—via the invention of the cyclotron—for $25. This work would help drive the atomic weapons research in the United States. Lawrence ended up winning a Nobel Prize and having two major research labs in the Bay Area named for him—Lawrence Livermore and Lawrence Berkeley National Labs.

Another Berkeley physicist, Robert Oppenheimer, furthered atomic weapons research during his tenure overseeing the Manhattan Project in Los Alamos, New Mexico. Both were pioneers of an outstanding Berkeley physics department.

Berkeley has also impacted the computer science field in significant ways. In the late 1970s a Berkeley graduate student by the name of Bill Joy did much of the work on a new variant of the Unix operating system called BSD (Berkeley Software Distribution) Unix. This software would go on to power hundreds of thousands of business computers, including those manufactured by Sun Microsystems, a company Joy co-founded in 1982. Joy's method of sharing changes made to the Unix software contributed to what has become known as the Free and Open Source Software Movement, which serves as a competitor to proprietary software makers such as Microsoft. In addition, computer science professor David Patterson made large processor and data management advances, while another professor, Michael Stonebraker, did groundbreaking database work.

Closer to the counterculture fringe, a host of Berkeley students who participated in the 1960s Free Speech Movement would go on to pursue computer technology. Some of these folks ended up at the Homebrew Computer Club, where they worked to create a personal computer for the average person.

THE WEALTH OF DIVERSIONS SILICON VALLEY HAS TO OFFER comes through in smashing fashion during warm weekends in the nearby small town of Woodside.

► WINDY HILL

MOST SILICON VALLEY RESIDENTS CAN MAKE IT TO WOODSIDE'S center in twenty minutes or less. Then it's just another twenty minutes of relatively easy mountain driving to reach the top entrance of the Windy Hill open space preserve.

It's hard to believe such a glorious expanse lies just a few miles from strip malls, corporate campuses, and intertwining freeways. The Windy Hill preserve stretches across 1,308 acres of grasslands and forests packed full of redwoods, firs, and oaks.

Good weather will make a Windy Hill hike more enjoyable, since the area lives up to its name. Without some strong sunshine, the main 8-mile loop around the preserve can be a chilling experience. You start out on the top of the hill with the sun's rays heating your body and rolling grasslands feeding your eyes. Then, after a couple of miles, you begin a steady descent to the cool valley floor. A winding trail takes you back up the hill through Sleepy Hollow–like forests and into the sunshine once again.

To reach the lower parking lot, take the Alpine Road exit off the 280 freeway and head south on Alpine Road for close to 3 miles. Then take a right onto Portola Road and drive about 0.8 mile to a parking lot on the left side of the road. The parking lot at the top of the hill is on Skyline Boulevard (Highway 35) and is about 2.3 miles south of Highway 84 or 4.9 miles north of Page Mill Road. You can find more information and maps of the trails at www.openspace .org/preserves/pr_windy_hill.asp.

Fantastic views of Menlo Park, Palo Alto, Mountain View, Santa Clara, and San Jose are available through much of the hike. Visitors can, for example, catch a bird's-eye take on the Stanford University campus from atop the hill. It's these views and the diversity of the trails that make the Windy Hill preserve such a surprising treat.

You can actually start your hike near the hilltop or at the bottom of the valley. More adventurous types can break off from the main circuit and access close to 13 miles of trails. Many of the trails are open to dog owners, bikers, and horseback riders.

► THOMAS FOGARTY WINERY

IF YOU'RE FEELING MORE OF A WINE-TASTING THAN A HIK-ING vibe, then drive right past the upper Windy Hill parking lot for about five minutes to reach the Thomas Fogarty Winery. This idyllic spot combines great views of Silicon Valley with some romantic gardens and a cozy wine-tasting room. The 325-acre estate, owned by a Stanford cardiovascular surgeon and inventor, sits up at 2,000 feet.

The winery is located at 19501 Skyline Boulevard; for more information, call (650) 851-6777 or see www.fogarty winery.com. You're urged to follow the directions from the vineyard's Web site as opposed to an Internet map service.

From this height you can take in most of Silicon Valley in one glance. The estate boasts about twenty-five acres of grapes with a concentration of Chardonnay and Pinot Noir and smaller areas dedicated to Merlot and Sangiovese.

There's also a main house where you'll find the tasting room. As of last check, the vineyard offered two different tastings at $6 and $12, respectively. Those prices let you sample about five different wines.

Just to the left of the main house is an entertaining area that can accommodate about 220 guests. The impressive views and vibrant gardens surrounding this area make it a popular spot for weddings and corporate events. The tasting room is open for business 11 a.m. to 5 p.m. Thursday to Sunday.

➤ ALICE'S RESTAURANT

AFTER HIKING OR SUCKING DOWN A COUPLE OF GLASSES OF wine, you may want to take in some lunch at the ultimate crossroads eatery: Alice's Restaurant. Now, this isn't the Alice's Restaurant of Arlo Guthrie fame, but it does have a counterculture element. Bikers come from around the globe to hunker down for a meal at this establishment. On most weekends, you'll see dozens of motorbikes lined up outside the restaurant and at a corner store and gas station across the street. Car enthusiasts also stop by to show off their sports cars. The Hell's Angels vibe is reflected in Alice's menu, which features BMW, Kawasaki, and Suzuki burgers. On the whole it's a no-frills type of place with all the diner basics and some out-of-the-ordinary beers to choose from.

> You'll find Alice's at 17288 Skyline Boulevard; it's right at the junction of Woodside Road (CA 84) and Skyline Boulevard (CA 35). Give the restaurant a shout at (650) 851-0303.

ORACLE, REDWOOD SHORES

WHILE FLUSH WITH HARDWARE GIANTS, SILICON VALLEY has never produced a software company on the scale of Microsoft in Redmond, Washington. The only coding company to even come close in these parts is Oracle.

While Microsoft was busy dominating the desktop, Oracle burrowed deep inside the data centers of business customers with its pricey database software. This strategy proved lucrative for Oracle

CLICK HERE **The Village Pub, Woodside**

WERE YOU THE TYPE OF SILICON VALLEY star chaser who wanted to catch Apple's enigmatic CEO Steve Jobs dining with U2 frontman Bono, then it's time to book a table at the Village Pub. This mainstay of the Silicon Valley elite has operated since the 1930s and gone through a couple of transformations. In the good old days, you'd find the Village Pub located in the upstairs section of a warm, rustic, almost homey building. The Pub changed spots a few years ago, though; that's when it was moved downstairs and renovated in a major way. You can still find the original bar, but everything else is pretty much new. The Village Pub has an elegant design with exposed rafters, blood-red velvet chairs, and wooden floors. Inside it feels like the most regal cottage you've ever encountered.

The staff and the food separate the Village Pub from the competition. We're talking attention to detail, personal touches, and *no-request-is-too-great*. Top that off with succulent Daube beef smothered with horseradish butter in a cauliflower mousse, truffled potato gnocchi with foraged mushrooms and a parsley root emulsion, or a killer hamburger, and you get the picture. And there's a more than-adequate-wine selection.

One of the best things about this pricey, sophisticated restaurant is that you can show up in jeans *or* a tuxedo and feel right at home.

You can find the Village Pub at 2967 Woodside Road in Woodside or reach it at (650) 851-9888. It's also on the Web at http://thevillagepub.net.

and its well-known playboy CEO, Larry Ellison. Oracle ranks as the second largest software company on the planet, and Ellison has managed to hover around and even briefly surpass Microsoft co-founder Bill Gates as the richest person in the world.

Anyone traveling down the 101 freeway past Redwood City will know the Oracle headquarters well. The company has operated out of a series of modern, circular glass towers here at 500 Oracle Parkway since the early 1990s. True database geeks have grown fond of claiming that one of the buildings—400—looks remarkably like the old Cobol programming language symbol for a database. Apparently, this was not intentional. Less geeky types will be more interested in the peaceful surroundings. A marsh runs around the Oracle campus, allowing ducks and other creatures to toddle about the grounds.

THE ACCIDENTAL **POWERHOUSE**

Oracle owes much of its success in the database market to capitalizing on an IBM mistake. Ted Codd, a researcher working at IBM's San Jose lab, published a landmark paper in 1970 detailing a more flexible and easier-to-use database model. For a variety of reasons, IBM failed to make the most of Codd's invention of the "relational database." Larry Ellison, however, became intrigued by the paper and decided to build a company around the relational database technology.

> You'll find the database giant headquartered at 500 Oracle Parkway, Redwood Shores; (650) 506-7000. No public tours are available.

Ellison and his co-founders, Bob Miner and Ed Oates, created Software Development Laboratories (SDL) in 1977 and started work building a relational database. The SDL coders came up with a product dubbed Oracle in honor of the code name the CIA had given to a project that Ellison and Miner had been building for a previous employer. In 1979 the executives redubbed the firm Relational Software Inc.; ultimately, in 1983, they settled on the name *Oracle* to remind customers of the company's flagship product.

When Oracle released its first product in 1979, it was well ahead of the competition—namely IBM. The Oracle software ran on Digital Equipment Corporation's popular mini computers and made use of the SQL database query language, which IBM had also invented and failed to promote ahead of competitors.

A diverse, vibrant database market developed through the 1980s and 1990s, although Oracle managed to secure a position as the de facto standard for businesses. Today the company battles with IBM and Microsoft for the majority of database sales and is still the major player in a multibillion-dollar market.

LARRY ELLISON
Attacking life with reckless abandon

LIKE MANY OF THE ELITE SILICON VALLEY companies, Oracle has a personality that seems to come directly from its founder and CEO Ellison. As a company, Oracle has often been criticized for being overly aggressive in its pursuit of sales and all too eager to sell customers software at exorbitant prices. Along similar lines, Ellison attacks life with reckless abandon, tempting fate in high-speed yacht races, jets, and racecars. And like his company, Oracle's chief pursues increased wealth with unrelenting zest.

Ellison has become a Silicon Valley icon as a result of his unmatched bravado and fierce competitive streak. Like Sun Microsystems' Scott McNealy and Apple's Steve Jobs, he has spent much of his career battling Microsoft and criticizing the company in the press. This rivalry has extended all the way to the "world's richest man" contest: In 2000 the combination of healthy Oracle shares and wounded Microsoft shares allowed Ellison to unseat Bill Gates as the planet's wealthiest bloke for a few weeks.

Ellison has also made a name for himself on the Silicon Valley real estate scene. Buying a $25 million pad and then off-loading it after a couple of years is not out of the ordinary. But well beyond the $25 million toys is Ellison's $100 million or so Woodside compound. In order to outfit this twenty-three-acre site just right, Ellison paid to have close to 81,000 cubic yards of earth shifted for ponds, waterfalls, and the like. He also imported hundreds of trees and boulders and thousands of tons of specialized stones. As you might imagine, the Japanese-style imperial villa is said to be rather impressive.

Ellison's rich tastes seem to have carried over to the San Carlos Airport next to Oracle's headquarters, which is often used by businesses and wealthy individuals traveling on corporate jets. The airport uses the three-letter code SQL as an identifier, which hardly seems a coincidence.

While one of the older elite Silicon Valley founder/CEOs, Ellison does not appear to be slowing down. In 2004 he married then thirty-four-year-old romance novelist Melanie Craft. In addition he still tackles outside hobbies with vigor and runs Oracle with his usual swagger.

WHILE NOT FANCY, THE HILLER AVIATION MUSEUM MORE than does the job for flight buffs looking to take in some history. The first thing that will strike you about the museum is its location, right at the northwestern corner of San Carlos Airport. Drive up to the museum and you're just about guaranteed to see a small craft or corporate jet cruising overhead.

The next thing that will strike you about the museum is its simplicity. Combine a gift shop with one large display room and a 747 cockpit sitting outside the back door, and you've got the whole she-bang. That's not to say that the museum skimps on the exhibits. The staff have actually managed to pack dozens of real aircraft inside the 53,000-square-foot facility, along with hundreds of photos and well-crafted displays.

> The museum is located at 601 Skyway Road, San Carlos. It's just a couple of minutes from Oracle's headquarters. More information is available at www.hiller.org or by calling (650) 654-0200.

A number of qualified firsts hang from the ceiling of the main display room. Look for the Avitor, the first powered airplane to fly unmanned (or -womanned, for that matter); the Curtiss Pusher, the first plane to land on a ship; the Little Looper, which was the first aerobatics plane; and a number of other pioneering craft. You'll also discover antique engines, a replica of an old Stanford wind tunnel, and modern craft such as helicopters and Boeing planes. Outside the museum is a 747 cockpit that visitors are free to walk in and check out.

Helicopter designer and builder Stanley Hiller opened the museum in 1998. The museum has started hosting an annual "Vertical Challenge" helicopter air show in honor of its founder.

Close to 50,000 people make their way through the museum every year. And a couple of evenings a month, speakers from nearby companies and universities come and talk about aviation. (You can

find more information on the events at www.hiller.org/upcoming
-events.shtml.) The museum is open daily 10 a.m. to 5 p.m. Adult tickets cost $9, while seniors and children pay $6. There's a big gift shop,
too: If you need a flight-themed present, you've found your place.
Huge aviation buffs will want to allow a couple of hours here, while
the simply curious can make their way through in an hour.

JOINT GENOME INSTITUTE, WALNUT CREEK

THE NEVERENDING QUEST IN SILICON VALLEY TO PRODUCE
cheaper, faster devices at a steady rate has carried over to the field
of genetics. Since 1997, the Joint Genome Institute (JGI) has proven
that it can crank through DNA sequences at a rate that doubles just
about every eighteen months. Advances in computing, sequencing,
and mechanical automation have put JGI on pace with the processor
industry's ultimate directive, Moore's Law: *The number of transistors
on a processor will double every eighteen to twenty-four months.* Such
a rate of progress pushes the JGI and other research institutes closer
to the goal of making it affordable and practical for every person to
receive a blueprint of their genetic makeup.

JGI visitors can see much of the equipment that makes such human
genome mapping possible. Lab tours begin with about a fifteen-minute
overview of JGI's history and genetics technology. Visitors will then go
into the experiment area and see the machines that pick out genetic
material for study, process it, and then calculate the sequences of letters that make up a sample. Many of the machines at JGI cost upward of
$300,000, and you're sure to be impressed by the quirky gear.

Today the institute works with additional labs such as Oak Ridge
National Laboratory, Pacific Northwest National Laboratory, and
Stanford University. Close to 240 people—managed by the Univer-
sity of California—work at the 60,000-square-foot lab.

JGI AND **THE** HUMAN **GENOME** PROJECT

The JGI may seem to have an unlikely backer in the Department of Energy. In the mid-1980s the DOE started posing the initial questions around whether it would be possible to sequence an entire human genome. Few researchers back then thought such a goal achievable in their lifetimes, given that it would have taken 1,000 years to map the genome with technology of the era.

Determined to improve the technology, the DOE and National Institutes of Health kicked off the Human Genome Project in 1990, expecting a $3 billion, fifteen-year effort. A few years later private groups began working along similar lines in a race to sequence the human genome first. The best-known such private effort came from former NIH worker Craig Venter, who started Celera Genomics and vowed to beat the Human Genome Project by four years.

Rapid improvements in the machinery used to complete mundane scientific tasks pushed all these efforts forward. The public Human Genome Project also received another helping hand with the creation of the JGI in 1997. The Walnut Creek lab—with an annual budget of about $66 million—combined expertise from Lawrence Berkeley National Laboratory, Lawrence Livermore National Laboratory, and Los Alamos National Laboratory.

> The lab is located at 2800 Mitchell Drive in Walnut Creek. You can tour the facility by contacting the public affairs office at (925) 296-5643. You'll need to schedule the tour—which lasts about an hour—in advance. For more information, see www.jgi.doe.gov/education/tours.html. JGI's genetic data is open to public access.

As it turned out, both the public and private efforts finished at about the same time, in 2001—four years ahead of schedule. By 2006 researchers had reached the point where they could sequence the equivalent of the human genome every month at a cost of about $10 million.

Chef Chu's, Los Altos

TAKE HEED, SKEPTICS. THE FORTUNE cookies at Chef Chu's can have a profound impact not just on your daily life but on the economic and social health of entire nations.

Okay, that may be overstating the situation a tad. But in a 2004 interview, then Intel CEO Craig Barrett declared that a Chef Chu's fortune cookie helped him take a position on the controversial subject of outsourcing—specifically, US companies hiring workers in China, India, and elsewhere for high-level jobs. "About two weeks ago, I was at Chef Chu's and opened my fortune cookie, and it said: 'The world is always ready to receive talent with open arms.' That's really what outsourcing is," Barrett, now Intel's chairman, told a reporter.

Chef Chu's has been influencing Silicon Valley decision makers since 1970. It started out as a small part of a strip mall, serving just twelve items from a takeaway stand. The stellar food, coupled with the popularity of Chef Chu himself, helped the restaurant expand and then expand some more until it gobbled up all of the other stores in the mall. In 1976 Chef Chu's completed the renovation on the building that stands today at the heart of Silicon Valley.

The two-story restaurant has a pair of major dining areas that allow it to pack in hundreds of guests. The atmosphere is casual; the lunchtime crowd varies from a few folks in suits to plenty more in jeans. But it's the food, not the decor, that will blow you away here. The vast menu offers up many items you won't find at a typical Chinese restaurant. If you want to meet the man himself, that can be arranged. There is a small private dining area where Chef Chu holds cooking classes on Tuesday evening. For $45, you can attend one of these classes, eat a scrumptious meal, and down some fine wine. Chef Chu also takes some lucky patrons on three-week gastronomical adventures through China, exploring a different region each year.

For such a large restaurant, Chef Chu's does a remarkable job of treating patrons like family. Guests receive plenty of attention, and staff get to know your habits over the years. Craig Barrett, for example, always relaxes in the same booth, while others plunk down at the bar to catch their afternoon dose of CNBC.

The likes of Apple co-founder Steve Jobs and Intel co-founder Gordon Moore can be found dining at Chef Chu's any evening, and workers from myriad high tech corporate campuses, along with Stanford University students, count the restaurant as a faithful standby.

Chef Chu's provides a grand respite from the Silicon Valley hot spots that take themselves way too seriously and have little to offer. This place has been plugging away for more than thirty years, keeping the technology crowd satiated and ready to face a frenetic world.

You can find Chef Chu's at 1067 North San Antonio Road or on the Internet at www.chefchu .com. Place your order by dialing (650) 948-2696.

To break down the cost reductions further, you need to examine a couple of DNA basics. "The human genome is made up of DNA, which has four different chemical building blocks," JGI tells us:

THESE ARE CALLED BASES AND ABBREVIATED A, T, C, AND G. IN THE HUMAN GENOME, ABOUT 3 BILLION BASES ARE ARRANGED ALONG THE CHROMOSOMES IN A PARTICULAR ORDER FOR EACH UNIQUE INDIVIDUAL. TO GET AN IDEA OF THE SIZE OF THE HUMAN GENOME PRESENT IN EACH OF OUR CELLS, CONSIDER THE FOLLOWING ANALOGY: IF THE DNA SEQUENCE OF THE HUMAN GENOME WERE COMPILED IN BOOKS, THE EQUIVALENT OF 200 VOLUMES THE SIZE OF A MANHATTAN TELEPHONE BOOK (AT 1,000 PAGES EACH) WOULD BE NEEDED TO HOLD IT ALL.

In 1989 it cost about $10 per letter of genetic code. By 1997 the price had dropped to $1 per letter; in 2006 it fell to 0.1 cent. It's a decline that would make processor manufacturers proud.

With one of the largest genetics labs on the planet, JGI also works to see how genetics information can speed advances in clean energy, climate change, and radiation safety.

ELECTRONICS ARTS, REDWOOD CITY

DESPITE A FEW ATTEMPTS, SILICON VALLEY COMPANIES HAVE struggled to capture a meaningful piece of the video game console market largely dominated by Japanese companies and more recently Microsoft. Valley companies, however, have done well in the lucrative video game software market. Electronics Arts sits atop the video game market as the first game maker to crack $1 billion in revenue. It now brings in more than $3 billion per year.

EA was the brainchild of early Apple employee Trip

While EA started in San Mateo, its current headquarters are in Redwood City.

Atari, Sunnyvale

WELL BEFORE THE HOME COMPUTER took off, a Silicon Valley upstart had managed to make a different kind of computing device a common element of living rooms everywhere. Nolan Bushnell, a talented University of Utah alum, came to Silicon Valley and started Atari in 1972 along with Ted Dabney. The company initially pioneered the coin-operated video game market, installing a Pong system at a Sunnyvale bar called Andy Capps. (That bar has since turned into the Rooster T. Feathers comedy club, located at 157 West El Camino Real.)

While on its way to becoming a video game powerhouse, Atari hired a young Steve Jobs—future co-founder of Apple—to do some work creating a video game. Apple co-founder Steve Wozniak helped Jobs with the project while he was also working on what would become Apple's first computer and showing it to the Homebrew Computer Club. It's said that Bushnell passed on buying the Apple product.

By 1977 Atari started an attack on the home video game market by delivering a console. This changed video game technology and the lives of millions forever. Atari experienced incredible demand for the console, arguably making it the greatest Silicon Valley success story up to that point. In fact, by 1980 Atari had become the fastest-growing company in US history and the major player in a multi-billion-dollar industry.

The glory days, however, didn't last long. Console competition, the rise of the PC, and badly done games started to wear on Atari's business as early as 1982. Then in 1983 a video game market crash occurred that resulted in Atari posting a huge loss. The firm never regained its cachet and watched as companies such as Nintendo, Sega, and Sony grew to dominate the console industry. The company that started the video game craze in earnest changed owners multiple times. Most recently, Atari has operated as a subsidiary of France-based Infogrames Entertainment and makes software only.

Atari founder Bushnell has gone on to found numerous companies and has been a player in the restaurant business. He opened the popular Lion & Compass restaurant in Sunnyvale and started the Chuck E. Cheese's Pizza chain in San Jose.

Hawkins, who started the company in 1982. At that time, the PC market was just getting going, but Hawkins and venture capitalist Don Valentine were convinced that games would soon become a hit on the computers. Valentine allowed Hawkins and a small team to work out of his Sequoia Capital offices, marking one of the first times a company was "incubated" by a venture capital firm.

Over the years, EA has managed to thrive with titles for both game consoles and PCs. The company has enjoyed particular success with its sports games for the game consoles and titles such as The Sims and SimCity for the PC. (EA obtained the rights to the simulation games and hired their creator—video game legend Will Wright—in 1997.)

Video games have turned into one of the most lucrative segments of the entertainment industry. They're now crossing into the music, movie, and advertising fields and are seen as a strong promotional tool by many media companies.

LAWRENCE LIVERMORE NATIONAL LABORATORY, LIVERMORE

FEW RESEARCHER CENTERS CAN MATCH THE SCALE AND scope of work done at Lawrence Livermore National Laboratory (LLNL). This high-security facility nestled amid rolling green hills has the stewardship of the nation's nuclear stockpile as its foremost goal. To ensure that decaying nuclear weapons remain safe, LLNL makes use of the most advanced supercomputing, laser, and bioscience technology known to humanity. The breadth of research done at the facility places LLNL at the forefront of numerous scientific fields. While just outside the Silicon Valley borders, LLNL feeds a wide variety of technology fields through its ties to leading scientists, universities, and top technology suppliers.

THE GOVERNMENT, UNIVERSITIES, AND large companies funded the vast majority—if not all—of the early computing work. That trend, however, changed in a major way during the 1970s as hobbyists began to wrap their heads around the idea of having a personal computer. The Homebrew Computer Club, more than any other hobbyist collective, drove the Silicon Valley push behind creating a computer that would be by individuals for individuals.

Unlike some of the staid tales of early technology work, the story of the Homebrew Computer Club's formation taps into the racier aspects of Bay Area culture—or rather counterculture. Colorful characters with a strong electronics bent saw basic computing components arriving for public consumption and figured that they had the tools needed to build personal computers capable of reeking a bit of havoc. If nothing else, these individuals didn't want to see a company such as IBM wall off computing from the masses. They wanted to make sure this new tool found its way into the hands of the Average Joe and then hoped to see what would happen from there.

The year 1975 saw the introduction of the MITS Altair 8800 personal computer kit. The system really didn't do much besides prove the validity of the personal computer concept. Still, flyers went up in March of that year inviting electronics fans to study the Altair at hobbyist Gordon French's two-car garage in Menlo Park. On a rainy night, about thirty people—some of whom had previously been meeting at potlucks—showed up for what would become the first Homebrew Computer Club gathering. "It was just all these guys standing around and looking at a computer on a table," according to one of its founding members, Lee Felsenstein.

A second meeting took place at Stanford's Artificial Intelligence Lab and a subsequent, larger meeting was held at the Peninsula School in Menlo Park. Organizers had been taking down the names and contact information of participants. The meetings continued, and the club grew and grew. Eventually, it made its way to a larger conference room at the Stanford Linear Accelerator (SLAC) where more than

100 people would show up for the sessions held every two weeks.

While some Homebrewers used the get-togethers simply to feed their interest in computers, others perceived the gatherings as a path to a greater calling. "The general idea emerged that getting control of technology in various forms was really the central task of the generation," Felsenstein said. "Not exclusive control but control." The quest to conquer computer technology was driven by the need not to compete with corporate researchers but simply to make sure the coming PC revolution wouldn't be owned by a corporate giant like IBM.

It wasn't. In the end, it was the *hobbyists* who in many ways managed to create and own the personal computing revolution. Dozens of companies can trace their beginnings or some of their work to the Homebrew Computer Club, including Apple.

Homebrew would continue until 1986. By then the PC industry had taken off in earnest, and numerous other clubs had sprung up around the devices. "The nature of the club changed," Felsenstein said. "After 1983, it became an old farts society. The same guys showed up again and again. It was just the same faces all the time."

Historians and journalists continue to dig deeper into the reasons that Homebrew proved more fruitful than other, similar clubs scattered around the country. Most point to the proximity of Intel, Xerox PARC, and other companies key to early PC technology. They also note the relatively compact nature of Silicon Valley as compared with, say, Los Angeles, which allowed word to spread quickly about the club and its discoveries.

Felsenstein has another explanation: "The image we had of ourselves was that of the tinkerer in the basement who had at least a shot at coming up with something that upsets everything else. There was definitely this feeling that we were pulling off something that was against the established order. It would have consequences. We believed that. We just weren't sure what the consequences were."

The sensitive nature of the work done at LLNL leaves the majority of the facility off limits to the public. That said, the lab has a very accessible and thorough tour program that visitors can tap. The tours take tax-paying citizens to some of the most compelling—and unclassified—spots on the 1-square-mile site.

BEHIND THE **TOP-SECRET** DOOR

LLNL opened in 1952 at the urging of Berkeley researcher Ernest Lawrence and Edward Teller, "Father of the Hydrogen Bomb." The scientists were convinced the United States needed a second site to complement the Manhattan Project and subsequent work done at Los Alamos.

Boosted by primary backing from the Department of Energy, LLNL began operations with the University of California managing the facility. Rather quickly the lab started churning out breakthroughs in warhead designs. This research would translate over time into pioneering work done in less violent but related fields such as biological and energy studies.

More recently the lab has been tasked not with creating new weapons but with making sure that nuclear stockpiles remain safe. To help study how weapons degrade without actually blowing them up, LLNL has turned to powerful supercomputers that can model the behavior of weapons systems and the material inside them. Since the late 1990s LLNL has owned some of the most impressive supercomputers in the world. These enormous systems can occupy an entire floor of a building and combine thousands of processors to crank away at a single task.

LLNL took its computing prowess to the next level in 2005 with an IBM-built system known as Blue Gene/L. This supercomputer—made up of an unprecedented 130,000 processors—obliterated the existing mark for the top-performing system. As part of a $230 million contract, IBM also provided LLNL with another powerful computer known as ASC Purple that has also ranked as one of the top five supercomputers on the planet.

To house the computers, LLNL built a $96 million facility equipped with specialized power and cooling systems. The building can deliver twenty-five megawatts of energy—about how much power it would take to fuel 25,000 houses.

Mark Seager, one of the leads behind the supercomputer projects, said that the cost and effort behind the systems has a large payoff. "The science we can do is revolutionary," he said in an interview. "We're actually able to take computation to a point where theory and experimentation merge, which is a rarity." In addition, the systems give the United States "a major competitive advantage" over other countries. The work done at LLNL, for example, has inspired Japan and China to pursue catch-up projects.

LLNL AND THE ACRONYM SOUP

Due to the classified nature of the work done on the supercomputers, most visitors cannot gain access to the systems. They can, however, see the National Atmospheric Release Advisory Center (NARAC), the Center for Accelerator Mass Spectrometry (CAMS), and the National Ignition Facility (NIF). (Hopefully, there's a LLNL researcher out there using all that computing power to create an acronym reduction algorithm—or ARA.)

NARAC provides a nice example of where LLNL's mission begins to diverge from the pure oversight of the nuclear stockpile. The NARAC facility has a type of command center designed to track the spread of hazardous material in the atmosphere. This mission has spanned from real-life incidents such as modeling the post-Chernobyl radioactive cloud to emergency scenario planning for the release of a dirty bomb at the 2002 Winter Olympics in Salt Lake City. Visitors can sneak a peek of the command center, which is packed full of computers, world clocks, and a high-end "live" map of the world, and see videos about how NARAC has helped out with a wide variety of events.

One of NARAC's shining moments came after the Chernobyl disaster. Governments around the world, including the Soviets,

The Discovery Center is located off Greenville Road on Eastgate Drive; its official address is 7000 East Avenue, and you can find it on the Web at www.llnl.gov. You can find more information on the center at www.llnl.gov/pao/com/discovery_center.html or by calling (925) 423-3272. More information on the tours can be found at www.llnl.gov/pao/com/tours.html.

turned to the information NARAC had gathered via probes in the atmosphere and at partner sites to figure out what would likely happen to the radioactive cloud.

CAMS has a more docile mission that centers around the study of biological material behavior. One of the key jobs performed by the CAMS staff is the dating of a wide range of materials. For example, close to 25 percent of the world's carbon dating takes place at CAMS. This LLNL unit works in conjunction with other labs, universities, and companies. The various organizations send samples to CAMS either for dating or for information on how the materials might be breaking down over time. This type of study has moved out of the realm of physicists and into the purview of geologists, oceanographers, and others in the earth sciences field. The tour will show you the funky CAMS nuclear probe that weaves around the facility in a mesh of tubes and wires.

Still, the most visually stimulating portion of the tour takes places at NIF. First off, the NIF building, best described at blah green, stands as the largest structure at LLNL. Connected to the huge facility are a bizarre assortment of multicolored tubes and power generators that look almost like growths.

The public cannot visit Sandia's California site. You can find more information about the lab at www.ca.sandia.gov/casite. It's located at 7011 East Avenue.

Inside NIF visitors will see a complex collection of lenses, mirrors, specialized glass, and lasers—lots of lasers. "Inside a 30-foot-wide target chamber, a gold cylinder the size of a dime receives energy from all 192 laser beams simultaneously: about 1.8 million joules over a few billionths of a second (about 500 trillion watts, which is nearly 1000 times the power generated in the US at any time)," the laboratory has said. "This cylinder then produces x-rays that compress and heat a fusion capsule inside the cylinder to temperatures and pressures approaching those in a nuclear explosion or in the Sun, igniting the fusion fuel in a self-sustaining reaction."

The controlled fusion experiment, described as creating a star on Earth, is meant to advance our knowledge of stars and energy and ultimately to aid national security by improving the understanding of how nuclear weapons work.

▶ LLNL DISCOVERY CENTER

TO TAKE IN ALL THESE SITES, YOU START OUT AT THE Discovery Center, which sits just outside of the LLNL fortress. This center is basically a small museum dedicated to LLNL and physics research. You'll find exhibits on LLNL's main mission of monitoring the nuclear stockpile along with less aggressive displays on the work being done at the lab in other scientific fields. The center is open to the public Tuesday through Friday 1 to 4 p.m., and on Saturday 10 a.m. to 2 p.m.

A court order requires LLNL to display an anti-LLNL exhibit produced by Tri-Valley CAREs (Communities Against a Radioactive Environment). Rather comically, the Discovery Center staffers have angled this exhibit toward a wall and placed it near the bathrooms. This is surely a coincidence and not some kind of symbolic gesture.

A small building just off the Discovery Center serves as the educational hub for students. School groups frequent LLNL on a regular basis. The students get to interact with LLNL scientists, who walk them through a brief history of the lab and then perform a Mr. Wizard–type show. The kiddos get to experiment with things such as designing circuits and freezing everyday items with liquid nitrogen.

Adults can set up a more formal tour after submitting their information to LLNL and going through a background check. This process usually takes up to two weeks (or two months for noncitizens), and LLNL looks for groups of between six and thirty people. The tours take place on alternating Tuesdays and Thursdays and last about two-and-a half-hours.

Overall, LLNL can be a tad intimidating. Heavily armed guards patrol the entrances to the lab, and a SWAT-caliber team of a classified size stands ready to eliminate any threat. (Keep that in mind if you're tempted to go crazy and hop on one of the hundreds of bright orange bikes littered about LLNL that the workers use for free transport around the facility.) The LLNL personnel, however, couldn't be more accommodating. Like most national lab staff, they treat those who take an interest in their work well and want nothing more than for people to gain an appreciation for science.

CLICK HERE   Maria Elena's

A POPULAR ALVISO ESTABLISHMENT with a major geek bent is Maria Elena's restaurant. At about noon every weekday, Alviso streets come alive as workers from Mountain View, Santa Clara, and San Jose descend on Maria Elena's for their Mexican food fix. You can't help but overhear technology chitchat while sneaking a beer or margarita.

The eatery's most famous dish might be the jumbo chipotle burrito. This bad boy demands a serious commitment to lunch. It's also pumped full of spice, so, if heat is your thing, cruise by for a meal.

If you're in a hurry, it's best to avoid the lunch rush. This no-frills eatery packs 'em in during the weekdays.

You'll find Maria Elena's at 1450 Gold Street, Alviso.

SANDIA NATIONAL LABORATORIES, LIVERMORE

WHY SETTLE FOR JUST ONE NUCLEAR RESEARCH FACILITY in your neighborhood when you can have two? Brushing right up against LLNL is its smaller satellite, Sandia National Laboratories. The main Sandia lab sits in Albuquerque, New Mexico, where thousands of scientists have worked over the years to turn the warheads developed by Los Alamos and LLNL into deployable weapons. Essentially, Los Alamos and LLNL supplied the parts that go boom, and Sandia figured out how to fire them.

Like LLNL, Sandia has since moved away from creating new weapons systems and toward making sure the nuclear stockpile degrades in a safe manner. And like its larger counterpart, it explores such areas as energy and supercomputing. Just a fraction of Sandia's 8,000 or so workers call Livermore home, and the California site is dwarfed by LLNL, which employs close to 8,000 workers and can swell to 10,000 staff during the summer when university researchers visit. Unlike LLNL, Sandia is run by Lockheed Martin.

ALVISO

EVEN STRUGGLING SILICON VALLEY SUBURBS CAN CLAIM A couple of impressive scalps. For proof, you should head out to sleepy Alviso. This tiny San Jose annex at the southern tip of the San Francisco Bay would seem to have little to offer these days. It's a pretty run-down town with a smattering of decaying houses and ramshackle stores. Unlike most of Silicon Valley, Alviso isn't clogged with traffic and doesn't give off much of a buzz.

But the town hasn't always been mired in such lethargy. In the mid-1800s it had plenty of stores, hotels, and pubs to support a healthy shipping trade. The boom-and-bust effect that seems part of this region's nature hit Alviso when San Francisco and San Jose started to dominate the shipping business, crimping Alviso's style. It would, however, enjoy a second run of success when a large cannery opened up at the turn of the century. Then the Depression hit, driving Alviso into the doldrums again. Throughout the cycles it maintained a reputation as a gambling and prostitution hub.

Alviso has managed to bumble along over the years, eventually being annexed by San Jose, and it functions today as an interesting tourist spot. You'll find the old cannery, some Victorians, and an abandoned marina more or less stranded in swamp. Many points in Alviso are actually more than 10 feet below sea level.

These rather gloomy circumstances make the business center at the edge of town really stand out. A number of companies, particularly those in the networking space, have set up shop at the expansive new buildings of this center. Networking player Foundry Networks is the leading occupant.

Still, the best-known Alviso-based company would have to be TiVo—maker of the popular TV recording device. You'll find the start-up at 2160 Gold Street; www.tivo.com.

DRAWBRIDGE

DRAWBRIDGE'S ONLY REAL CLAIM TO FAME IS ITS POSITION as the Bay Area's lone ghost town. During the early 1900s Drawbridge—named because it boasted two of the structures—managed to survive on the back of a healthy hunting and gaming industry.

Its location away from larger towns also provided pleasure seekers with a lawless getaway.

By about 1940, though, people had managed to pollute the area enough to drive animals away and make the marshy land more or less

You can find more information at the US Fish and Wildlife service Web site www.fws.gov/desfbay.

uninhabitable. In the years since then, what's left of Drawbridge has sunk deeper and deeper into the ground.

At its peak, Drawbridge had about 400 residents and close to a hundred houses, most of which were built on stilts. It officially gained ghost-town status in 1979 when its last resident went looking for a livelier home. There are still a couple of run-down houses on display, although you can't really get to them. The best information on the town is available at the Fremont Visitor Center, which offers occasional educational sessions on Drawbridge.

⏻ APPLE COMPUTER, CUPERTINO

THE HISTORY OF SILICON VALLEY IS LITTERED WITH DYNAMIC duos who started companies from scratch and managed to become giants in a few short years. Hewlett and Packard, Google's Brin and Page, Intel's Noyce and Moore, and Yahoo!'s Yang and Filo all come

to mind. No pairing, however, has secured broader appeal or more attention than the founders of Apple Computer—Steve Jobs and Steve Wozniak.

THE STEVES

The Apple story covers all the basic Silicon Valley clichés in spectacular fashion. You start with a pair of local

You can see Apple's glam Cupertino headquarters by visiting 1 Infinite Loop. You can also see the garage where Apple started at 2066 Crist Drive, Los Altos. Don't expect a marker or any Apple fanfare. You'll just find a typical, one-story suburban house.

STEVE JOBS UNPLUGGED
"I had been rejected, but I was still in love."

HE HANGS OUT WITH U2 SINGER BONO, used to date Joan Baez, and has reinvented himself as many times as Madonna. Steve Jobs may be the closest thing Silicon Valley has to a rock star.

Few would have guessed that Jobs would turn into such a flashy multibillionaire. Throughout his early years, he tended toward what most would consider counterculture pursuits. Jobs attended the left-leaning Reed College for a few weeks before dropping out and auditing classes such as calligraphy. Next he went off to India, hunting down spiritual enlightenment.

Eventually, however, Jobs's entrepreneurial tendencies took over, and he looked to make the most of friend Steve Wozniak's engineering prowess. The two Steves started Apple, making history as computer pioneers. In short order Jobs then was unceremoniously booted from the company, started another computer firm, and returned to Apple. In many ways, the Apple CEO's life mimics that of the boom, bust, and boom again Valley. Such ups and downs have fueled the Jobs legend.

Yet even more than his business prowess, it's Jobs's personality that stands out. To the so-called Apple Faithful, he's a kind of quasi-deity, while critics portray him as a moody, egotistical control freak. To get a sense of the man, here's a glimpse at the oft-quoted speech he made to the Stanford graduating class of 2005:

I DIDN'T SEE IT THEN, BUT IT TURNED OUT THAT GETTING FIRED FROM APPLE WAS THE BEST THING THAT COULD HAVE EVER HAPPENED TO ME. THE HEAVINESS OF BEING SUCCESSFUL WAS REPLACED BY THE LIGHTNESS OF BEING A BEGINNER AGAIN, LESS SURE ABOUT EVERYTHING. IT FREED ME TO ENTER ONE OF THE MOST CREATIVE PERIODS OF MY LIFE.

HOW CAN YOU GET FIRED FROM A COMPANY YOU STARTED? WELL, AS APPLE GREW WE HIRED SOMEONE WHO I THOUGHT WAS VERY TALENTED TO RUN THE COMPANY WITH ME, AND FOR THE FIRST YEAR OR SO THINGS WENT WELL. BUT THEN OUR VISIONS OF THE FUTURE BEGAN TO DIVERGE AND EVENTUALLY WE HAD A FALLING OUT. WHEN WE DID, OUR BOARD OF DIRECTORS SIDED WITH HIM. SO AT 30 I WAS OUT. AND VERY PUBLICLY OUT. WHAT HAD BEEN THE FOCUS OF MY ENTIRE ADULT LIFE WAS GONE, AND IT WAS DEVASTATING.

I REALLY DIDN'T KNOW WHAT TO DO FOR A FEW MONTHS. . . . I WAS A VERY PUBLIC FAILURE, AND I EVEN THOUGHT ABOUT RUNNING AWAY FROM THE VALLEY. BUT SOMETHING SLOWLY BEGAN TO DAWN ON ME—I STILL LOVED WHAT I DID. THE TURN OF EVENTS AT APPLE HAD NOT CHANGED THAT ONE BIT. I HAD BEEN REJECTED, BUT I WAS STILL IN LOVE. AND SO I DECIDED TO START OVER.

boys going to Homestead High School in Cupertino and sparking a friendship. Rather than finishing off a college education like the rest of the drones, the Steves dropped out of their respective schools—Reed College for Jobs and UC Berkeley for Wozniak. Reunited in California, Jobs and Wozniak began to develop the dynamic that would serve them well for years to come: The gifted Wozniak would create engineering marvels and the charismatic Jobs would sell them.

An early example of this partnership came when Wozniak designed his own version of the infamous Blue Box—a device used by "phone phreakers" to make free telephone calls—and Jobs sold the device. Later, Jobs would take a job at Atari and have Wozniak help him out on tough engineering projects such as designing the game Breakout.

While working for Hewlett-Packard, Wozniak started to take Jobs to the Homebrew Computer Club meetings held at the Stanford Linear Accelerator, which is when the pair started to dream big. This club brought together electronics enthusiasts on a quest to create a type of personal computer. By most accounts, Wozniak was the most talented engineer of the bunch and impressed the crowds with his early motherboard designs. In 1975 he built what would become the Apple I. It was a type of hobby PC inaccessible to the mass market but still much better than existing PC kits. Jobs and Wozniak discussed the system with Atari and HP but didn't get any takers. So Wozniak quit his job at HP and founded Apple with Jobs on April 1, 1976. Again in the true Silicon Valley tradition, the Steves worked out of Jobs's family garage in Los Altos and sold their first computers to the Byte Shop in Mountain View.

APPLE II, LISA, AND MAC

Apple truly "ignited the personal computing revolution," as it likes to say, in 1977 with the release of the more advanced Apple II. These early Apples were far from user-friendly for the average consumer. Nonetheless, more than two million of the systems were sold as small businesses and enthusiasts bought the products out of curiosity or in hopes of developing some useful software to run on the computer.

As the 1980s rolled around, IBM started to get its act together and entered the PC market. IBM's presence combined with a not-

SILICON VALLEY SOUNDBYTE

The Apple Cult

IT'S HARD TO DESCRIBE THE PASSION Apple engenders to those outside technophile circles. Insiders, though, know the Apple Faithful all too well. It's not a stretch to describe Apple's biggest fans less as enthusiastic consumers than as religious zealots. True backers consider the company's computers—and its operating system in particular—as symbols of their decision to choose a better life than the masses on Microsoft Windows machines.

Much of the fanaticism stems from a love for the company's co-founders, Steve Wozniak and Steve Jobs. Wozniak is a hero to engineers, while the charismatic Jobs is more of the inspired prophet for the merry band of Apple aficionados. When Jobs speaks at a conference, for example, throngs of Apple fans line up outside the auditorium and then rush in once the doors open, hoping to get the best seat. Throughout Jobs's speech they hoot and holler in fits of enthusiasm as the CEO unveils new products. Jobs usually saves the best product for last, sending the crowd into rapture as he says, "And one more thing."

Such love for Jobs can seem confusing to outsiders. There are just as many stories painting Jobs as a ruthless, selfish egomaniac as there are celebrating his vision, strong will, and creativity.

Nonetheless, the Apple Faithful have been known to do just about anything for their leader. Some spend hours in computer stores trying to promote Macs to consumers, despite not being on the clock. In addition, reporters who utter a single negative word about the company will receive hundreds of threatening e-mails almost the instant their piece hits the wires.

Without question, this adoration has helped Apple gain far more than its fair share of media attention over the years.

A pair of books detail the Apple passion. Those interested might want to check out *The Cult of Mac* by Leander Kahney or *iCon* by Jeffrey Young and William Simon.

terribly-impressive Apple III proved troubling for Apple. Meanwhile, though, Jobs had found what he believed to be the next big thing in personal computing during a 1979 visit to the famed Xerox PARC research lab. The PARC team had developed what is widely considered the first PC, called the Alto. This system used a mouse and sophisticated software such as SmallTalk and a graphical user interface (GUI) with icons and windows that all proved inspiring to Jobs. He then initiated the "Lisa" project to create a state-of-the-art computer with a GUI. But brewing internal conflicts resulted in Jobs being kicked off the Lisa project. So he commandeered the other GUI-based project then in the works: "Macintosh."

It may seem strange that Jobs, a co-founder of Apple, could be kicked off anything. Apple, however, had already brought in adult supervision in the form of CEO Mike Scott and early investor Mike Markkula. The temperamental, aggressive Jobs didn't always get his way around these managers and would, in fact, eventually be asked to leave the company.

At $10,000 the Lisa proved a flop in 1983, but the Macintosh restored Apple's luster in 1984. The computer was really the first mass-market PC with a GUI. In the following years Apple would become well known for creating attractive, useful software. The company's strategy allowed it to play well with educational institutions and companies doing large amounts of graphics work. The firm struggled, however, to compete with IBM and its allies Microsoft and Intel in the corporate PC market. In fact, Apple's share of the computer market dropped down into the low single digits by the late 1990s. The company had gone through a couple of CEO changes and lost its original swagger. A group of loyal customers always referred to as the "Apple Faithful" in news reports stuck with the company through these hard times. They often critiqued Microsoft for pinching Apple's ideas and were aggressive in their support of Apple products. Apple is nothing short of a cult for these folks.

THE RETURN **OF** JOBS

In 1997 the Faithful's messiah returned when Jobs was brought back into the fold after Apple had acquired Jobs's computer start-up NeXT. Jobs would be reinstalled as CEO after Gil Amelio was shown the door by Apple's board.

Jobs worked to resurrect Apple's products using his trademark attention to design. And Apple, in fact, did put out some good-looking products, including colorful computers and laptops. Despite the flashy gear and grand marketing campaigns, Apple's market share continued to hover in the single digits.

Then came the iPod.

In 2001 Apple released the portable music player that would reinvigorate the company on an unprecedented scale. The tiny white device tripled Apple's sales. It also helped Apple promote its iTunes music and TV show store, which has placed the company at the intersection of old-line media companies and technology makers. Apple's computer market share remains quite low, but strong iPod sales have cured any financial ills at the company.

Steve Jobs also extended his media mogul role in 2006 when Disney acquired his moviemaking company Pixar, making Jobs the largest Disney shareholder.

Drive the Valley:
Best Routes for Seeing It All

TOUR DE FIRSTS

LET'S GALLOP PAST ALL THE FAMOUS "FIRSTS" THAT TOOK
place in Palo Alto and Mountain View with a driving tour that takes
you about as far back into Silicon Valley history as you can go.

You're going to start out at 913 Emerson Street in Palo Alto and
locate the historic marker for the Federal Telegraph Company. It was
here that the vacuum tube amplifier was invented between 1911 and
1913. From this spot, you can drive or walk to the HP Garage by heading down to Addison Avenue (0.1 mile) and taking a left. The garage
where Bill Hewlett and Dave Packard started their company is at 367
Addison Avenue (0.2 mile). Palo Alto considers this spot the "Birthplace of Silicon Valley."

Next, hop back in the car and set out on Addison toward Scott
Street. Go 0.3 mile and take a left onto Alma Street. After about 3.3
miles, you'll follow the ramp toward Los Altos, go 0.2 mile, and then
turn right onto San Antonio Road. Stay alert, because after 0.3 mile,
you'll stop at 391 San Antonio Road—Mountain View's version of the
"Birthplace of Silicon Valley."

With any luck you'll be looking at a grocery store, which used
to be the home of William Shockley's transistor lab. Shockley was
responsible for collecting the likes of Robert Noyce and Gordon
Moore in one place and starting the region's focus on producing
semiconductors out of silicon. Workers from this lab would go on to
found Fairchild Semiconductor, Intel, and countless other companies.
There's a historic marker on the sidewalk outside.(As of this writing,
the Shockley site is in flux with a fruit stand closing in early 2007 and
plans being made to construct a new grocery store at the site.)

Speaking of Fairchild, you're next stop will be the company's first headquarters. Here Noyce invented the integrated circuit that would go on to become the basis for processor technology. Take a right out from the Shockley site and get going on San Antonio Road toward California Street. You'll go about 1.3 miles and then take a left onto East Charleston Road. You'll soon see a low-lying building on your left; next to it is a car repair shop. The historical marker is out front of the building at 844 East Charleston.

All told, this shouldn't take you more than an hour. If you're feeling peckish afterward, consider backtracking a short distance for a meal at the famous Chef Chu's Chinese restaurant. Head back toward San Antonio Road and take a right. You'll travel right past the old Shockley lab and, after about 1.6 miles, end up at the intersection of San Antonio and El Camino Real. You'll see the large Chef Chu's to your left across El Camino Real, at 1067 San Antonio Road. The restaurant has fed generations of Silicon Valley workers. Tell them we sent you.

Those looking for an extended day out can head from Chef Chu's to the start of the Mountain View Tour (below) by taking a right onto El Camino Real and driving 1.7 miles to Shoreline Boulevard. You'll then take a left onto Shoreline and head to the Computer History Museum—about 2 miles down at 1401 Shoreline.

MOUNTAIN VIEW TOUR

THIS TOUR STARTS OUT AT 1401 SHORELINE BOULEVARD, Mountain View. This is the home of the Computer History Museum and a former Silicon Graphics Inc. (SGI) building. If you're visiting during the week, check the museum Web site to make sure it's open—the facility has limited weekday hours. Saturday is really your best option.

You'll likely spend an hour or two at the museum, which will be the most time-consuming part of this tour. Then hop back in your car; you can also walk if you have any interest in hoofing about 5 miles.

Take a right back onto Shoreline and cruise about 1.6 miles to Crittenden Lane, where you will make a right turn. Just before you get to Crittenden, pay attention to the redbrick buildings on Stierlin Court. Those used to be SGI buildings as well. Drive to the end of the street, 1500 Crittenden Lane—the old headquarters of SGI and an office complex for start-ups.

Walkers might want to retrace their steps and then take a right back onto Shoreline, heading toward the golf course. If you veer off to the right in the large, open parking lot, you'll find an entrance to local trails with maps provided.

Otherwise, drive or walk back down Crittenden toward Shoreline, where you make a left. Continue just about 0.7 mile and then take a right onto Amphitheatre Parkway. On your right you'll see the great white tent of Shoreline Amphitheatre; up ahead lies the Googleplex. The official Google headquarters are at 1600 Amphitheatre Parkway, although you'll notice there are Google buildings everywhere. Cruise around the surrounding area to gain a sense of Google's empire. All the buildings you've visited so far once belonged to SGI.

From here you'll want to drive the rest of the tour, so hop back in your car, head out of the Googleplex, and get back onto Shoreline, making a right turn. Drive about 0.5 mile and take a left onto La Avenida Street. Half a mile down on your right will be the Microsoft Silicon Valley headquarters. At the end of La Avenida, you'll also find an entrance to the Stevens Creek Trail, if you do happen to be up for more walking.

From the Microsoft headquarters, head back toward Shoreline and take a left. You're going to bear right onto the US 101 freeway heading south. Travel about a mile and take the Moffett Field exit toward Moffett Boulevard. As you head down Moffett, the NASA Ames center will come into view. Take a right before you get to the guardhouse and park near the large white tent. That's the Ames visitor center.

From here, head out of NASA Ames back up Moffett toward the freeway. Instead of getting on the freeway, though, continue on Moffett for a couple of miles. It turns into Castro Street, putting you in the middle of downtown Mountain View and its myriad dining and shopping options.

Take a right onto Villa Street if you want to stop into the Tied House (954 Villa) for a burger and a beer.

SANTA CLARA **AND** SAN **JOSE**
HEADQUARTERS **TOUR**

START THIS TOUR AT INTEL'S HEADQUARTERS, LOCATED AT 2200 Mission College Boulevard in Santa Clara. Turn into the complex and park in the visitor area just outside the Robert Noyce building. Signs around the campus will point you toward the Intel Museum, which takes about an hour to explore.

When you're ready, take a left out of the Intel headquarters back onto Mission College Boulevard and travel about 0.4 mile before taking a right onto Agnew Road. Keep going on Agnew for 1.2 miles to reach the Sun Microsystems headquarters at 4150 Network Circle. You're free to park here and check out the historic buildings that used to be part of the Agnews asylum.

Take a right back onto Agnew Road, travel about 0.3 mile, and turn left onto the Montague Expressway. Keep going on Montague for 0.7 mile and then turn right onto North 1st Street. In about 1.6 miles you'll reach 2211 North 1st Street—headquarters for eBay's PayPal division and a more impressive site than eBay's main office.

Head out of the eBay offices and make a U-turn; you want to be heading back down North 1st in the same direction you came from. Travel about 2.7 miles to West Tasman Drive.

At this point turn left to see Cisco's official headquarters at 170 West Tasman. Then make a U-turn and travel along West Tasman

Drive for about a mile for a look at Cisco's massive campus in its entirety.

When you've had enough of Cisco, head back to North 1st Street and travel away from eBay's headquarters. Keep going, passing under Highway 237 to end up on Taylor Street. Look to your right to see the headquarters of TiVo at 2160 Gold Street.

You're now in sleepy, historic Alviso. Have a drive around to see some of the old Victorian houses. If you're hungry, be sure to stop at Maria Elena's for a burrito. It's located at 1450 Gold Street. All told, you've traveled about 11 miles on this route.

SAN JOSE TOUR

SAN JOSE MAKES LIFE PRETTY EASY ON VISITORS BY putting many of its main attractions right next door. You'll want to pick out your San Jose stops based on whether you have children in tow and what kind of attention span you and the kids can maintain. Those of you with wee youngsters will probably want to start at the Children's Discovery Museum, located at 180 Woz Way. If your kids are seven and up, you might prefer to begin at the Tech Museum of Innovation at 201 South Market Street.

You can park right by the Children's Discovery Museum. The downside is that it's somewhat separated from the rest of downtown San Jose, though we're only talking 0.5 mile. If you want to start at The Tech, park just about anywhere in downtown San Jose. A number of lots are located in walking distance of the museum.

After you've done the museum bit, you can head across the park—the Plaza de Cesar Chavez—to the San Jose Museum of Art, next to the well-known Fairmont Hotel. Or take a right onto West San Fernando Street. At the corner of 1st and San Fernando, you'll find historic marker 952—the site of the first radio broadcasting station, KQW. Keep going down San Fernando, and you'll see San Jose State University open up on your right. It's well worth a look.

There are plenty of dining options nearby, if you want a snack. In the afternoon you might want to hop in the car and catch a late tour at the Winchester Mystery House, then pop across the street to Santana Row for dinner.

STANFORD TOUR

FOLKS TOURING IN AND AROUND THE STANFORD UNIVERSITY campus have a number of interesting options to choose from. If you plan ahead, for starters, you can sign up for a tour of the Stanford Linear Accelerator located at 2575 Sand Hill Road, Menlo Park. You'll need to go to the SLAC Web site (www.slac.stanford.edu) to schedule your tour. The drive to SLAC along Sand Hill Road takes you past countless venture capital company headquarters.

If atom smashing isn't your thing, we recommend that you start out at the Cantor Arts Center; it's on the main Stanford campus at Lomita Drive and Museum Way. You can park right by the museum and check out the Rodin Sculpture Garden on your way into the building. At this point, a Stanford campus map will come in handy. You can download one off Stanford's Web site or pick one up on campus. The Cantor Arts Center is very close to the Science and Engineering Quad, which holds the main science and computer science buildings. You'll find structures named for the likes of Bill Hewlett and David Packard and Microsoft chairman Bill Gates. You can spend quite a bit of time walking around Stanford's scenic campus.

If you'd like to get in some serious walking, head to the intersection of Stanford Avenue and Junipero Serra Boulevard. Park on Stanford and head into "The Dish"—a wide-open area with trails that stretch over a few miles. If you're hoping to grab a bite or do some shopping, follow the signs to Palm Drive. This road will turn into University Avenue and deposit you into the heart of Palo Alto.

The headquarters for PARC and SRI are just a couple of miles from Stanford's campus, if you're interested, as is Perry Avenue (where author Ken Kesey used to hold drug-infused parties while penning *One Flew Over the Cuckoo's Nest*). You can also hit the core of the Stanford Research Park by traveling to HP's headquarters.

SAN FRANCISCO TOUR

SAN FRANCISCO HAS SO MANY OPTIONS THAT IT'S DIFFICULT to tell you where to begin. Here, however, is one route that will provide a pleasant day out.

Start off at the Exploratorium located at 3601 Lyon Street. You'll probably spend an hour or two here and at the surrounding Palace of Fine Arts.

Star Wars buffs or those wanting a bit of a walk can head to the Presidio and the Letterman Digital Arts Center, headquarters of director George Lucas's Lucasfilm. The Presidio is essentially across the street from the Exploratorium, although it might not look that way depending on where you park.

If you're driving, take a right out of the Exploratorium parking lot onto Marina Boulevard and then, after just 0.2 mile, take another right onto Broderick Street. Travel 0.5 mile, turn right onto Lombard Street, and go through the Lombard Gate entrance into the Presidio. You'll see the Lucasfilm headquarters on your right and will have several parking options. You're free to walk around the grounds and the Lucasfilm land.

Another option after leaving the Exploratorium or the Presidio sends you across Marina Boulevard to the Chrissy Field and Golden Gate National Recreation Area. Again, you can park and walk around on the edge of the water. The Wave Organ is located at the end of Yacht Road behind the boats. The Green Street Lab and the California Academy of Sciences can be reached by car in about fifteen minutes from any of these points.

If you're sans children and looking for an afternoon pint and a bit of adventure, cruise over to the corner of Geary and Larkin. You'll be just one block from both the Edinburgh Castle (950 Geary) and O'Farrell Street Bar (corner of O'Farrell and Larkin). These pubs are in the colorful Tenderloin District of San Francisco, which has a high homeless quotient and a lot of character.

■ ■ ■

Suggested Reading

What the Dormouse Said: How the 60s Counterculture Shaped the Personal Computer Industry by John Markoff. Penned by the top *New York Times* technology reporter, this book delves into the intersection of the Bay Area's leftist leanings and passion for technology. It doesn't have a lot of sex, but it does have some drugs and rock and roll—and a lot of computers. Markoff makes the best attempt to date at tackling a difficult subject.

The Man Behind the Microchip: Robert Noyce and the Invention of Silicon Valley by Leslie Berlin. This is the definitive biography of Noyce, co-founder of Fairchild and Intel. It's a great read and covers Noyce's role as one of the founding fathers of Silicon Valley. Berlin's book stands as one of the best-researched biographies you'll find and provides a sense of both Noyce's engineering prowess and his charismatic personality.

Crystal Fire: The Birth of the Information Age by Michael Riordan and Lillian Hoddeson. One of the most detailed accounts available of the creation of the transistor at Bell Laboratories in 1947. The authors trace the story of inventors John Bardeen and Walter Brattain and their boss William Shockley, who all went on to have a huge impact on Silicon Valley.

Dealers of Lightning: Xerox PARC and the Dawn of the Computer Age by Michael Hiltzik. This book covers the evolution of the Xerox PARC laboratory by looking at both the people and the motivations behind the lab's creation,as well as detailing how Xerox failed to capitalize on many of its inventions. The prose stalls at times and doesn't always hold your attention, although the book does a fine job of trying to come to terms with the PARC experiment.

Backfire: Carly Fiorina's High-Stakes Battle for the Soul of Hewlett-Packard by Peter Burrows. Written by *BusinessWeek's* star technology reporter, this tome explains the confrontation between HP CEO Fiorina and some HP veterans when the company went through its acquisition of Compaq. It's one of the best dives to date into Fiorina's character.

Cities of Knowledge: Cold War Science and the Search for the Next Silicon Valley by Margaret Pugh O'Mara. Penned by a Stanford history professor, this volume uses the academic's lens to distinguish the factors that have led to Silicon Valley's success. The author spends a lot of time examining the academic and social underpinnings of the Valley and the federal policies that shaped the region. A dry but informative read.

Done Deals: Venture Capitalists Tell Their Stories edited by Udayan Gupta. The title says it all about this collection of interviews with Silicon Valley venture capitalists. Close to thirty people are interviewed. You're not likely to discover any great insights here, but you will get a better picture for the venture capital game.

The HP Way: How Bill Hewlett and I Built Our Company by David Packard. You don't get more classic than this, the HP story told by one of the company's founders. It will take just one or two sittings to digest this history of how HP came to be, how Hewlett and Packard ran the show, and how Packard believes a company should function.

Making Silicon Valley: Innovation and the Growth of High Tech, 1930–1970 by Christophe Lécuyer. A rare look at the electronics pioneers who made Silicon Valley possible, this volume starts off at the turn of the century, looks at 1920s and 1930s electronics makers, and then stretches to cover HP and Fairchild Semiconductor. It's a pretty dry and academic affair, but still one of the best-researched books on Silicon Valley's technology beginnings.

Droidmaker: George Lucas and the Digital Revolution by Michael Rubin. This is an ideal book for any technophile with a *Star Wars* fetish. It tracks Lucas's creation of the in-house graphics technology machine that eventually turned into Pixar and fell into Apple co-founder Steve Jobs's ownership. More than that, however, it tracks the rise of graphics technology in painstaking detail. This book doesn't have as polished prose as some of the others on this list, but it's a true gem.

Surf the Valley

The Duck Rabbit: www.theduckrabbit.com/siliconvalley. This site serves as the online companion to this book and includes photos and more information on the topics covered.

The Register: www.theregister.com. Europe's most popular technology-focused Web site. Expect biting analysis and comic takes on high-tech happenings. Do a search for "Into the Valley" for an ongoing collection of stories on local events.

Slashdot: www.slashdot.org. The ultimate geek site. Millions of technophiles visit Slashdot every day to catch up on technology news collected from multiple sources around the Web.

Good Morning Silicon Valley: http://blogs.siliconvalley.com/gmsv. The daily virtual newsletter for the Silicon Valley set. Best headlines on the Internet.

Dvorak Uncensored: http://dvorak.org/blog. The musings of well-known technology writer and Silicon Valley veteran John Dvorak.

Wired: www.wired.com. In-depth technology news and feature stories from a talented collection of writers.

Nerd TV: www.pbs.org/cringely/nerdtv. An ongoing series of interviews with Silicon Valley luminaries done by PBS host Robert Cringely.

IT Conversations: www.itconversations.com/index.html. A wide variety of interviews with technology personalities.

Stanford's Silicon Valley Archives: http://svarchive.stanford.edu. A virtual collection of the documents Stanford has collected over the years relating to the Silicon Valley.

Computer History Museum: www.computerhistory.org. The site of the Computer History Museum in Mountain View. You can search for a wide variety of content, including online versions of exhibits and interviews.

PARC Forum: www.parc.com/events/forum/archive.php. A collection of past presentations done at the PARC research center in Palo Alto. Topics range from processor design to energy conservation.

HP History: www.hp.com/hpinfo/abouthp/histnfacts/garage. One of the more impressive corporate history sites. You'll find every last tidbit about HP.

General Santa Clara County History: www.cr.nps.gov/nr/travel/santaclara/intro.htm. A site produced by the National Park Service with a decent overview of the area and some historical links.

Silicon Valley History: www.siliconvalleyhistory.org. A Web site with a wealth of photos tracing the agriculture, people, and technology in the area.

Index